Too Good for the Rich Alone:

The complete guide to tax-exempt bonds for the middle-income investor

TOO GOOD
FOR THE
RICH ALONE

*The complete guide to
tax-exempt bonds
for the middle-income investor*

by

James F. Reilly

PRENTICE-HALL, INC.
Englewood Cliffs, New Jersey

*Too Good for the Rich Alone: The complete guide to tax-exempt bonds
for the middle-income investor*
by James F. Reilly
Copyright © 1975 by James F. Reilly
All rights reserved. No part of this book may be
reproduced in any form or by any means, except
for the inclusion of brief quotations in a review,
without permission in writing from the publisher.
Printed in the United States of America
Prentice-Hall International, Inc., London
Prentice-Hall of Australia, Pty. Ltd., Sydney
Prentice-Hall of Canada, Ltd., Toronto
Prentice-Hall of India Private Ltd., New Delhi
Prentice-Hall of Japan, Inc., Tokyo
10 9 8 7 6 5 4 3 2 1

Library of Congress Cataloging in Publication Data

Reilly, James F
Too good for the rich alone.

1. Securities, Tax-exempt—United States.
2. Bonds—United States.   I. Title.
HG4936.R4   332.6′323   75-11658
ISBN 0-13-925081-6

This book is dedicated to
the memory of Louis S. Lebenthal,
whose book *The ABC of Municipal Bonds*
first introduced me to
the wonderful world of tax-free bonds.

———————————————

Preface

I have been active in the bond markets for over twenty-five years and I have always been perplexed by the aura of mystery that surrounds the tax-exempt bond market. This sense of mystery extends not only to investors, but to many people in the securities business as well. Indeed, many of the top partners or executives on Wall Street (and the other famous financial streets throughout the nation) almost dread questions about tax-exempt bonds.

This aura of mystery and confusion extends even to the press. Except for reports about the "rogues" of the business, financial writers have little to say about tax-exempt bonds. Read the question-and-answer columns and you will see what I mean.

This book is an attempt to tear down the "veil of mystery" that surrounds tax-exempt bonds. I have tried to write in a way that any potential investor can understand. This is a must because the tax-exempt bond business has a language all its own, as you will see.

I have divided this book into two parts. The first part will tell the story; the second part will contain supporting charts, tables, etc. These charts, etc., are meant to be self-explanatory. I want you, the reader, to always know what I am talking about.

Two of the most frequent questions about tax-exempt bonds are, how did they begin and why? The last question is a philosophical one and is fairly well loaded. I will not touch upon that one until much later.

Local bonds are as old as man's ability to govern himself. England is an example of how popular local bonds are.

Their local bonds are sold in the City and also at some of the borough halls. All Europe has bonds although the control is more central than here. This is why our local bonds are different: Our local areas are free to make their own financing decisions. (This is not true even in England.) But the big difference is that our bonds are *tax-exempt*. Our neighbor Canada has autonomy in its local financings, but its bonds are taxable.

Local bonds were introduced in the colonies and, strange as it may seem, one issue in the Massachusetts colony was sold for the purpose of building a steel mill. Thus industrial-revenue bonds are not as new as many would think. However, the establishment of the tax-exempt principle did not occur until the early 1800s when that famous pacesetter, Chief Justice John Marshall, made a landmark decision that was to have a lasting effect on the relationship between the federal government and the states.

The case before the Chief Justice was *McCullough v. Maryland*. The nub of the case was that McCullough, who worked for the Bank of the U.S. in Baltimore, had tried to tax some notes which had been issued by the state of Maryland. Justice Marshall established the principle of mutual tax reciprocity. This meant that states could not tax the bonds or notes of the federal government, and neither could the federal government tax the bonds or notes of a sovereign state. This principle was extended to include the local towns and cities of those sovereign states. Thus tax exemption got its earliest boost before there were income taxes.

The men who built the railroads in the early nineteenth century saw local bonds as a solution to some of their problems. Railroads going nowhere with no towns to stop at were not what they had in mind. They needed towns and thus towns were built. The money came from bond issues. (Unfortunately, many of these issues defaulted since the railroads sometimes went another way because of some natural block or because the promoters had a new idea.)

These ill-fated financings led to many safeguards, some of which are still in practice. The most prominent one was the retention of attorneys to render opinions that the bonds were legally issued.

Local financing moved into the twentieth century with little or no change except that there were many more financings as our states and cities grew. However, what did they have to finance? Paved streets were not needed. Schools and public buildings (such as Boss Tweed built in New York in the late nineteenth century) and parks were the usual expenditures. We had not yet begun supplying hospitals, public transportation, or (heaven forbid) public assistance.

It was not until 1913, with the adoption of the 16th Amendment to the Constitution, that the tax-exempt status of local area bonds began to have some significance as Congress voted an income tax. Yet the income tax was relatively small, so that local bonds were hardly any better an investment than taxable ones except in the matter of security.

The years after World War I, prior to the great Depression, spawned many of the authority-type projects that we see about us today. It was in the early twenties that Seattle broke the mold with an electric power system backed by local bonds. We also saw the birth of the Port of New York Authority, which sold bonds to build the George Washington Bridge and the Holland Tunnel. This type of financing changed the face of the bond business as we financed projects via special revenue authorities without the use of tax dollars.

The Depression had the same effect on local areas that it had on business. There were some defaults, but relatively few when you consider how badly the local areas were hurt. There were many refunding issues, which in effect kept the original issues from defaulting. However, the local areas on the whole have had a proud record. (Remember Richmond, Virginia, sent its interest money to England and thence to New York during the Civil War so that its bonds would not default.)

Local areas had no chance to begin new projects as the Depression was overcome by World War II. All local improvement came to a complete standstill. Local bonds had become so unimportant that municipal-bond men had the same draft priority as the manufacturers of artificial flowers. The only way that many bond houses could stay open was for their key personnel to take defense jobs at night.

With the end of the war, there was an upsurge of local issues. First, we had the various bonds issued by states to grant their veterans a bonus for their service. Interest rates on these issues were as low as 1½ percent. This was a holdover from the war, when all rates were controlled by common action of the Treasury and the Federal Reserve System. This marriage came to an end in March 1951, when interest rates were decontrolled—in other words, the free market was reestablished.

When we talk about bonds, especially tax-exempt bonds, we find that almost everything dates from March 1951. Rates started to move up, slowly at first, to the level we know today. Income taxes were getting higher and higher so people were looking for new investments that would help them to legally avoid paying federal income taxes. Local, state, and city taxes were coming into their own.

Volume of new issues of tax-exempts has shown a dramatic increase from the early fifties to the $24 billion or so of bonds issued in 1971. See Appendix 1.

Today volume is still going strong, and investor interest, especially the small investor's, is running higher than ever before. There are some problems on the local level, and many bond firms have had financial problems. But tax-exempt bonds are here to stay.

Over the years, I have helped to create changes in tax-exempts. Many changes have now been adopted and are considered neither daring nor radical today. These include tax-free funds, industrial-revenue bonds and the notion of widening distribution of these bonds to individual investors.

There are still many new problems to be solved, but there are also many bright, alert young men and women around today who are solving them and keeping the tax-exempt bond industry alive.

Not every investor has to be a tax-exempt investor. However, there are many who should be, but just do not know about them. That is what this book is all about. I mean to help you decide whether you can be and should be an investor in tax-exempt bonds. And I also want to show you how.

Contents

Preface / vii

1 "I Wish I Could Buy Tax-Exempt Bonds" / 1
2 Getting to Know Them Better / 8
3 "How Can I Tell if It Is a Good Bond?" / 12
4 That Wonderful Apparatus—The Municipal Secondary Market / 20
5 The Dollar-Bond Markets / 26
6 Caveat Emptor / 31
7 The Businessman's Risk / 40
8 The Protectors / 46
9 How to Read an Ad and a Prospectus / 54
10 The Rating Game / 59
11 What About Those Moral Obligations? / 64
12 The Building of a Tax-Free Portfolio / 69
13 The Industrial-Bond Revolution / 76
14 How About Tax-Free Funds? / 85
15 Some Definite No-No's / 92
16 What About Those Defaults? / 98
17 The Anatomy of a Bond Issue / 105
18 The Mechanics of a Bond Delivery / 111
19 All About Bond Insurance, Discounts, Calls, Tenders, Etc. / 116
20 Tax-Exempt Bond Math Made Easy / 122
21 How to Become a Bond Expert by Reading the Papers / 127
22 What About the Future of Tax-Exempt Bonds? / 133

Appendices

1 Tax-Exempt Bond Volume for the Past Fifty Years / 137
2 Who Owns the Outstanding Tax-Exempt Bonds? / 138
3 The Tax-Exempt Bond Glossary / 139

4   An Offering List / 144

5   A Sample Page From the Blue List / 145

6   The Blue List Retrieval System / 146

7   The Mechanics of Getting a Bid / 147

8   The Principal Dollar Bonds in the Tax-Exempt
     Market / 148

9   A Typical Legal Opinion / 149

10   Typical New-Issue Ads / 151

11   Understanding the Official Statement / 156

12   Tax-Exempt Bond Ratings / 213

13   The Tax-Free Fund Glossary / 214

Too Good for
the Rich Alone:

The complete guide to
tax-exempt bonds
for the middle-income investor

"I Wish I Could Buy Tax=Exempt Bonds"

I can't count the number of times investors have sheepishly said to me, "I wish I could buy tax-exempt bonds."

My answer invariably is, "Why can't you?"

Their answer, just as invariably, is exactly what I expect it to be: "I'm not rich enough."

If I am on my best behavior, I will say, "I have a surprise for you. I think I can show you this is not true."

However, if I've had a tough day and am not interested in attempting even a surface politeness, I'm more apt to say, "You're crazy." And it's even more likely, since my days seem to be tougher than ever lately, that I will say something a lot stronger.

If you have a middle income, tax-exempts are something you should know about because they very probably will fit into your investment picture. I repeat, if you are of middle-income, tax-exempts are something you want *in* on.

To be very specific, if you have an adjusted gross income that puts you in the 32-percent tax bracket (which means

$20,000 for a married couple or $16,000 for a single person), tax-exempt bonds can be your cup of tea. There is a further bonus if your state has an income tax and you buy bonds issued in that state, because you benefit from tax-exemption increases. For instance, if your state tax is added to your federal tax, your bracket could be 40 percent. If you purchased an 8-percent bond of an out-of-state issuer, the equivalent yield you would have to buy in a taxable maturity would be 11.6 percent. If you purchased a bond issued in your state, the equivalent yield would have to be as much as 13.3 percent. These numbers make a great case for home-state buying.

Anyhow, if you're in the 32-percent bracket, you retain only 4.08 percent of a 6-percent yield. If you're lucky enough to get 10 percent, you keep only 6.8 percent. And keep in mind that there is practically no risk in tax-exempts. If you bought something that was yielding 5 percent with the expectation of making a capital gain of 15 percent a year, only to find six months later that the market had taken a dive and 40 percent of your principal had disappeared, you may possibly want to hear more.

More is what I'm about to give you. Banks, insurance companies, and some of the rich have long recognized tax-exempts to be a very sweet investment indeed. But it hasn't been to their interest to spread the word, and so they haven't. In fact, it would not be far from wrong to say that they prefer to keep tax-exempts a secret. Everybody talks about competition being such a great thing, but nobody wants it in his own business. (I won't insult your intelligence by attempting to explain that one.)

So if you're still with me, let's look at this wealth of information that has made you feel that tax-exempts are out of your league. We will take up the arguments one by one, and I think I can show you that they add up to one big bunch of nothing.

You probably have looked at many of the ads in the *Wall Street Journal* on tax-exempt bond issues and were convinced that no one wanted you to buy. The ads gave little or no information. There was no explanation of why the bonds were being sold, but the yields were listed. You may have called your broker, only to hear, "The bonds are not for you." For whom were they? They were for the banks and the insurance companies. If you asked for a prospectus, he said that he would try and he hoped that the bonds would not be sold before he mailed the prospectus to you.

You may also remember that whenever there was a large issue with a great deal of publicity, the bonds were often sold out within one day. By the time you called, the salesman or woman was saying that the bonds were now priced 101 even though they came out at 100. You were trying to buy the wrong bonds. Had anyone told you about the secondary market and the many varied bargains for sale there?

Your toughest job has undoubtedly always been getting past your salesperson. You say that you want to buy tax-exempt bonds and he or she wants to know why. You are of the opinion that the customer is always right. However, this genius who has led you down one dark road after another now decides you need some protection from the obscure recesses of the tax-exempt market.

The salesperson might well say, "After all, the pension funds do not buy them any more." What he or she does not tell you is that these funds are tax-exempt themselves and should not be buying tax-exempt bonds. If you were lucky enough to hold a tax-exempt certification from the government, I would also advise you to pass them by.

The real reason that this salesperson does not want you to buy the tax-exempt bonds is because he or she is sure never to see that money again. It is not polite to talk about "churning," but this is the device that wide-awake salespeople use to earn commissions over and over again on the same dollars of the client. Most salespeople look on tax-exempt purchases as very final. What better endorsement could you get?

Then you probably have heard the oldest knock there is against tax-exempt bonds—"You know that there's not much of a secondary market." I will show you in Chapter 4 how big a lie that is.

You may also have received the knowing look and the whisper about "those defaults." There is no doubt that there have been defaults, but so very few when compared to the billions of bonds outstanding. (See Chapter 16.)

There are also some people who have been scared away from tax-exempts because "they" (whoever "they" may be) are going to repeal the exemption very soon and you will lose your investment. There is not a chance that tax exemption will be repealed in the near future. It is a constitutional question. The question is not going to be decided by the IRS (although it would like to decide it). However, let us concede that the tax exemption may be removed at some future time. The removal would apply only to future bonds and not to those outstanding. This, in effect, would give you what the bond business calls a museum piece, and its value would increase as time went on because of the lack of supply.

You can also be scared off by the philosophical approach. Every time someone writes about the tax system and the possibility of tax reform, tax-exempt bonds get a pasting. The idea of tax-exempt bonds seems to bring out the crusader in these people. They have been egged on by many secretaries of the Treasury (since the time of FDR, because he hated tax-exempt bonds) and people like William McChesney Martin, the former chairman of the Federal Reserve Board, who once said that he could not go along with a system that allowed people to loll on beaches and clip their tax-exempt coupons.

Thus the crusade against tax-exempt bonds goes on. The charges against tax exemption are always vague, but they are put forth in such a way that is supposed to appeal to the less-moneyed people. You are supposed to be indignant at this further "excess" of the rich.

The politicians usually fall in line. They hurry to add amendments to various legislations. It is a good thing that there are some people in Congress who know that the principle of tax exemption is not for the rich to get richer but to insure that the local areas (your community and mine) are able to sell bonds to provide the improvements that you need without having to petition Washington for them.

These charges have tended to keep some would-be

buyers off-balance. Thus one of the best-developed myths about tax-exempt bonds is that they are special and are reserved for the banks and the rich, synonymous terms to many people.

Several years ago, an investment banker had a chance to learn if the wealthy really did have a corner on the tax-exempt market. It was at a dinner in Palm Beach, Florida, with an accumulated wealth of about $300 million among the twenty or so people there. Some had more millions than others, but they were all very wealthy. His poll showed that not one tax-exempt bond was owned by that group.

Does this mean that tax-exempt bonds are not considered a good investment by wealthy people? No, it just means that there are gimmicks in the tax laws such as oil depletion and various housing write-offs.

Tax-exempt bonds have remained a secret for too long. Sure, trust departments bought them and some individuals also found them. However, there were always many more people who never found them or who believed that they could not buy them.

Actually, the Palm Beach story shows that the person who is in the 32-percent bracket cannot compete with the wealthy in their write-off situations.

In addition to the lack of enthusiasm of the leading investment bankers, there was also a feeling in the industry that advertising was immoral. It was all right to advertise an issue without the ratings and without mentioning any of the security features of the bond. Thus, this "tombstone" advertising, basically showing off to each other in the business rather than appealing to the investing public, became the prevailing kind.

The reasoning was that the privilege of tax exemption should not be handed out. It was good to let the banks and the insurance companies get the benefits of tax exemption, but ordinary investors need not apply. Most of the bankers and the insurance-company people could not have cared less. They were all for opening up the market.

However, some of the knights in shining armor who posed as the leaders of the tax-exempt industry thought it was better to keep tax-exempts under wraps. It must be said that they did a marvelous job for many years. It was a big secret. In fact, it was so much so that most of their colleagues within their own firms did not really know what a tax-exempt bond was, or what its possibilities were.

Therefore the investors who came into tax-exempts in the early fifties would have to be called pioneers. They got very little help from the salesman who was stock-oriented and who did not see any prospect of churning the accounts of clients who bought tax-exempts.

Then some people came along and started to advertise the fact that they wanted to sell tax-exempt bonds. The industry's comments were restrained, but disapproving. Such words as "crude" and "crass" were mentioned at their luncheon tables. Nowadays, many bond people are reproducing the same type of advertisement and using the "crass come-ons" of the lure of tax-exempt income.

Despite all the obstacles placed in their way, many individual investors have found out about tax-exempt bonds. Part of the credit is due to many firms in the industry who have worked on the art of communicating with investors. The committee at the Securities Investment Association (formerly the Investment Bankers Association) has done a fair job with varying results. At times this committee was more interested in maintaining the status quo of the business or setting up rules for regulation.

Just so you do not think that there are only a few individual investors involved in tax-free bonds, I am reproducing a table (Appendix 2) that shows a breakdown on the holders of tax-exempt bonds. Notice that I have also broken down bank holdings because many of the bonds that are purchased by banks are on behalf of their trust accounts.

While the figure of 26.5 percent of all outstanding tax-exempt bonds being held by individual investors does not look small, it should be higher. The responsibility for its lack of growth belongs to the industry and even to the issuers. The officials of the local areas (whether they be governors or mayors) have sometimes shared the feeling that they were participating in a private society. Now many of them realize that with the increased volume they must do something to help in the distribution of bonds.

Yet when New York City (to take one example) runs a junket for buyers, they invite institutional buyers from all over the nation. But the basic buyer of New York City bonds over the past several years has been the individual investor, and no one even runs an informal meeting for him. I am not saying that trying to attract institutional investors to New York City bonds is bad. It is an excellent idea. What I am saying is that local areas should also try to sell themselves to their own residents who are investors as well as taxpayers.

The job of figuring out whether a yield that is tax-free is sufficient when compared to a taxable situation always bothers investors. Over the years many types of tables have been developed. One thing that has annoyed me was the fact that most of these tables relate to single taxpayers. But most tax-exempt buyers are married and therefore need a table that refers to a joint return. In fact all of these tables have bothered me because they can go out of date very quickly with changes in the tax laws.

The formula for instant figuring of equivalent yield is contained in Chapter 20. All you need to know is simple long division and it can be done.

As you will see as you read the subsequent chapters, there is nothing mysterious about tax-free bonds. They can be an excellent investment; they can be an important part of your overall portfolio. You may never buy more than $5,000 worth of bonds, but you ought to know what you are buying. You are not buying a U. S. Savings Bond. But you do help promote the type of local, noncentralist government that has made this country great.

There are many decisions to be made, but they are not difficult when you have decided what your goal is. You may find that your situation demands diversification even for the limited amount of dollars that you have to invest, and this might mean that you should be looking at the tax-exempt funds. However, the main point is that there is ample room for all kinds of investors under the very large tax-free-market umbrella. Therefore you do not have to wish that you could buy tax-exempt bonds—*you can.*

Getting
To Know
Them
Better

It is easier to deal with bonds when you understand them. Therefore, this chapter will spell out most of the definitions. I am going to give you a list of the various types of bonds plus a glossary (Appendix 3). This glossary can be important, because if you hear or read a word that throws you, just refer to the glossary. Much of the material in this chapter comes from a booklet entitled "Tax-Exempt Municipal Bond Guide," published by a long-time colleague of mine, Mr. John M. Nash, and his company, The Financial Government and Public Affairs Communicators, of Washington, D.C.

It seems as if there are hundreds of types of bonds in the tax-exempt market, but basically there are six different types of issues.

General-obligation bonds are backed by a pledge of the issuer's full faith and credit for prompt payment of principal and interest. Most city, county, and school-district bonds have the further distinction of being secured by a pledge of unlimited *ad valorem* (property) taxes to be levied against all taxable property. In most cases, if taxes are not paid the delinquent property is sold at tax sale, giving the bondholder a superior claim above mortgages, mechanics' liens, and similar encumbrances. Since general-obligation bonds are geared to tax resources, they are normally analyzed in terms of the size of the resources being taxed.

Limited and special-tax bonds are payable from a pledge of the proceeds derived by the issuer from a specific tax, such as an *ad valorem* tax levied at a fixed rate, a gasoline tax, or a special assessment. Occasionally a bond will be secured by the first $250,000 each year of a tax which annually yields $1 million, thereby giving unusual ability to withstand a weakened economy. Limited and special-tax bonds are frequently bargain-priced.

Revenue bonds are payable from the earnings of a revenue-producing enterprise such as a water, sewer, electric, or gas system; a toll bridge; airport; college dormitory; or other income-producing facility. They are usually analyzed in terms of their earnings, historical or potential, compared with bond requirements. They have built up a good record over a long period of time, and are sometimes considered to be better than the general obligations of the same issuer. The yield is generally higher for this type of bond.

There are bonds issued by authorities and agencies which can be created by a state or local government. The purpose of an authority is to fill a need that cannot be filled via general-obligation financing. Thus when a bridge, tunnel, or toll road is needed, an authority is usually formed. Authorities have been used to build water and sewer systems, electric power plants, gas systems, hospitals, baseball parks. In most cases the idea is to have a self-liquidating project, thus relieving the taxpayers of liability. Some authority issues need subsidies from the state or local unit. This type of authority is usually set up to avoid inflating the debt of the issuer. It should be noted that authorities are the most criticized of all issuers.

The reason for this is the autonomy that some of these authorities have. In some cases there is little control by the local body that created the authority in the first place of what is built or how a project is run. Authorities have their value. The problem occurs when the authority will not recognize its true place.

Lease-secured bonds are backed by a pledge of a fixed dollar amount by a party other than the issuer to make payments to the issuer over the life of the bonds to cover the principal and interest requirements on the tax-exempt bonds. Normally the payment is made pursuant to a lease-and-trust agreement.

These bonds are the types that we use when we set an industrial-bond issue. It is also a way that some public bodies have of using the "lease-back" theory to build city halls, libraries, etc., and to pay back by the lease-payment method.

"Double-barrelled" is a term applied to tax-exempt bonds which are backed by a pledge of two or more sources of payment. For example, many special-assessment or special-tax bonds are additionally backed by the full faith, credit, and taxing power of the issuer. Similarly, one occasionally finds a bond secured by the joint pledges of several parties, any one of which would give adequate protection.

You do not find too many double-barrelled situations around today, but if you come across one, take a good look at it—it might be a very rewarding situation.

Over the years I have seen municipal-bond issues for convention centers, marinas, baseball stadiums, roller skating rinks, swimming pools, golf courses, campsites, motels, factories, bus terminals, wheat silos, ski lifts, CATV networks, airplane hangars, airport terminals, sugar mills. . . . I could go on and on.

I have no idea of what new types of issues will be introduced, but whenever a community needs something it will ask, "Can we float a bond issue?" Sometimes they can, and sometimes they cannot, usually depending on the state's laws.

I do not intend to get into any deep discussion of what is a proper and what is an improper use of tax exemption. However, this might be a good place for a short discussion of the basic test for any tax-exempt bond. It is contained in the two words "public purpose."

I know that some of the issues described above might

make you think that they did not qualify. Well, just hold on. How about that roller skating rink? Actually, it was built for all of the people in a town and is nonprofit; thus it has a public purpose. Golf links are the same, so long as they are public and open to all. The CATV situation was for a college in Indiana, in a town shut off from decent TV reception because of the terrain. Public purpose means that the project must do something for the community, such as adding jobs, increasing the area's net worth, furnishing enjoyment to the local citizens, or, of course, providing services as an airport or a bus terminal does.

I have never been a believer in stadiums, because most of these structures are built to accommodate the local entry in a professional football or baseball league. It is usually a matter of subsidization, but even the boosting of a team is thought to be public purpose in some areas. In fact the Congress thought so too, and specifically named stadiums as being exempt from any restrictions they put upon industrial-revenue (lease-back) bonds. But I have accepted the fact that we have had our stadiums for many hundreds of years, and today's politicians continue to subscribe to the theory that the populace can be satisfied with stadiums (whether for baseball or for men fighting lions).

I must confess that I have always been obsessed by issues that meet a vital community need. However, I must also confess that some of the lesser-rated priorities (at least in my judgment) could be called better risks. I point this out because an investor should be an investor and not be carrying a banner. Let your causes be separate from your investments. The best thing about tax-exempt bonds is that there will hardly ever be a project that will not outrage the most devoted believer in causes.

I also think that it is good objective thinking to accept the bond attorney's opinion as to whether a bond is tax-exempt or not. As long as you have that opinion, you are safe. What I am getting at is that there is no reason for you to make a concentrated effort to find out if the tax exemption is really there or not.

3

"How Can I Tell if It Is a Good Bond?"

Investors usually need a course in the art of buying tax-exempts. It is no different than finding out about art or music. You need some instruction. Now you may be a great art collector and a wonderful judge of property. In fact, you may be (or may have been) the craftiest of stock buyers, but what do you know about buying tax-exempt bonds?

The basic problem is that there are so many of them. Not only are there many issues, but each issue can have up to forty or more different maturities. This is why so many people shy away from the tax-exempts. The problem starts with the salesperson who handles your securities. He or she sometimes does not understand the subject, and this is a sure sign that you will never get to understand it either unless you are very persistent.

You start with the idea of earning tax-exempt dollars consistent with quality. This seems to be inconsistent to some people who insist on knowing what you really want —yield or quality. The disbelievers are usually bond salesmen or women. Unfortunately, not many bond salespeople know very much about bonds. This is especially true in the houses that do not specialize in bonds, but it is also true of many bond houses.

I have always resented lazy bond salespeople because they are dangerous. The crooked bond seller can be weeded out, but the lazy one hides under the guise of being prudent. Unfortunately, these people seem to be in the majority.

These are people who think that the selling of an AAA bond to an investor when excellent bonds are available in lower ratings constitutes doing a good job.

What happens is that an investor requests a good bond. There are many good bonds available in the A and even Baa (BBB) ratings. These are credits which have never had a problem as far as a default is concerned. However, the lazy salesperson retreats to the AAA bond and the investor can lose as many as fifty basic points in yield.

To put it more strongly, the investor may get a 6.5-percent instead of a 7-percent yield. On a $10,000 investment you would lose $50 tax-exempt income each year. Who needs that?

The only time that a lazy salesperson helps you is when the prices of bonds are low. That is when you should be buying high-grades.

This is not inconsistency. This is being adaptable, and this is one talent that a tax-exempt investor needs. You need not possess any degree in economics to have this talent, but there are a few strings attached. You must know what is going on in the financial world. A brief glance at the *Wall Street Journal*'s bond column would help. Each Monday they run an index—a simple averaging of yields—which gives you the relative position of the market. If that index is over 6 percent, then you know that the market is at a low point and you should be looking at high-grade bonds. If it is below 5 percent, then you know that it is at a high point and you should be looking for the best value that also has yield.

Many people have a problem because some uninformed salesman or woman somewhere along the line convinced them that only general-obligation bonds are any good. There is a lot to be said for the notion of the full faith and credit of a community, but you first have to ascertain that the community is credit-worthy. You might find that a revenue bond is just as good or better, and you will be earning more yield (*i.e.,* tax-exempt dollars).

Many investors assume that their investment goals are similar to those of insurance companies and banks. There is only one point on which your aims are the same as an institution's: in the hope that the investment works out. However, there are very few other goals that can be matched. For instance, banks usually have to make short-term investments, but you do not unless it makes you comfortable. Insurance companies usually need AA bonds or better. You do not need them unless they are so cheap that you cannot pass them up.

No, their investment goals are different from your own. However, you can join them in their search for quality. There are some excellent A-rated situations and many Baa (BBB) bonds that have never had a default. Check that out. It is always a good item to check, and the information can be obtained in minutes. For instance, the cities are never given high ratings, but I believe that some of our city bonds will do just as well over the years as those of our suburban communities, which will ultimately be subject to the same problems as our cities.

What about unrated bonds? An unrated bond does not necessarily mean that the security of that bond is not good. In some cases the bonds have not been presented for a rating or the rating agency has some rule that prohibits it from rating this type of bond.

Look at unrated bonds very carefully. Read the official statement. If you do not feel competent to make a judgment, call your attorney and/or your accountant.

What I am trying to say throughout this chapter is that you should feel comfortable. That may not sound like good security advice, but it is good advice for believing that you have done the right thing. Feeling comfortable might mean that you pass up some higher yield and fall back on a lower one where you understand the situation.

For many years I have been advocating the four *W*'s when buying tax-exempt bonds. This is about as basic as a non-professional can get. I also add two *H*'s so that the formula becomes $4W + 2H$. Here they are and here is how you should use them in your appraisal as to whether to buy a bond:

Who—This could be the most difficult of the *W*'s because it makes you ask yourself which bond you should buy. If you have ever seen a Blue List (a publication printed each market day that lists most offerings being made by dealers and dealer banks—not available, however, to individual investors), you would know that an average issue has about 144 pages and carries a total of $650 million worth of bonds. The question of *who* could also be turned around to ask yourself if you should be buying tax-exempt bonds. If you are in the 30-percent bracket and you can find an attractive yield, *they are for you.*

What—Should you buy a general-obligation bond or a revenue issue? We find that most people have made up their minds that they will stay in the general-obligation area because they know they have the credit of the issuing government behind the bond. Some are dubious about revenue situations because they see that the most prominently defaulted issues are the revenue bonds. We say that you *should not* close your mind to revenues. However, if you feel more comfortable (a recurring word in this book), then you should stay with the general-obligations. It should, however, be noted that some of the finest tax-exempt bonds outstanding are revenue situations. In fact, there are some cities whose revenue bonds are rated higher than the general-obligation bonds of the city.

When—This looks like an easy one to answer, but if you were to make a poll of other investors, you would find that the problem of maturity bothers them most. They are confused—and you may be too—as to what constitutes a short-term or a long-term investment. *The one thing that the maturity of a bond should not be confused with is what you believe your life expectancy to be.* Life expectancy has *nothing* to do with an investment. There isn't much anyone can do if you feel that a five-year investment is long term. I do not consider anything under twenty years as a long-term investment. In fact, you will also hear opinions that a thirty-year maturity is a long one and that twenty years is an intermediate one. The most important thing to remember is that *very few bond investments are held to maturity by an individual.* You may buy a twenty-year bond today and sell it in five to ten years because you can make a profitable switch or even a long-term profit. In the matter of maturity, you will have to first settle your investment priorities. If you are in the tax-exempt market until the equity market gets well again, then you should be in dollar bonds, where you have a quick marketability. If your ideas of maturity tend to make five years a long-term situation, leave your money where it is. Just remember that after you have picked the rating and the bond you want, the amount of yield to be earned will depend on how long you initially cared to risk your money. Remember, however, that you must pay capital-gains tax on bonds sold prior to maturity when those bonds are sold at a price greater than the one you paid.

Where—The location of your bond is important, especially if your state has an income tax. It means that if you buy bonds in your state, you will be preserving all of your yield. Otherwise you could be paying state taxes on your out-of-state bonds. The importance of location might also make you more comfortable if you are familiar with the city or area where the bonds are issued. I think about my uncle, who became interested in tax-exempt bonds, but only for those projects he knew about or could see. As he never left New York, he bought only New York State, New York City, Triborough Bridge, and Port Authority bonds. He could go to the various projects and see them in action. He could follow the gyrations of the various politicians. He certainly impressed upon me the value of knowing intimately all about the bonds you buy.

The addition of the two *H*'s is also important to the formula. They are *How* are the bonds backed? and *How many?* The first *H* is the most important, because it gives you the reason for buying. No matter how much yield you receive, it means nothing if the security of the bond is not sufficient. General-obligation bonds are easy. The bonds are backed by the good faith and credit of the community, city, or state involved. When you consider revenue bonds, you are looking at a more difficult subject. There are many ways that a revenue bond can secure its revenues, and you must know what makes revenue flow to the bonds of your project.

Understanding credit (*i.e.*, security) means understanding an official statement (prospectus), explained in Chapter 9. You may find that this subject is beyond you. Do not feel inadequate or stupid. Rather, get the advice that you need.

That second *H—How many*—is something that only you know about. However, there is always the matter of "putting all your eggs in one basket." Do not be like the man who put no more than $5,000 in any one name. This would have been enough for a small investor, but this was a wealthy individual who was investing a total of almost $500,000. He should have been investing in lots of about $50,000, because there is some value in large blocks.

There is nothing that bothers a small investor more than the fact that his or her $5,000 investment does not mean as much as a $50,000 investment or larger. However, as good as tax-exempt bonds are, we have to face the fact that the volume buyer runs the market. Large bond issues are controlled by the big buyers. However, this should not bother a small investor. There may be a problem when you sell your bonds. The seller of $50,000 bonds might do a point or two better than the seller of $5,000.

This irritates the small investor, but the irritation is not worth it when you consider the benefits of tax exemption overall. As time goes on, more individual investors will buy bonds and the small blocks will be worth more in the secondary market.

The art of buying bonds demands some study. The most important thing demanded is the no more than ten minutes of your time required each day to read the bond column in the *Wall Street Journal* and any other information that you can find on bonds. I must warn you that some of the people who answer the questions in the Q & A columns are liable to be vague, if not actually misleading. However, there is no substitute for reading, and most of this reading can be enjoyable. I write a weekly column in the *OTC Market Chronicle*, and there are many other bond people who are also writing.

Many firms also put out interesting bond letters. As you learn more, you can advance to the bank letters and those published for the pros. Referring to the glossary will make you knowledgeable enough to understand all the special terms they use.

The way to invest your funds is via an offering sheet or list. It is just a listing of a company's inventory of bonds (I am reproducing an offering list of Lebenthal & Co. of New York City as Appendix 4, which gives you all the information you will need about the bonds being offered for sale except that information which must be found in an official statement [prospectus] or other documents). Always ask for the offering list. Do not take suggestions over the phone.

However, after the purchase your diligence should not end. It is not enough that some "expert" has advised you to buy the bonds. It is also his or her duty to supply you with progress reports. If you do not receive them then write to the issuer and identify yourself as a bondholder. If you do not get satisfaction, write to the trustee bank. All of this information is in the official statement. This procedure should be followed on all revenue bond purchases.

When you buy general-obligation bonds, your best way of checking them is to ascertain whether the town or city has retained its bond ratings. This is something that you should check out with the salesperson. Actually, they should give you any information that might affect the rating so that you can decide whether to retain the bonds or not.

One problem that new investors have when considering the purchase of tax-exempt bonds is that they often let a salesperson fit the dollars they have to a bond. For instance, the new investor may have $12,000. The salesperson sees a bond that sells for 80, and sells the investor $15,000. (A bond with a face value of $15,000, selling at 80 points on 100, sells for $12,000.) However, the coupon may be low, and the investor may only get a 6-percent yield when the level should have been 7-percent. Buy only yield. Matching dollars can cause you to lose money.

Chapter 21, on how to become an expert in the money market, is not written facetiously. It is easy to become knowledgeable, and, when you consider how poorly some of the economists have done over the past several years, you may prefer to become your own expert. This does not mean that you should forego the advice of others, especially of those with competence in these areas.

This also doesn't mean that I am ruling out all salespeople as advice-givers. There are many experienced people in the field who do an excellent job for their clients. What I am saying is that you should gain some independence so that you can stand on your own and make some of your own investing decisions.

---

4

*That Wonderful
Apparatus—
The Municipal
Secondary Market*

The most often repeated wheeze about tax-exempt bonds is that there is no market for your bonds when you want to sell. Those of us who have been carrying the torch all these years call it the big lie. However, we all must admit that the story gets better circulation than the one I am trying to tell in this book.

I would say that the big lie got its credence in the days when the stock market was booming and when no self-respecting salesman would put his client in bonds when there was money to be made in stocks, to say nothing of the commissions the salesman earned.

In August of 1974 the president of Morgan, Stanley & Co. implied that there was no market for tax-exempt bonds. That indicates how much we still have to do. Why, when over $324 million long-term bonds had been sold, did he make such a statement? It was a typical corporate bond man's attitude, combined with resentment that this end of the business had grown so when formerly it was restricted to the back rooms of investment banking houses.

(Years ago, I used to emcee some of the bachelor dinners

on Wall Street, and, as part of a routine, I would dream up congratulatory telegrams for the honored guest. One sure-fire "message" was, "Dear Future Son-in-Law. Glad to hear that you are really a bookie and not a municipal bond man as rumored. Now I feel my daughter's future is secure.")

Many of us in the business may have become self-conscious. But we have identified ourselves too long as municipal bond men only to get a knowing smile and wink as people said, "Too bad you guys can't sell bonds when a customer wants to sell." Actually the secondary market for tax-exempt bonds is the best-organized and best-disciplined market we have.

The truth is that you can always get a bid in the tax-exempt secondary market. There is one problem that has to be recognized: the problem of time. The bids are not instant, especially in the case of bonds that are not well-known, but there are bids. Can every market make this claim?

What is the secondary market? It is a combination of things. It is the group of traders who sit at desks of dealers and dealer banks all over the country. It is a group of brokers who work with the above traders only and never do business with any institutional or individual investors. It is the Blue List, which is a listing of the bonds available in the market. It is the Munifacts machines around the country (operated by the *Daily Bond Buyer* organization, the industry trade paper), that also helps the secondary market by listing offerings.

Indeed, it is a vast network of people with many different outlooks, thus making it a wide area of interests. It is no different from any other market. It is an auction market where the seller has to find a bid. In this market, the seller has the choice of going direct (via his broker, of course) to a regional dealer or specialist in a particular bond using a broker who will funnel back the highest bid of many. The seller also has the option of asking a dealer to place his or her bonds in the Blue List, where some prospective buyer might see them. In the latter case, the seller is usually putting a price on the bonds rather than looking for a bid. The point is that the tax-exempt market has many sides.

The real picture makes you wonder who first thought up the big lie.

Here is the best proof I know of how well the secondary market works. It was the crunch of 1966, in the month of August. (A crunch is when the financial system loses its liquidity.) This was very rough on bids, and the various other markets, such as the corporate and U. S. treasuries were having a tough time getting bids. I wanted to know what, if anything, was happening in the tax-exempt market. I called Jack Kenny, the founder of J. J. Kenny & Co. Jack is the dean of the brokers. On that hot, forlorn August day, he looked at his pads and told me that his firm (and this did not include any other municipal broker) had traded $5 million in bonds. Actually that was a drop in the bucket, and Jack was not happy, but blocks of corporate and treasury bonds were not moving on the worst day the market had seen in many years. I will not pretend that the prices were great, but bonds were moving, and that is sometimes more important than the price.

The market works because of men like Jack Kenny who perform the brokerage duties for the municipal-bond business and are known only to people in the business. They do no business with you or with any other investor, individual or institutional. They are restricted by an unwritten code (to which all adhere) to do business with dealers and dealer banks only. Their charge is usually $1.25 per $1,000 bond. They can get more on certain odd-lot and other situations. What they do for this nominal charge is really something.

The Blue List is an operation that is now owned by Standard & Poor's. However, many years ago it was started by an enterprising young bond man named Roald (Rollie to the industry) Morton, with the help of another man who is still active on the dealer side of the market, Bill MacKay.

What they did was to set up a municipals version of the Pink Sheets (The National Daily Quotation Service) where dealers could advertise bonds for sale. The Blue List, however, has become more than that. After Rollie Morton's retirement, the present president of Standard & Poor's, Brenton Harries, developed some new systems that have made the Blue List more than just a sales sheet. The most important of these systems has been the one called the Blue List Retrieval system. This allows a bond house to ascertain what is available in any Blue List by various categories. The subscriber (the Blue List is only available to dealers and dealer banks) can find out, for instance, the AA bonds in $50,000 (or $10,000 or $5,000 for that matter) lots due in a certain maturity. This information is flashed to the subscriber in a matter of seconds.

The Blue List is more than a place where your bonds may be placed by your dealer or dealer bank (if you want to sell). It is also a source of record. We all watch the Blue List volume. When the market is heavy, the Blue List is thick, and has, at times, been the largest list of liars assembled under one cover. This is when the market gets rough, and the dealers do not know at what price they should list their bonds.

Therefore the Blue List becomes an important factor in the day-to-day market. The totals that are shown in the Blue List are the factors that determine the state of the market. I have reproduced a page of Blue List offerings in Appendix 5. Appendix 6 shows the Blue List Retrieval system and how it works.

One of the sad things about these great assets in the tax-exempt market is that you, the investor, cannot deal directly with either municipal bond brokers or the Blue List. As I wrote earlier, the municipal broker only does business with dealers and dealer banks, and the Blue List can be subscribed to only by the same group. However, the fact that you know about them and what they do for you in the marketing of your bonds can be a solace.

In addition to the Blue List and the broker, we cannot forget the regional bond dealer who makes bids for the bonds in his area. Most of these dealers are connected to the large markets by teletype systems and are also on the various brokerage teletype systems.

Back to the brokers. They are fascinating people. They are the product of an evolution that began over fifty years ago, and they have grown in stature as well as in business. The first brokers were almost itinerant peddlers. They went from office to office seeking to broker bonds. Then

they found that they needed telephone trunk lines to protect their clients, the municipal bond dealers. They were on
their way.

It was in those formative years that they developed the
relationship which has become more sophisticated, but yet
remains basically the same as the ones that were established
in the twenties. It is a relationship of trust. The dealer bares
his soul to this man called the broker, and the broker works
to find him a buyer for his bonds. No client has ever received as confidential a hearing or a better execution. The
basic thing to remember is that while the transaction is on
behalf of a dealer, it might be your bonds that are for sale.
This is why the bond broker is important in this narrative.
He is someone with whom you have no contact, but on
whom you must depend if you are selling bonds. In fact, if I
had bonds to sell, I would demand that the bonds be given
to a broker.

I do not want to give the impression that J. J. Kenny & Co.
is the only broker. There are others, including Drake &
Company, Inc., Chapdelaine & Co., Inc., and Harry Downs
& Co., Inc. However, I think that Jack Kenny deserves a lot
of credit for harnessing computers to his end of the business without really letting the computers run the show.
Appendix 7 will give an idea of how a transaction evolves in
the Kenny office once a bid has been requested. This appendix gives you a complete rundown, from start to finish,
on one particular trade. You will see how many bids were
made for the bonds, etc. This should give you the feeling
that yes, there is a secondary market where you can sell your
bonds when you choose.

It seems to me that once you have established that there
is a secondary market that is operative even when the
government and corporate markets fall away under the
pressures of a crunch or some other crisis, then you have
established that it is safe to buy bonds.

The secondary market has one other important advantage for the individual investor. This is the fact that the
investor who buys bonds in the secondary market is usually
better off dollarwise than the investor who buys in the
primary market.

It is no secret that most of the bidding on the primary issues in the tax-exempt market is fiercely competitive because of the competitive-bidding regulations that prevail in most issues. One aspect of these bids does not lend itself to the best interests of small bidders: The bidding revolves around the ideas of the banks, who are interested in the earlier maturities, and the insurance companies, who are interested in the longer maturities. There is rarely any thought given to what the individual investor is thinking about. To be utterly frank, it does not matter at this point (except if it is an issue that has a low rating and is pointed toward the individual market) what you and other individual investors think. To win the issue, the bidders must have a feel for what the institutional buyers think.

This is why I have always advocated that individual investors concentrate on the secondary market rather than the primary one. This gives you a chance to look at the whole market and an opportunity to be selective both as to bonds and as to price. Do not forget that the secondary market is not under any price restrictions. This is very important, as it means you have the entire list of outstanding bonds to choose from.

We are then back to the question, "How do you operate in this market?" It seems to me that the investor has several ways to go. You can get a list of offerings from your salesperson. You can direct your bank or broker to find a bond within certain specifications (rating, maturity, location, purpose, and, of course, amount). Using this system, and following the ideas that I have prescribed elsewhere in this book, you should be able to find the bonds that will fit your portfolio and your income needs.

5

The
Dollar=Bond
Markets

Although I always decry those who make a mystery of
tax-exempt bonds, I nevertheless see dollar bonds as a sort
of a mystery that I have been trying to unravel for many
years. Why do people buy them when there are better buys
yieldwise? Let us define what a dollar bond is.

A dollar bond is born when an issue has a "balloon"
maturity of about twenty to forty years (or maybe more).
Serial bonds with limited amounts cannot become dollar
bonds. After a new issue (usually a revenue issue) is sold and
delivered, the term bonds (or the balloon maturity) become
dollar bonds; the trading is then conducted in dollars.
There are firms and brokers who specialize in this market.

Trading in dollars makes it easy to list the issues in newspapers such as the *Wall Street Journal, The New York Times*
and many other dailies around the nation. I will discuss
some reservations on this dollar trading later in the chapter.

The one thing that sets the dollar markets high in the
estimate of many investors is the fact that many of these
issues are listed in the papers mentioned above. There is a

26

great feeling in being able to find the quote each day on the bonds you own.

The investors in this market are a breed unto themselves. What really made the dollar-bond market was the need of many investors to find shelter when they were temporarily out of the stock market. They therefore found the shelter and earned tax-exempt dollars while being sheltered.

Dollar-bond traders are also a separate breed. They have the instincts of a stock trader in that they trade supply and demand without any real interest in the background of the issue. Of course they are cognizant of reports of slackening revenues, but basically they trade the supply and demand.

Twenty-five years ago there was only one dollar bond: the New York City 3 percent bonds due in 1980 (known as the 3's of '80). The traders of that day would gauge the market based on what the 3's of '80 were doing at that particular time. Today, this issue is just another New York City bond drifting toward maturity.

The world of dollar bonds changed in the early fifties, when the turnpikes (or toll roads) became a leading preoccupation of the tax-exempt market. The issues had to be term maturities to justify pay-outs, and thus a new market was born. It was soon discovered by the people who habituated the stock market. They found that they preferred investing in this part of the tax-exempt market rather than getting a low return in banks or letting the money lie idle in checking accounts when the stock market was in the doldrums. They also preferred trading to be in dollars rather than in yield to maturity. These people were not interested in the yield twenty-five or thirty years hence. They were interested in current return, and the use of dollars rather than yield was convenient.

Over the years, the dollar-bond market has given the tax-exempts much direction. It has indicated what the shelter investors were doing at a particular time. It has also been a barometer of what has been happening to the various toll projects revenuewise. This was shown in early 1974, when we were beset with the energy crisis. It was also apparent when the legislatures of New York and New Jersey passed enactments that would allow the Port Authority of those two states to spend money on mass transit. Whipped up by Wall Street opposition, the investors became unhappy and many of them dumped their bonds.

They accepted the thoughts of the Wall Street people that the passage of this legislation violates their rights as bondholders. This shows that bondholders in this type of market are very sensitive to the "doomsday" type of speech or article. It also proves that bondholders separate their do-gooding from their investing.

Actually, when the toll-road bonds were initially traded, there were some rough days. The roads opened, but did not immediately do as well as the feasibility engineers said they would, and some of the more conservative investors got out. However, in the course of the changeover, the equity investors noticed that this was probably the fastest municipal market available for the quick selling that they were used to in the equity markets.

Then, too, newspapers such as *The New York Times,* the *Wall Street Journal,* and many others across the country began to carry quotes on these bonds, which meant that these were the only bonds in the tax-exempt market where you could follow the daily progress of your investments. Other issues are not reported this way for obvious reasons—the vast number of issues plus the maturities within them.

In Appendix 8, I list the most prominent issues that are traded in the dollar-bond market. Although dollar bonds originated as toll-road bonds, you will see that the list includes public utility bonds and even some bonds that have the backing (or moral backing) of a city or state. The majority, however, are still roads or bridges depending on toll revenues.

The defaulted situations are not on this list. Nevertheless, many of these issues are actively traded. They are traded *flat,* which means that you do not have to pay any interest when you buy, and you cash in the coupons (with interest on the late interest) when they have enough funds to pay out the coupon.

Some of the most famous defaults are in this market.

Some examples (in chronological order) are the West Virginia Turnpike, the Chicago Calumet Skyway, and the Chesapeake Bay Bridge and Tunnel. What makes their inclusion in this market valid is that they are in the process of working out their problems.

It is interesting to speculate on the future of dollar bonds, assuming the equity markets were to continue in the doldrums. It seems that many new investors have come into the market drawn by the allure of the quick sale when needed. It is also possible that the shelter people are still there waiting for the equity markets to reverse their trend.

I have always considered the dollar-bond market to be more emotional than the rest of the tax-exempt market. I assume that this is because of the emotionalism that is rampant in the equity markets. Another thing that always bothered the purists of the tax-exempt market was the fact that the dollar-bond market did not always go along with the rest of the market. It could be flying high when the tax-exempt market was sinking, and vice versa.

Many (myself included) have been shocked at the lack of interest in yield by some of these investors. Therefore we wonder whether these bonds will have to qualify more in the yield area, or if their ready marketability will make up for the differential that has always existed and still does. If this is indeed a new ball game, and the switching aspect from equity to bonds and back will not be a factor any more, then the concept will have to be rethought.

It would certainly make sense for this market if dollar bonds were placed in proper perspective. The bearish thing about it is that it would probably be bad news for the equity markets, and that is not good. As far as the tax-exempt market is concerned, however, it would bring the bonds in the dollar markets into line with the remainder of the market. I am also saying, I fear, that it could mean adjustments in prices from present values. A look at this market shows that money-market factors have not been as weighty as the energy crisis or bad news from a project.

Switching over to the positive side, a rebirth of equity-market confidence could mean a rebirth of the dollar market as the former machinery becomes operative again.

Coupled with those who enjoy ready marketability and like to read daily quotes, this could mean that the dollar market will return to being its independent self.

Aside from buying these bonds when they were originally offered, I have never considered the dollar markets as bona fide investments. Rather, I have thought of them as temporary investments to be used as a bail-out. It would take a realistic policy in pricing to change my mind. This, of course, would depend on whether enough new investors (less the equity-market shelter people) have entered the market. It could also be that some of the shelter people have become permanent investors in this market.

While anything connected with the money market has to involve questions, we may be finding that the dollar-bond market is going to have to deal with the same problems they have ducked over the past years because of the peculiar status of the market. The questions as I see them are, will there be an adjustment in yields? and would this mean a price problem for the present holders of these bonds?

6

Caveat Emptor

There is one misleading idea that many people have about tax-exempt bonds: You cannot be cheated because the bonds are being sold on behalf of local governments. This is naïve. You must take the same precautionary measures that you would apply in buying any other security. Let me make it plainer—you have to know with whom you are dealing. If you do not want to do this, forget about buying bonds. You will be taken just as easily as the people who have been sold the Brooklyn Bridge.

Some people think that the fact that these bonds are issued by governmental units makes them immune from fakery. The truth is that this is no protection, especially when the bonds are of the revenue variety. This is not a knock against revenue bonds. It is a warning to investors to know what they are buying.

There has been some fraud over the many years of municipal-bond history. There have been relatively few frauds when compared to other areas of the security business; however, this is no balm because tax-exempt bonds are not thought to be subject to fraud. The sad truth, however, is that we have many thieves preying on investors.

One of the reasons could be that there is no regulation to speak of in the tax-exempt bond business. The basic theory of tax-exempt bonds is that the bonds are issued by local

31

areas without regulation from the federal level. This should
not, however, stop an investor from checking out what he
or she buys and from whom they are buying.

Let us face one fact. Investors almost surely get into
trouble when they are greedy. This has been demonstrated
time and again. The most recent cases involved the tax-
shelter oil deal, or Oklahoma and a Mexican bank certificate of deposit. Many prominent people who had access to
good advice were caught in these webs, and it makes one
wonder how the small investor can avoid the pitfalls. One
can write and talk about this angle until one is blue in the
face, only to find that someone has jumped the fence and
done exactly what one warned against. After a while, one
just chalks it up to human nature.

As the saying goes, "Figures do not lie, but liars figure,"
and this is true in the tax-exempt business as well. There are
too many so-called bond houses (but really boiler shops)
around the country that are waiting to fleece would-be
tax-exempt bond purchasers. I do not say that you have to
deal with New York Stock Exchange firms, but I do say that
you had better have a good idea of with whom you are
dealing. There is no doubt that when there is a serious
fraud, it usually involves small investors.

I was very much surprised years ago when I found that a
prominent law firm in Chicago whose influence spreads all
over the nation had approved an issue that was nonexistent.
To compound this, the bonds were sold to an insurance
company. Thus there were two very sophisticated entities
being deceived. The fact that a law firm that has been
approving tax-exempt bonds for many years could be so
deceived may seem incredible to you until you have looked
at the system.

I can create an issue of bonds in a nonexistent town, but
in an existing state and county. I can take the details of that
issue to a bond attorney who has been involved in that
particular area. I can tell him that the bonds are already
sold to the XYZ Insurance Company (which, indeed, they
were). Bond counsel will then look at the laws of the state
and the county to see if I followed every rule. This is the
easiest part of the swindle. There are no mistakes on my

part—I concoct a perfect issue except for one thing: It really does not exist.

A strange thing that I have uncovered in my research is that frauds involving nonexistent towns, etc., have never been sold to individual investors. They have usually been sold to institutional investors such as banks and insurance companies. The record shows that many prominent institutions have been caught, and this is not reassuring. The frauds on individuals are usually perpetrated with real issues. However, most of these real issues have very glaring potholes to begin with.

An easy mark for fraud is the industrial-revenue bond. One example is a group of issues that emanated from an industrial district called the Northwest Industrial District of Oklahoma. It was built on the remains of an old Air Force base in northwestern Oklahoma. The people in the area thought that all of their problems would be solved if they attracted industry to the area.

As any industrial recruiter knows, there are all kinds of industries and many kinds of people in these companies. Some of them make a career of going from place to place and failing. It may seem surprising that such companies cannot be detected, but then you forget the zeal of the average community, especially when faced with a great unemployment problem or a situation that spells decay.

Strange as it may seem, although this particular industrial district in Oklahoma had officers of banks as its officers, it found some of the companies that I have described. In fact, even more curiously, *all* of the companies they found or that found them were of that ilk.

Now the basic thing that a company seeking finance through industrial-revenue bonds must have is some history and a net worth. I maintain that it should have at least as much net worth as the amount of bonds it has issued. Thus if a company is issuing $1 million in bonds it should have a minimum of $1 million in net worth.

The problem in this industrial district in Oklahoma was that the companies involved were new, and they had no net worth. In checking out the situation, this writer found that the authority members were outstanding people in the community. (A local bank president was the head.) It did not seem wrong to them that the bonds were sold at seventy cents on the dollar. They thought that this represented the risk factor involved since the companies were "start-ups."

What they did not know was that the underwriter (who has not been seen since) sold the bonds through other dealers and the bonds were sold at 100 to individual investors all over the country. In other words 30 points, or $300 per $1,000 bond, was split up by all these middlemen before the investor received the bonds.

Now the story becomes involved. The bond underwriters in question were not known to the usual bond community. However, they were known to a bank in the South that financed the operations and took a major share of the profit. This is reminiscent of respectable businesses backing up Mafia-type operations. This southern bank was not linked to anything in the deal except for providing the cash to transact the deal. If you were to look for any direct evidence that this bank was involved, you would not find it. However, the author of this book has interviewed people who sold the bonds, and has ascertained a connection.

The story has a lot of ramifications. Bondholders found that they were holding worthless paper, and they looked around and found no one to blame. The only people who could be "blamed" (the quotation marks around the word *blamed* are there because the bond counsel traditionally only passes on the legality of an issue) by the bondholders were the attorneys who gave a legal opinion. The reason they were sued is simple: They were the only ones who could be "blamed" or found.

I come back to my original thesis that investors must take some precautionary measures. They cannot expect to be protected by the law when these bond situations are so vague. They must come to realize that their own greed has to be the largest factor involved.

Greed is also a factor when investors get taken in by shoddy bond dealers. The factor of greed is always present, and the crooked bond dealer is aware that most investors will take a higher rate of interest and not ask any questions. Thus they know that they can come to an investor with a very weak security and sell it on the basis of yield. Now yield is good consideration, but it does not overshadow security. Security is the basic criterion. If you do not have security, then you have nothing. All the yield in the world will do you no good if that bond does not pay out, and the only way it can pay out is if the bond has security.

Most of the crooked people in the bond business are individuals. It is rare that a firm begins with the idea of selling bad bonds. The trouble starts when a firm gets overambitious (when it is small and undercapitalized) and hires hot-shot salesmen.

Part of the problem deals with inexperience. Some of the people in the bond business in the high pressure bond houses became used to the idea of selling bonds to their customers almost on a carte-blanche basis. The average level of experience for some of these bond people was less than two years, which does not seem consistent with the $50,000 or more in commissions that they were earning.

People who bought these bonds violated rules that are basically very simple. You can only conclude that they were driven by greed. They saw a rate of interest higher than is normally obtainable, and they grabbed it without looking at anything. My investigations show that some investors did not see a prospectus or any other information about the companies involved in the bad issues.

When an investor acts like this, you could very well think that he is entitled to anything that might happen to him. This is true. However, we should not condemn him because of his foolishness. The big problem is that tax-exempt bonds gained a bad reputation. The people who lost their money will be down on tax-exempts for a long time to come. They will not take into consideration their own ineptitude. They will act like poor investors and will put themselves in the "widow-and-orphan" class. *My aim is to make sure that something like this does NOT happen to you.* What should you be looking for?

1 • Know the bond dealer. Check him out through your bank or through a regulatory body such as the NASD (National Association of Security Dealers)—there should be an office near you.

2 ● If it is an industrial-revenue issue, find out what the security is and check out the net worth of the company or find out if the company has put up any additional security.

3 ● Find out the exact costs of the issue, and find out what the bond dealer has paid for the bonds. Anything over 10 percent (which is also too high) should be rejected. In some issues, however, the 10 percent covers all legal expenses, etc.

4 ● Check out the trustee bank and find out what safeguards it has set up and whether it has checked out the company and its principals.

You cannot have any inhibitions when you are buying bonds. Do not be afraid to ask the necessary questions. Do not be fearful of hurting a salesperson's feelings—although I do not advocate being boorish. However, I do not think that you should choke up and hold back if the question is legitimate and helps you understand the issue better.

This also applies to finding out about the company and the salesperson who are trying to sell you the bonds. These people are paid very well (no one is trying to cut their commissions) and they should be willing to supply you with any reasonable information.

There is no doubt that many firms and salespeople resent what they consider prying questions. If they do, you should find another company willing to tell you what you want to know—whether it is about the bonds being offered or about themselves. I think you will find that you will have no problems and you will never be caught in the misrepresentation net.

The feeling of being overwhelmed is the biggest problem that most investors have. Add to this the human weakness of hating to admit that we do not know something about a particular subject. You can also add the naïve belief many people have that no bad tax-exempt bonds can be issued, and the idea that all issuers protect themselves from bad issues, so that you, the investor, are protected as well. This nonsense is also perpetrated by many salespeople. There is a selling slogan that is used in the business, which describes tax-exempt bonds as second only to U. S. Government securities as far as safety is concerned. This is generally true. . . . But there may be times when bonds such as

industrial-revenue issues, might not qualify for that impos-
ing description.

It is true that most tax-exempt issues that have problems
eventually work out. In today's market, however, there is a
breed of people hustling bonds that may be just as worthless
as some stock floated during the boom days of the OTC
market. You have the means of seeing that this does not
happen to you if you insist on the right information.

When it comes to buying anything but rated bonds you
should have some extra help, such as your attorney or tax
accountant, in your corner. I know that some people will
wince because their lawyers and accountants are sometimes
thought to be too stodgy. I realize that some of them would
not recommend a bond under AAA or with a longer maturity than six months. I would agree that this is not the sort of
"expert" that you need. You need someone with an open
mind. Such a person is not too hard to find. I cannot
understand why some people will take some glib excuse for
the lack of printed information on an issue. For instance,
one investor was told by the salesperson that "the issue is too
old for the prospectus to have meaning." The investor
accepted his word that "everything is doing great. . . . I
even spoke with the president of the company this morning
and he told me so." If you accept this kind of assurance,
then you are in trouble.

There is no reason why a salesperson cannot supply you
with an official statement (this is the municipal description
of a prospectus), or at least with an updated report concerning the project. In the case of an industrial-revenue bond,
the most up-to-date information is the balance sheet of the
company. Nothing else really matters, because the balance
sheet contains the whole story of how well or how poorly
that company is doing. The balance sheet is the most important part of the official statement on any new industrial-
revenue bond issue. The official statement may describe
the city or county and the economic area, but *the credit is 100
percent dependent on the company itself.*

If you have one of the following problems, most of what I
am trying to warn you about will not mean much:

1 ● If you are looking for a tax dodge as well as tax exemption by using "hot money," or trying to buy bonds under an assumed name by trying to pay for the bonds in cash, you should be warned that it does not work. If you also refuse to give your Social Security number, you certainly will have problems. If the salesperson who is handling your account suggests that you need not give your Social Security number, then he or she is the one for you to watch very closely.

2 ● If you are serviced by a lazy or stupid salesperson, then you have a problem just as serious as if the salesperson is dishonest. I would hope that some of the questions that I suggest just ahead will help you to ferret out stupid salespeople, too. These people can cause you to lose money by letting you buy very highly rated bonds, when a lower rating would have been adequate; also their lack of knowledge of the bonds that they are selling could cause you serious loss.

There is another interesting situation that you should know about. There are many undercapitalized firms who will use your money to finance their operations, especially in new-issue situations. They do this by requesting that you send your money a week before delivery of the bonds. This allows them to clear your check and to accumulate the money they need to pay for the bonds that they have purchased. Thus you become their partner with no profit to you, and they usually pay no interest.

I suggest you write the following letter to the salesperson who wants to sell you tax-exempt bonds. If the questions therein are answered, you will have a fairly good idea of with whom you are dealing. (Do not forget that this is just a suggestion—you may want to phrase it far differently):

Dear Mr. (or Ms.) Salesperson:
You have asked me to become a client of your company. I would like to do so if you can answer some questions about your company and yourself.
They are as follows:

1 ● Can you send me a balance sheet or a D & B report on your company? (Note: some companies may object to a balance sheet, but they should be able to give you bank or other references.)

2 ● Please supply me with a list of the officers of your company.

3 ● How long has your firm been in business?

4 ● Does your company belong to a regulated group such as an exchange or the NASD?

5 ● Are investors protected with investor insurance?

6 ● Has your firm or any member of it ever been cited for a violation involving clients or their accounts?

7 ● If I pay for new-issue securities, what safeguards do you have to protect my payment in case the delivery is not made either to you or to me?

8 ● What are your criteria for hiring new salespeople?

9 ● Does your company have a continuing educational program for its sales personnel?

10 ● How long have you been in the bond business?

11 ● What was your previous experience?

12 ● What is your academic background?

13 ● Are you personally registered with the NASD?

These questions should not be regarded as an invasion of privacy. However, you will find that some salespeople will resent them and may drop you as a potential client, which will be good news for you. Actually, many firms have such material ready to mail to their prospective clients. There could be a question as to whether this letter puts the small specialty firm at a disadvantage against the larger firm. This could be, but I feel that if the small firm answers with a spirit that impresses you with its sincerity, the so-called advantage of the large firm disappears.

I do not advocate that you deal with a firm because of its size. In fact some large firms do not do as good a job with individual investors because their emphasis is on the institutional investor. You have to make up your mind based on the following requisites:

1 ● The reliability of the firm.

2 ● The type of service that they can give you when they are requested to supply official statements, performance records, and other pertinent data.

3 ● Are you and the person who is trying to sell you bonds congenial? This does not mean that you have to be old buddies. It does mean that you should have mutual respect, and that there are clear-cut channels of communication open.

7

The Businessman's Risk

No one seems to know how the term "businessman's risk" originated. It became part of the bond jargon in the early sixties as speculative issues came to the fore in greater numbers. There were other projects which basically were unproved issues. However, these bonds were not all bad. In fact most of them are well-regarded in today's market. The problem was that they were new and the market traditionally shrugs off anything new and makes it pay some sort of penalty, usually in the pricing.

Thus every high-yielding bond is not as bad a deal as some of the writers who conduct those Q & A columns in your favorite newspaper would have you believe. I recently saw one where an investor said that he could get a high rate of interest on a tax-exempt. The response was "Back off, you are looking for trouble." The "answer man" is a likeable old hack (although stern in print) who never leaves his house in the suburbs, and who has never studied the subject too well. He got into the Q & A game years ago, and is an example of how little one has to know about securities to write about them.

His answer did everything but suggest that the questioner call up the Better Business Bureau. His yardstick (and that of many other people) is that a bond whose yield is much higher than most other bonds has to be suspect. This is not always true. (Although the bonds that have defaulted, it must be said, have usually been of the higher-yield variety.) The point that I am making here is that there are many good high-yielding bonds available.

Where does price or yield come into the picture? There is usually a differential of at least 2 percent between the Baa- or BBB-rated bonds and the so-called businessman's-risk bonds. Of course in a very tight money market when Baa or BBB bonds begin to sell at 8½- or even 9-percent yields, there isn't much room for a differential because usury laws prohibit very high rates. Therefore most of these projects stay under wraps until rates return to more "normal" conditions.

It is also true that many of the bonds that are well-regarded today began as businessman's-risk bonds. In fact most of the bonds of the state of Florida were considered high-risk at one time, not to mention those of Alaska and Hawaii. So were some assessment bonds in Orange County, California. When they were first put up for bids, all the banks and prominent dealers snubbed them. They were left to some dealers who sensed that the bonds had value because they represented land. Now everyone bids on these bonds when they sell, and institutions have them in their portfolios. The same is true of some airport bonds, and there are countless underpriced (at least when they were originally offered) issues in the pollution area. Then there are the small bond issues of small towns that the big underwriters do not bid on. These become yield bonds too, because they are small in amount.

Remember another basic rule: The market always makes a new issue go through an initiation period. This is true even if the new type of bond has a good rating. Of course ratings do not always do the trick. New York City has an A rating, but its bonds sell at a much higher yield than other comparable A-rated issues.

I do not urge that you buy businessman's-risk situations as a matter of course and fill your portfolio with them.

However, I do recognize that many investors look at the high yields with envy, and would like to have some. Therefore what I am doing again in this chapter is giving you some guidelines on how to approach these bonds and still be happy at a later date.

First, the more bonds that you have in your portfolio, the more chances you can afford to take. Now, if $10,000 in bonds will be your entire investment in the tax-exempt market, I would say that you should be in something very comfortable. However, if you have followed a circumspect course in investing in tax-exempts, and have accumulated several blocks, I think that you would not be getting too far off-base by buying some higher-yielding bonds.

Of course you must stop, look, and listen. Remember the "Caveat Emptor" chapter; you do not want to stumble into a bad deal, nor do you want to be hoodwinked by any unscrupulous bond dealer.

There is one type of high-yielding bond that I think merits special attention. I am not saying that I would rush out and buy any such issue just because it is available. However, they are coming along in fine style these days. They are the hospital and nursing-home bonds (sometimes called health-care projects). The best type of health-care projects are nonprofit ones. This may sound confusing, but keep in mind that there are many private institutions funded via industrial-revenue bonds that are tax-exempt. There is nothing wrong in this procedure, except that I have not seen too many issues that look good when they are using the credit of their sponsors, because not many of these sponsors have healthy-looking balance sheets. Sometimes this is because the sponsoring company has a string of nursing homes. Thus when you total the bonds outstanding (or mortgages) against the net worth of the sponsor, it does not always measure up to the one-for-one theory. (That theory insists that the total net worth of the company equal the amount of the bonds being issued.)

The counter argument to this approach is that even though those sponsors are the guarantors, the basic dependence in such issues (nursing homes) is on the third-party pay. These are the payments made by federal, state, and local agencies on behalf of the elderly people in these homes. However, I insist that the profit-oriented (as differentiated from church and real nonprofit groups) sponsor think only about that profit. Some of these sponsors will walk off and leave a project if it is not working out or if it is not spinning off enough profit.

This is true of hospitals, too. In these days of higher wages and costs, the problem is whether or not an institution can make it. To you, this has to mean whether it can make enough money to pay its overhead plus the principal and interest due on its bonds. Look at the bottom line and worry whether your bonds are going to be paid or not.

There will be more nursing homes than hospital financing in the future and this is why I have picked them as the example for this chapter. There are actually getting to be too many hospitals. This is not true in all areas, but there is no longer the big need of, say, five years ago.

Then most hospital financing was done via corporate bonds (that is, taxable bonds), but when one of the largest underwriters of such bonds, Ziegler & Co., of West Bend, Wisconsin, turns more to tax-exempt issues, you know that there has been a big change. One of the differences between a taxable and a tax-exempt issue is that the tax-exempt issues can be funded up to 100 percent of the costs, whereas most corporate issues were funded up to only 75 percent of the project cost.

The most important document in any revenue-bond issue, whether it be a hospital, health care, or any other type of revenue bond, is the feasibility report. (See Chapter 8, "The Protectors.") The most important part of any feasibility report is the conclusion: whether the issue will earn enough revenues so the bonds can be paid. I have seen many wishy-washy reports that actually sidestep the question. The only thing that you are interested in is whether the bonds will pay out. However, some of these reports are so written that you can take either side of the question. If this is true of any report you see on a new issue, pass the issue by. Do not even bother to find out why the language is vague. Let it be vague but do not try to read between the lines.

Also, make sure that the producer of the report is a nationally recognized company. If you do not recognize the name, or cannot find any background material on the company, pass the deal by. Most companies will give a rundown on themselves in a report—except for some of the larger CPA firms whose names are almost household words.

The basic investment question in a feasibility report is coverage. You cannot be interested in an issue that can just meet its debt service after all expenses are paid. You must have more than that. You need at least one-and-a-half times the total debt service (and the highest debt service). If the debt service is $100,000 per year, there should be $150,000 left after all expenses. This is minimal. To go any lower would be taking a chance.

Always remember: Unless certain facts are laid out very clearly you should avoid the issue. The coverage factor is one. The other is whether the report maker has considered the rising costs of wages and prices in the years ahead. You must assume inflation will continue to some degree. Not to do this makes any report meaningless.

We now get to the part about knowing the people. Know who the sponsors are and who the bond underwriters are. There are too many good people in the latter category for you to do business with some fly-by-night. Just as important are the sponsors. Some of the sponsors in health-care issues who hide under the guise of "churches" are just people using the church (often a very obscure sect or sometimes a very vague connection with some well-known sect) as a means of making you think that the project is respectable. These things are easy to check out if you have the time, and you should make the time when investing.

There is one thing that I cannot say too often: Buy bonds of the projects that you know. This is especially true in a small issue (small being anything under $1 million in bonds). I would never buy a bond of some place that I had never heard of.

There are so many high-yielding bonds available you do not have to reach out as though there were a shortage. You can make some excellent investments in high-yielding businessman's-risk bonds.

There are many detractors of these bonds—perhaps the salesman or woman who covers your account, or possibly your banker who does not handle them. I look on all their no-no's as being constructive, because they will make you think and read before you make a decision. This is also an area where you should have your attorney or accountant do some work.

A few years ago I talked to a woman who was always complaining that her attorney would not give her permission to buy the bonds she wanted. I checked into her situation and found that the attorney was 100 percent right. However, I know of many other lazy attorneys and accountants who just say no so they will not be accused of making a mistake. If you have one of these, get rid of him.

Occasionally some elderly investor interested only in tax-free income and not so concerned about the principal acquires some of these bonds. This is not good investing, but it is a fact of life. Many elderly men who pursue this policy argue that it will be up to their heirs to worry about the soundness of the project. Thus if they see several years of capitalized interest (the setting aside of funds for interest for a year or more when the issue is originally financed, thus making the interest for a stated period a sure thing) plus debt service (similar to capitalized interest, except that a reserve fund for debt service is extra insurance in case the project has some problems), they are ready to go.

Summing up this chapter on businessman's-risk bonds, it seems to me that the purchase of these bonds depends quite a bit on how well you are doing financially. They should not be your only investment in tax-exempts, but should be an adjunct to your portfolio. However, at the same time you do not have to think that all buyers of businessman's-risk bonds are high rollers. You can administer the same tests to this type of bond as any other tax-exempt. The key word here is objectivity.

8

The Protectors

There are people in this business whom I call your protectors. As tax-exempt bonds are free from most regulation, I am not referring to the SEC (Securities and Exchange Commission) or the NASD (National Association of Security Dealers), although the latter organization has authority to regulate the selling practices. The people I refer to are in the private sector. They are the bond attorneys, the feasibility experts, and the bank trustees. The people in the public sector who can be counted among your protectors are the various public officials such as the city attorneys and the courts.

You may wonder why you need protectors. I am not suggesting that the bond deals are crooked. In any transaction, however, whether it be the selling of bonds or the buying of a home, safeguards must be taken. These procedures may often be tedious, but you cannot afford to be bored by them.

The first protector you encounter in a revenue-bond issue could be the engineer whose job it is to declare an issue feasible or not feasible.

There is some debate as to whether all of these engineers do such a good job. This is because there were many toll-road issues sold in the fifties that never worked out according to the feasibility reports. These were usually traffic reports.

46

Feasibility engineers are also used in other projects where people must be counted. Hospitals, for example, or nursing homes, or ski slopes all need these services.

The feasibility report gives an investor an unbiased look at a project. It would be silly to pretend that there has not been criticism or even hints of hanky-panky on some of these reports. It has been suggested that some reports were inspired by a golf-partner sort of relationship. The implication is that the feasibility people will ask the issuer what kind of report is needed, and then prepare it.

Feasibility studies can get off to a false start and never get back onto the road. The problem haunting the feasibility report makers is that they must deal with people. If a representative of a feasibility report maker asks you or me whether we will use a bridge or go to a motor speedway, we all invariably say yes, but frequently we never do. Such reports have to look very silly eventually.

Must we avoid feasibility report deals based on popular response? Not all. However, we should never be afraid to pay attention to our gut feelings. A feasibility report should be a part of your decision, but it does not relieve you of the responsibility of making the decision, nor does it relieve the underwriter of his obligation to delve into all of the facts about an issue.

Make sure that none of the people connected with an issue have been seen walking on water. This is a highly problematical business. They are putting together information for you and me. Sometimes the results can be great, and in some cases they can be just horrible.

One last word. Know the feasibility firm; check out their record; ask the underwriter on which other issues the firm has given opinions. If all of this seems like too much trouble, avoid the issues where feasibility is a major factor.

There is another important protector, or should I say protectors? These are the raters. (See Chapter 10.) While there may be controversy about how ratings are determined, there is no doubt in my mind that the raters should be included in the group that I have dubbed the protectors.

What goes on behind the scenes of a bond issue may also seem very tedious. If you ever go to a bond closing (where the bonds are delivered to the underwriters), you might have a hard time staying awake while the attorneys pass around documents and quibble about the wording in various clauses. All of these people have a function, and it is to protect you, the bondholder. In fact, knowing that this great array of talent has been involved in the bond issue should make any bondholder feel more secure.

The key man here is the bond attorney. Bond attorneys have an interesting history. They have been around for about one hundred years, but most of us were not aware of them until John Mitchell became front-page news. The newspaper stories told of how much money Mr. Mitchell had made in the practice of bond law. What they did not tell us was how important the work is that John Mitchell and other bond attorneys have done over the years.

It has been said that bond attorneys *make* law as well as interpret it. Most bond attorneys would deny this, but when you consider the nature of their job the making of some law is almost inevitable. Governor Nelson Rockefeller turned to John Mitchell some years back and asked for a device whereby New York State could put its moral obligation on a bond issue without issuing it directly itself. The reason he asked this was that he had to get around Arthur Levitt, the state comptroller, because Mr. Levitt was not being cooperative. John Mitchell did his job, and New York State led the way (despite Mr. Levitt's protests, discussed in Chapter 12) in issuing bonds with the so-called moral obligation.

The nation's bond attorneys have been in the forefront of new legislation on bonds. The leading attorneys in a state (which means the ones that give opinions on the bonds of that state) will usually write the legislation for new laws, or at least point out the holes that they find in the proposed law or laws. You can see, therefore, that these men (and a few women here and there) are held in the greatest respect. To my knowledge, I do not think that any legal opinion issued by a bond attorney has ever been reversed. This is especially true in some of the industrial-revenue financing, where it has been rumored that the IRS has upon occasion disagreed with the opinion, but has held its tongue. They might let it be known that they would not stand for a second issue like it, but the first one has always stood.

How can a man or a law firm be the means of getting an issue to be called legal or vice versa? It all started out over one hundred years ago, when the railroads were making their big move across the country. So many towns were built and financed illegally that investors began to look for legal help. The principal investors of those days hired outstanding attorneys to decide on the legality of the issues. The investors rather liked the idea and felt secure, and that, after all, is about 90 percent of the sales process.

As time went on the cities, counties, and communities began retaining the bond attorneys themselves. They not only received the legal opinions, but they also had someone to lean on for advice in the consideration of new issues. This is still the case today. The bond attorneys work on a contingency basis—*i.e.*, if there is no bond issue, they don't get paid—and only when the bond is issued are they paid. The many meetings and phone conferences that they attend or participate in are sort of "on the arm."

It is well to remember that even though the bond attorney is hired by the municipality and has a close working relationship with the underwriter, he and his firm are your attorneys. He views the transaction as if he were acting for one bondholder.

Many public officials have suggested that legal opinions by private firms be abolished and that the work be taken over by the staffs of the attorneys general of the nation. I do not think that this makes sense. Most of these offices are understaffed, and these are times when no one is looking to increase the costs of any level of government. Actually the bond attorney's fees are very small when compared to the expense of marketing the bonds. In other words, the bond salesmen get the big money, not the bond attorneys.

The job of the bond attorney is an intensive one. It is in many respects similar to that performed by the attorney who acts for you on the closing of a home sale. He must check out all the new laws. He must see that no court decisions have been rendered that would tend to make the bond issue not legal. In the industrial-revenue bond area, he must check to see if the issuers and the sponsors are conforming to the many and tangled regulations set up by the IRS. The various decisions by the courts are as important as the basic law, and his opinion is in trouble if he misses an important court decision.

Another of the important jobs of the bond attorney is to write the lease (where needed) and the trust indenture. The latter document basically sets the ground rules for the project and instructs all parties (the trustee, etc.) as to their duties. There is no doubt that some of this work (as has been noted by critics) is boiler-plated (which is really the art of copying or duplicating). However, each issue has its own problems which cannot be boiler-plated. The bond attorney can show his ingenuity in the lease and can show his respect for the bondholder in the indenture. In the majority of issues, this is just what he does.

Another of the bond attorney's jobs is to examine the bond itself. In actuality, it is the bond attorney who composes the form of the bond. It is also his job to ascertain that no litigation is pending against the financing in question. If there is any, he will not issue his legal opinion. He will also not release his opinion until the treasurer of the issuing body has furnished him with a receipt showing that the bonds have been paid for.

On the other side of the coin, no underwriter will ever pay for the bonds until he knows that the bond attorney has issued an unqualified opinion. This is important for a bondholder. Never buy a bond where a bond attorney has issued a qualified opinion. It does not happen too often, but it can happen.

One of the great bond attorneys was a man named David N. Wood. He wrote the bond-attorney section of a book entitled *Fundamentals of Investment Banking,* which was published by Prentice-Hall many years ago. Wood cited a legal opinion in the paper of a bond opinion issued in 1899:

WOOD & OAKLEY
Lawyers
Chicago

June 12, 1899

I HEREBY CERTIFY that I have examined a certified copy of the record of the proceeding of the Common Council of the City of Prescott, Arizona, passed preliminary to the issue by said City of its Water and Sewerage Bonds to the amount of Seventy-Five Thousand Dollars ($75,000) dated December 15th, 1898. And in my opinion, such proceeding shows lawful authority for the said issue under the laws of the Territory of Arizona now in force.

I FURTHER CERTIFY that I have examined the form of bond prepared for the said issue, and find that same to be in due form of law and in my opinion the said issue to the amount aforesaid is valid and legally binding upon the said City of Prescott, and that all of the taxable property in said City is subject to the levy of a tax to pay the same.

Chas. B. Wood

Today's legal opinions (which, by the way, are usually printed on the bonds, making it easy to ascertain the legality instead of the separate opinions that used to be hard to find) have much more detail. You will notice that the bond numbers are referred to in the opinion issued by the firm of Reed, McCarthy & Giordan of New York (Appendix 9).

An important aspect of legal opinions is that no delivery of bonds is good without one. Thus an older bond, issued before they started printing the opinions on the bonds or where the opinion was too long to be printed on the bonds, has to have the legal opinion attached to the bonds to make it a good delivery.

A very important function in the bond-issuing process is the continuing job that must be performed by a bank trustee. In my opinion, this is one of the badly neglected components of the bond business. There are too many banks that have the necessary trust powers and can legally act as a trustee, but do not do a good job. This is another job that has been set up to protect the bondholders. I do not think that all bank trustees do a poor job. But if even one bank trustee is not doing a good job, then some bondholders are at least potentially in trouble.

The selection of bond trustees is not a very reassuring process. The most important factor in selecting a trustee is the amount of influence that a bank has in a particular area. The fact that the bank buys a good deal of the area's bonds is also a consideration. In many cases the ability of the bank to act as an advocate for the bondholder has never been tested. The only time it will be tested is when there is a problem with an issue.

From my studies of how bank trustees act when the chips are down, I would have to say that the majority of them do not act fast enough. They become bogged down and look for the officials of the project to do something. This is not what they were hired to do. But most of these banks never dream that they might ever be called upon to do any unpleasant jobs.

I believe that poor bank trustees can be made into good trustees. It takes constant prodding by bondholders and by underwriters. If you do not receive information that should be sent to you, scream for it—you will be making that particular bank into a better trustee. Most of the trustee banks that do a bad job do so because they think of their assignments as just a routine clerical situation. Some trustee banks just do not know what their job really is. This is a damning indictment because it means that they have not read the indenture that was drawn up by the bond attorney.

The protectors that you have on the public side are the city and county attorneys and the courts. The local attorneys usually do not want a bad issue to be sold. They feel that it is their job to protect the publicly elected officials from bad deals. Thus they are defending potential bondholders. There are all kinds of attorneys, however. There are some very good ones, but when they are bad or lazy they are awfully bad.

Most local attorneys do an excellent job and are great at playing the devil's advocate. These incorruptible people make your job as an investor easier. It is the lazy people who do more damage than the crooked ones.

In the end, the courts are the bondholder's best friend. In many states where revenue-bond issues have to go before the courts, the bondholder is given the full protection of the devil's-advocate system because the district attorney or the county attorney has to argue against the issue. The judge then decides whether to approve it. This is the system used in the state of Florida, and it works out very well there. I would advocate it for every state.

The bondholder is therefore not without friends, especially as far as the bond attorney and the courts plus most public officials (local attorneys) are concerned. They are usually in good hands with most trustees. However, there is a disturbing number of trustees that like to handle the funds of the project and get the money for paying out the interest and other expenses, but will not rise up and take a stand when the project has problems. However, if people keep writing and talking about it, the situation will improve. This is what the bondholder needs. Always remember that you have a right as a bondholder to make your ideas known to a trustee. If you speak up, you will be heard and heeded.

9

*How to
Read an Ad
And a
Prospectus*

Past experiences have shown me that reading tax-exempt ads and tax-exempt official statements (this is the tax-exempt equivalent of the word prospectus) are not the favorite sports of most investors.

Now, an ad is not essential to buying a tax-exempt bond. In fact, most tax-exempt bond issues are not advertised, and this is no great loss. I say this because most of the ads printed in the *Wall Street Journal* and other publications do not give you much of an idea what the issue is about, anyway. Also, most of the ads that are run are for the successful issues, and they do not have any bonds available when you get around to calling. The only ads that really say anything are the selling ads. Be careful of this type of ad because some of them sell too hard, and make more use of the yield they offer than of any information on the issue.

Over the years I have come to feel that tax-exempt new-issue ads are not really meant for investors. They are run for the purpose of impressing the competition within the industry or to make the senior officers of the underwriting firm happy. (Of course, there is also the ad agency and their 15 percent commission to be considered.)

It has been my experience that the ad agencies have no control over the content of the ads. Many have tried but failed to brighten up these aptly named "tombstone" ads. The ads as you read them are a mixture of what the lawyers and the industry group, the Securities Industries Association have ordained. The latter group came up with the real winner in advertising ideas—not showing the ratings. This is still adhered to by many.

Outside of stating the name of the issue, and the fact that the bonds are tax-exempt, the ad doesn't do much more than show the amount, the coupons, and the yields. So what's wrong with that? Well, most people cannot translate yields to dollars too easily, although I hope to remedy that situation somewhat in Chapter 20. There is also the fact that those facts are not much to go on, and in the absence of other information would provide a poor reason to buy the bonds.

There is rarely any information about the credit or the security involved, although this is or at least should be very important to you. Some underwriters do unbend a little. I have reproduced four ads in Appendix 10.

The tax-exempt people have started to use the media and have come up with some tantalizing ads. Of course there are a number of "straight" ads, where you know what you will be looking at in case you are tempted to fill out the coupon or make that call the ad insists you should. In fact, some of the old-line companies are now advertising in advance of issue, wherein they explain the issue and ask that you send in a coupon to receive a full prospectus. But the bucket-shop boys merely want to say, "We have 9-percent bonds!" When you call, they will want to sell them to you right over the telephone. Who ever heard of anyone asking for an official statement (or prospectus, if you will)?

Some situations stand up and cry out for exposure and this is one of them. Any attempt of bond dealers to try and sell you bonds on the basis of a come-on ad and yield is unconscionable. However, if you, the investor, do not resist, then chapters like this do no good at all.

Reading an official statement is not as difficult as many people think it is. I've heard many people say, "This is fine for the lawyers, but what about us lay people?" Many of these documents are becoming easier to read because the underwriters know that the people who will read them will not be just the pros, but ordinary people. Even the governor of a state once complained to me about the complicated language in an official statement. He was an attorney, and he felt the language was absurd.

I have reproduced an official statement in Appendix 11. It is very complete, and I have tried to be as explicit as possible without boring you to death. There are certain situations, however, which cannot be glossed over. There are certain passages that are important for you to read.

It is necessary that you understand the importance of an official statement. Everything that you need to know about a bond issue is contained in it. It is also the place to confirm what the salesperson told you about the issue in his or her sales pitch. If you do not find a reference to what he or she claimed, then you know that you have the wrong issue, to say nothing of the wrong bond salesperson.

Some official statements translate the yields to dollars, but most still do not. Of course, if it is a 6.5-percent coupon at par, then that is a 6.5-percent yield and needs no translation. However, a 9-percent coupon at a 6.8-percent yield might throw you a curve—in fact, it would make an old pro run for his basis book.

What are the most important items to check out in an official statement?

1 ● The ratings.

2 ● Whether the bonds are tax-exempt in your state as well as federally.

3 ● When are the bonds callable, and at what rate.

4 ● The date of the issue and the due dates.

5 ● Who or what backs up the bond.

6 ● The disposition of funds—look to see that too much money is not being spent on underwriting fees, etc.

7 ● In revenue-bond issues, check to see if ample reserves are set aside.

8 ● Check to see if additional bonds can be issued—if they

can, check under what circumstances—additional bonds can dilute your investment.

9 ● Any good official statement has a layman's version of the indenture and the lease (this applies in revenue-bond issues especially).

10 ● If it is a revenue-bond issue, look for some projections—these projections may not pan out, and no one can be held to them, but at least you can find out what the project hopes to accrue in the way of revenues—remember, it's the revenues that pay off your bonds.

11 ● Also look at the table that shows how the bonds will be paid off and whether there is a chance of an early pay-out.

12 ● A feasibility report should be printed *in full* if there is one available.

There are parts of an official statement that are not important to you, but must be included for full disclosure. This is an important situation. Full disclosure is required in every issue. If you see an issue that has an official statement that is not as complete as the one in Appendix 11, then you should not bother considering it. You are entitled to know everything about an issue. You may get the excuse that the underwriter was trying to make it easier for you to read. Do not be taken in by this so-called concern.

The matter of disclosure is getting to be a very sticky situation. Understand that the tax-exempt industry has been free of regulation since its inception. Recently moves were made to bury the business under SEC controls. However, the business was never free from the fraud provisions of SEC regulations, though many bond dealers acted as if this were not so. Of course this might have been because not much pressure was brought upon them for more complete official statements.

Some of the official statements that used to be issued on tax-exempt bonds contained the minimum amount of information that could be given. However, there were few bad deals. The marginal issues have increased, however, and we also have more "bucket shops."

How does this lack of disclosure work? Well, a case in point was a 1972 health-care-project issue. The developer in this issue had connections with one of the firms that ordered a feasibility report and, through members of his family, also owned the bond underwriter. There was nothing wrong in this situation (although some bondholders might have been scared off if they had known about it). *The wrong was committed in not making the disclosure.*

You may wonder whether this is not hypocritical. In many cases the use of a developer who has connections with the contractor may be beneficial to the project. Of course the feasibility report should be by a very neutral third party.

What all of this discussion leads to is that full disclosure is to your benefit. So look to see that it is there. Do not take verbal assurances. Demand that everything about the issue be in print.

10

The Rating Game

I will begin my discussion of rating with a statement I made to the Joint Economic Committee of the Congress of the United States on July 11, 1968 on the subject. Upon review, I find that I still have the same feelings today.

> I have been asked about the present rating systems and my opinion of them. I, of course, have been on record for many years as a critic of the system, but I have never been a critic of the integrity of these people. It is important to make this distinction. It is sometimes very upsetting to me and others to read statements maligning these agencies.
>
> I am a critic of the system and not of the people who run it. I believe that they are excellent technicians. In fact, if we ever formed a new rating system, I would prefer that the personnel that would comprise the cadre of such an organization be drawn from the present people in the rating agencies, if they were available.
>
> It is important to fix the role of the rating agencies in the right perspective. You hear many questions such as, "If we have had such few defaults in municipals over the past twenty-five years, why do we need ratings?" The simple answer is, "Who will determine what the worth of a bond is if we do not have a neutral third party."
>
> The issuer is naturally biased on the worth of his issue

because he thinks his issue is the best ever. The underwriter wants to sell the bonds.

Therefore, the investor who does not have the time or background to investigate a credit has to have someone give him an opinion as to value. This is the value of the rating agencies.

You must know what the rating agencies mean when they give a rating. Appendix 12 is a rundown on the Moody's and Standard & Poor's ratings.

How do the rating agencies figure out how to rate bonds of the local areas? I am going to quote from "The Rating Game," a study sponsored by the Twentieth Century Fund and written by John Stevenson. (I am quoting liberally from this study because it is a good one and it contains a lot of my material, spoken and written, from over the years.)

> Basic analysis of the bond issue depends on the nature of the security. In the case of general-obligation bonds, prime importance is attached to various measures of debt to wealth, population, and governmental revenues. The economic base of a community, the stage of its development, its sociological character, and the quality of its government are also leading factors. Last, the analysts examine the exact nature and strength of the legal obligation that the bonds represent.
>
> Revenue-bond analysis stresses the limited, but often very complex, relationship between project revenues and the obligation to pay back the money raised from the sale of the bonds. Most important in the debt contract are the various covenants that govern the conduct of the borrower in providing for full payment of the debt service and proper maintenance of the project's earning capacity. Of course, the credit must also measure the underlying strength of demand, the public necessity of the project, and the threat of competing or substitute facilities that might diminish the market.

You may say, "That's fine, but what does that all mean to me? I just want to know what the rating is." True, but most of us still want to know the rationale for a certain action. John Stevenson's statement above covers all the factors that enter into a rating. It gives us a better idea of what a rater is up against. It also points out how ratings can vary because raters would not be human if they did not differ just as economists do.

John Stevenson touches on one important area to the individual investor in his summary of the borrowers that have caused the most commotion in the tax-exempt market. These are the big-city and the small-town borrowers. They are as opposite as can be, but they also have certain similarities. Here is another excerpt from "The Rating Game":

> Two groups of borrowers—big cities and small, unrated local borrowers—have caused much of the contention about the impact of the present rating system. Critics of the rating agencies have felt that the low marks given by the raters either have been too severe or, by increasing the cost of borrowing, have worsened municipal financial problems.
>
> The agencies, for their part, have been unswerving in their defense of the investor, concerned only with aiding him in his investment decisions. The trend in the postwar period has been to downgrade the older, declining eastern cities, and one major urban school district is considered to be so precarious that it is no longer of investment quality. On the other hand, for most, the decline in creditworthiness may have halted, a development signaled by the upgrading of New York City at the end of 1972.
>
> Because the rating agencies have become more lenient about rating certain classes of revenue bonds, the problem of the large unrated bond has subsided. But the problem continues for small towns, especially since it commingles these who choose not to be rated and those who feel it either unnecessary or expensive.
>
> Either rated or unrated, smaller governmental units pay demonstrably higher rates of interest. This is defended on several grounds: higher risk of default; irreducible fixed costs of borrowing that drive up the per-dollar cost of selling bonds; the difficulty of getting information; and limited secondary-market interest in unknown credits. None of these phenomena seems illogical or out of line with the experience of other financial markets. However, efforts by several state and industry groups have shown that such handicaps can be minimized by organized efforts.

If I have any quarrel with "The Rating Game," it is that the study did not come to grips with the problem of the urban areas except in a limited way. Nor did the study ever face the problem of how cities use their tax receipts. I have always been obsessed with the idea that it was more important that a city use its dollars well than show full investment of those dollars. In this regard, we seem to be honoring thrift as opposed to good management. If I have any problem with raters it is that they are sometimes very much like those economists who think that the old-time-religion brand of economics is not replaceable. I worry whether they have the flexibility that rating bonds requires.

Despite all the words and definitions, you may still question whether the bonds you buy will default or not. It is not a bad habit to assume a pessimistic attitude, the traditional stance of an investment banker. The investment banker usually takes the role of the devil's advocate, and so does the rating agency. So should you.

There is always the question of what link there is in ratings and defaults. Most studies have shown that there is not much evidence of any connection at all. The record shows that since the Depression most defaults have been in the nonrated areas. The rating system might get a real test if we have another Depression.

There is also the question of how ratings affect the pricing of bonds. This is a definite fact. Tax-exempt bonds comprise a business of comparisons. The bonds of a certain city rated A are compared to the most recent city which was also rated A. There is always the problem of quality within a rating bracket. In other words, there are AAA's which are deemed better by the market than others. However, this is where the market apparatus of supply and demand takes over once the rating is established.

It is rare to see the market upgrade a bond from where the raters have placed it; however, it is possible that the market will *downgrade* a bond. New York City is an example of this. A combination of bad publicity and a very high volume brings this about.

I have given as much detail on ratings as you need to judge what you buy. No doubt those who buy rated bonds have a great deal more to rely upon than those who pick the unrated situations. This does not mean that the unrated issues are bad, but the investor does have a rationale for picking a certain issue when it is based upon a rating.

There are a number of issues that are now being passed over (such as hospital and nursing-home issues) because the agencies do not see proof of continued third-party pay which involves the paying of the principal and interest of the issue. Here we have to make some independent judgments, because regardless of proof that this kind of aid will have to continue, no rating agency will see it since there is no legislative fiat that future congresses and state legislatures will continue the aid. This is where a sense of history and social progress must take over. It is also why you can never completely rule out an unrated bond.

As one who has created considerable discussion over the years about whether rating agencies did the right thing in certain issues, I still believe that your lot as an investor is a better one because they are there.

The best thing that has happened to the raters is that they have become more commercialized by charging for their ratings. When this was first thought of in 1968, there were those who worried that the ratings were in danger of losing their value. There was never any chance of that. Now the issuers pay for their ratings whether they like them or not. The truth is that no issuer ever likes a rating. They always feel that they should be at least two notches higher.

There is always the question of whether an investor is not better off with a lower rating for a good bond. It would be great if all the AAA bonds were rated BBB from a yield viewpoint, but this is where the rating system makes sense. The bond under review is considered from the standpoint of security and not of value. Thus the system tries to reward those issuers who do the right thing. Of course the best of all worlds, for an investor, is to buy a bond that begins with a low rating and improves by the time you are ready to sell it.

11

What About Those Moral Obligations?

An investor wrote to me some time ago asking why I was against moral-obligation bonds. He thought that I was engaged in a political vendetta. He had purchased some bonds that his salesperson had told him carried the moral obligation of a state. He told the salesperson of my remarks, and was told that I did not know what I was writing about. In addition, the salesperson had asked whose word his client would take, mine or the governor of the state?

I have never claimed that any of the bonds that carry the so-called moral obligation are about to default. What I am concerned about is some future time when perhaps things may not be so good. What will happen to the moral-obligation bonds when the direct debt of the state demands payment, especially if there are limited funds to pay out with?

This is sometimes called scare stuff, but this is exactly how investment bankers approach any bond issue, even those in which they have great confidence. You should always approach an investment from the negative side. It does not necessarily mean that you are down on the issue, but that you are looking at the investment with your eyes wide open.

The moral-obligation craze began in New York State. I am going to quote an old friend of mine, Arthur Levitt, the comptroller of New York State for the last twenty years or so. At first his opposition was thought to be political because he was the only Democrat in high office in New York State for many years.

However, when you analyze what Arthur Levitt has done in New York State, you will find that he is a strictly nonpartisan comptroller running on the Democratic ticket. Levitt criticizes anyone, if he thinks something is not right fiscally, whether that someone is a Democrat or Republican.

Indeed, his fiscal attitude might have brought on the moral-obligations phase. Governor Rockefeller wanted to do projects outside the usual channels, and not involve approval by the state legislature and a vote of the people. He retained John Mitchell, the prominent bond attorney, to find a way around the snag. Thus the moral obligation was born. Up to September 30, 1974, the amount of such bonds and notes outstanding amounted to almost $3 billion.

Now New York is not the only governmental unit doing this. The federal government is another practitioner of this form of bookkeeping. It floats about $1 billion or more of notes each week for various federal agencies, and it keeps them out of the federal budget.

New Jersey is another state that went to the moral-obligation route when it was financing its sports complex, regarded as necessary because the New York Giants needed a place to play. You will find other instances of the so-called moral-obligation bond in other areas of the country as well.

In May of 1974 Arthur Levitt made a speech in which I think he summed up this matter fairly well. Here is an excerpt from that speech:

> The problem is that, by various schemes, a great deal of our public financing is done by various agencies whose debt is not subject to the vote of the people. This is the so-called "back-door debt" you have heard about so often.
>
> I will not bore you with all the details. It is enough to say that there are lease-purchase schemes amounting to about $3 billion. To complete the picture, we must consider other commitments arising either because the state has directly

guaranteed the debt of certain public authorities or has undertaken a so-called moral commitment. These have almost quadrupled during the decade, adding several more billions to our debtlike commitments.

For all of these reasons, I am concerned not only about the magnitude of our debt structure, but also about its proliferation into unwieldy and distorted forms. I have recommended that the legislature consider the following actions with regard to state programs financed by the incurrence of debt:

—No debt proposition should be put to the people unless they are advised fully of the specific projects to be undertaken and the rate of expenditure incurrence.

—All programs currently financed through borrowings (direct, indirect, and other debtlike commitments) should be reviewed and placed within a scheme of priorities so that expenditures may be planned accordingly.

—*No further programs should be undertaken with the support of the "moral-commitment" clause.*

These steps must be taken if we are to keep faith with the people.

There are many articles being written about back-door financing. Many investors found out for the first time that they did not have as good a bond as they had thought. If they had read the official statement, as I suggest in Chapter 9, they might have seen a disclaimer that would indicate that getting the money from the state to one of these corporations might not be as easy as it seemed if the state legislature of some future date does not go along.

The investor is also up against another problem, however; in fact, several problems. Some of the ads run by very prominent firms well-known for their integrity seemed to indicate that these bonds were the obligations of New York State. Arthur Levitt finally got the industry to include in their ads wording that indicated the bonds were "not an obligation of the state of New York."

I am not sure that all salespeople have gone along on this, because my investigations show that some of them still talk about these bonds as obligations of New York or New Jersey. They do it with that knowing wink face-to-face or that voice inflection on the phone. There is no way of knowing how many people are sitting with these bonds, thinking that they have direct obligations of New York or New Jersey.

My fear about these bonds is not for now but for tomorrow, when priorities could become tougher and tougher to set. I am not sure that a legislature twenty years from now, faced with tough decisions on budget, etc., will go along and continue to subsidize these authorities. This can be regarded as a bearish outlook, but when you consider the changes of the past twenty years, you must take the possibility seriously.

I see nothing wrong with buying these bonds, but I do worry about the bonds being sold to investors under false pretenses. To be fair, however, I must say that some of the moral obligations issued, such as for the Albany Mall by Albany County, depend on the state to pay rent. This has to be considered a very binding contract because the state will pay rent as long as it is viable.

There are also some bonds that have fairly binding contracts because, again, these contracts are between a locality and an authority such as the New York State Dormitory Authority. These involve state aid, and are legal and binding contracts.

However, the project that is bound by nothing but an understanding that the state will step in if all does not go well has to be considered a bond that cannot enforce its obligations. You must decide before you buy if this is what you are buying. If you already own bonds of this type, you owe it to yourself to check on them. I am not advocating that you dump them. If, however, you bought them under a misapprehension as to what their true security is, then you might ask yourself whether you should hold on to them.

As this book was being set in type, the problems of the New York State UDC bonds (Urban Development Corporation) pointed up very vividly what I have written here. Steps were being taken to make sure that there would be no more "moral obligation" bonds. However, it would seem to me that they will make their appearance again because they are an excellent (I am being facetious) way to avoid budgetary problems. In the meantime, there are still millions of these bonds outstanding which may cause problems before they mature. It means that those who own them should reconsider their retention and those who are looking to invest should be careful that every City and State bond they buy (unless it is a revenue situation) is a *General Obligation* of the governmental unit. In other words, be very diligent.

12

The Building
Of a
Tax=Free
Portfolio

Many people do not worry about building a tax-exempt portfolio because they believe that they are buying their tax-exempt bonds on a one-shot basis. However, if circumstances permit, you will probably find yourself adding to that portfolio at least once. You want to avoid a hit-or-miss portfolio.

In September of 1974 we got a look at the tax-exempt bond portfolio of Nelson Rockefeller, exhibited at his confirmation hearing for the vice-presidency.

Here is the Nelson Rockefeller tax-exempt portfolio:

NEW YORK STATE BONDS
$3,000,000—N.Y. State Housing Finance Agency
 3,550,000—N.Y. State Power Authority
 1,000,000—Port of N.Y. Authority
CALIFORNIA BONDS
 1,000,000—Metropolitan Water District
 250,000—Sacramento Municipal Utility District
CONNECTICUT BONDS
 805,000—Hartford, Conn., Public Housing Authority
FLORIDA BONDS
 3,000,000—Florida Turnpike Authority

MISSOURI BONDS
    445,000—Poplar Bluff Public Housing Authority
MONTANA BONDS
    320,000—Helena Public Housing Authority
NEW JERSEY BONDS
    1,000,000—New Jersey Highway Authority
PUERTO RICO BONDS
    2,000,000—Puerto Rico Water Resources Authority

$16,370,000—TOTAL

We do not know the maturities of these bonds except in the cases of the Florida Turnpike, New Jersey Highway, New York State Power, and New York State Housing Finance. However, from the valuation which was made as of August 30, 1974, it looked as if most of the bonds were long-term.

Mr. Rockefeller, a New York State resident, had 59 percent of the portfolio in bonds that would receive a New York State tax exemption (including the Puerto Rico bonds, which are exempt in all states due to its status as a commonwealth). Did Mr. Rockefeller have enough local tax exemption? I do not believe so. In New York State, where there are many issues to choose from, I would have had more in New York State issues. You might ask, What about diversification? That might have been a factor, but I really do not see that as a very important factor when you look at the portfolio.

My reaction to his portfolio is that he could have used more yield. Although 62-percent A and Baa is good, a man in his position could have used 75 to 80 percent of the lower ratings. Using Moody's as a barometer, his rating classifications were as follows:

Aaa	15%
AA	23%
A	43%
Baa	19%

However, this was a judgment of the people who bought the bonds, and there ain't a clinker in the lot.

However, I would say that this is the kind of block buying that takes place when a large trust or group is involved, and, from what I have been able to find out, the buying was usually done on an across-the-board basis. I think this is fine for the Rockefellers and some others who buy in family or business groups.

Of course this is the way that bonds are often purchased by the trust departments of banks. They make a decision on a particular bond, and buy it for those who have money and for those who they think should have the bonds. While I am sure that many trust departments give each account as much attention as possible, I still have always worried about this mass-production method of bond selection.

Each investor's problems are different, and this is why a small or average investor is better off in many ways with a firm that watches out for his interests. If the investors know which direction they would like to go, this helps.

You cannot have the huge portfolio that Nelson Rockefeller has, and you cannot buy the same way. In fact, if I were giving marks on his portfolio, I would not give it a passing grade—it has no problems, but it has no imagination, either. You must be careful of many things, such as liquidity. This might mean not putting all of your eggs in one basket.

Now, let us tackle one of the big questions: How long? If there is anything about tax-exempt bonds that bothers people more than length of maturity, I am not aware of it. There is something about the maturity of the bond that worries many investors. There is also no consensus about what is considered long. Long-term can be one year, or it can be forty years. Actually the latter is right, but I would never be able to convince some people of that.

I discussed maturity under *When* in Chapter 3, but it comes back into focus when you talk about a portfolio, since if you do not consider maturity, then you cannot begin the work of putting a portfolio together.

Suppose you select a program that begins short and goes out as far as twenty-five years. This is the way it would work. For instance, the investor has $50,000 and he or she decided to buy A-rated bonds in five bond amounts and five-year increments. This means $10,000 in bonds per year. It is not a large amount, but it is not exactly an odd lot, even though some of the pros might think so. Here is what we would do, assuming we are investing in 1975: We would have $10,000 each of bonds (rated A) of locations in your own state (if there is a state income tax), due in 1980, 1985, 1990, 1995, and 2000. This gives you an average life of fifteen years. It also gives you a runoff every five years.

I have always found this to be the most successful of portfolios because it gives you the best of all worlds. You are not too long on the average life of the bonds, and you can diversify as to coupon. It also usually works out well as far as average yield is concerned.

If the twenty-five-year situation (until 2000) bothers you, you can shorten up by having $15,000 in bonds in the fifteenth and twentieth years with $10,000 in the fifth and tenth years. This also accomplishes the job and makes you comfortable.

If you are fortunate enough to have $100,000 for investment, you can use $20,000 a year under the first plan or $25,000 per year under the second. The $25,000 amounts would certainly be attractive if you were looking forward to the secondary market.

I think that most people know how to figure out average life. You multiply the amount of your bonds by the number of years to maturity. You add all those figures and divide by the amount of bonds, and you have the average life of your portfolio.

If you have $100,000, you might want to strip your bonds $10,000 every two years, which would also get you to 1995. This would give you some great runoff possibilities. This arrangement would give you an average life of eleven years on the bonds. Of course this would be reduced each time a bond matured, unless, of course, you have replaced a maturing bond with longer bonds.

There is always the person who has what is best described as a bunch of cats and dogs in his or her portfolio. If the strength of the bonds is okay, they usually have a hodge-podge of maturities. I happen to think that an orderly portfolio is the best, and not because of neatness alone. Actually, the only neatness I worry about is whether the portfolio can be productive. My experience has been that any portfolio that is all over the place is usually not productive.

This means that you might have to switch some of your bonds. The first thing to do is to get an evaluation of the bonds you now own to see if you want to sell them and replace them with others. You might want to tax-swap them, although you most likely would be trying to change maturities more drastically than the tax regulations allow under tax-swapping. Read Chapter 15 very closely. I talk there about some no-no's, and two of the subjects covered involve tax swaps and evaluations.

We started at the top with the Nelson Rockefeller portfolio, and now we are talking about relatively small ones. However, they are all big to the individual investor, since he has worked hard to build up the portfolio and he needs it to work well. No one can afford the old win-a-few-and-lose-a-few attitude. You did not see it in Mr. Rockefeller's portfolio (and not just because he is used to winning), and you should avoid it in yours.

This does not mean, however, that if you are so disposed (and have an adequate amount of capital), you should not go for a high-yield situation once in a while. However, don't just throw $10,000 (or whatever amount is involved) into the air and let it fall on some issue without checking it out. You should show the same due diligence with this situation as you would on any other issue. Do not let the salespeople know that you are taking a flyer or they may help you fly higher than you really want to go.

Remember that the above paragraph is predicated on your having the money to lose. It is not for the widows-and-orphans grouping, nor is it for those whose portfolio represents their life's savings.

The one thing that I think of as being important in setting up a portfolio is to remind you again that you should be comfortable with it. If there is anything that bothers you about any bond or even about the subject of tax-exempt bonds, just *do nothing* until you have it squared away. *Just be comfortable* in what you are doing, and you will see how this automatically makes you do the right thing.

I have now spent almost an entire chapter telling you how

to put a simple portfolio together. But how about that time when you are ready for retirement? Perhaps you will still have profit-making situations that will keep you in a high bracket. However, most of us have a rapid change in salary from the ages of 64 (or even younger) to the retirement age of 65 or whenever we do decide to retire.

This is why it is a good idea to put that portfolio in shape, so that it can be dismantled easily. This also means that as you approach retirement age and have a fairly good idea of what the economics of your retirement will be, you should arrange your portfolio so that it is maturing when you are retiring. This is relatively easy, but it does mean that you have to keep a close eye on those maturity dates.

I am not saying that you have to do all of this yourself. If you can get competent help from your salesperson, that is fine and you should consider yourself lucky. I recommend that you do the principal thinking and let others work out the pick-and-shovel details of what has to be done. In this way, the building of a portfolio can be fun because it is a challenge. It is something that you should do and not leave to a trust department (unless you are afflicted with Nelson Rockefeller's problem of too much money to invest), or to a salesperson. I believe that you can do this job yourself if you have been intelligent enough to make that much money up to now.

I am going to talk about estates now, even though many of us do not care for the subject at all. However, it involves one of those things that eventually happens to all of us, and the owner of a portfolio cannot ignore the fact if he or she wants to do the right thing for his or her heirs.

Over the years, I have met many investors (and this is in the over-60 age group especially) who buy bonds for immediate income and profess not to care if the bonds fail years in the future, so long as they get their nontaxable income. Granted that a person can do anything with his own money, but if he is interested in leaving a viable estate he can still have his income and a good portfolio, too.

If the investor has sufficient assets to buy long bonds, he can get that high current income and know that his or her heirs will have good bonds which might be held until maturity or could be traded for others or, for that matter, even sold.

One of the problems that haunt many people is the fact that their heirs might sell the bonds as soon as they are buried. Therefore some of them put clauses in their wills that prohibit the selling of their bonds. This is bad business, as I have seen estates stuck with bonds bought in 1950 at 1.5 percent which do not mature until 1980.

I would be remiss if I did not touch upon the short-term investments that look so good when money is tight. This kind of investment can be classified under that great overall heading, the good-and-bad-news syndrome.

The good news is getting all of that tax-free income for such a short time. The bad news can come when you wait too long, and the tight money market subsides and your notes are not yet due for payment. This can all be avoided. For one thing, you can sell your notes, no matter how short they are. If they are a month away from maturing, any good bond dealer will take them and hold them until they can be redeemed.

However, the prevention care for this may be found in Chapter 22. I want to assure you that it does not take that much background to find some of the answers. Just as any of us can see a thunderstorm approaching, or knows that a rainbow heralds the end of a storm, you can also detect the changes in the bond market.

13

The Industrial-Bond Revolution

The industrial-bond era in the tax-exempt bond business has brought about major changes in the attitudes of the bond business and in the investing habits of individuals as well. The important point is how these changes have affected the individual investor. Still, the background of how industrial bonds came into being and how they became such a controversial issue is also important and interesting for any study of the problem.

First, let us look at the origin of the industrial-revenue bond and define just what an industrial-revenue bond is. The bonds originated in Mississippi. The officials of that time (the late forties) understood the basic problem of the region—the decay of certain areas because of the lack of industry. They needed to develop payrolls or their towns would die.

The familiar pattern of these places was that the young people, after receiving their basic education, would leave either for the universities (never to return) or for the urban centers where work could be found. These were places that thought they had no future, only a past.

This is the way it began. It evolved over a period of years. Other states picked up the idea, but the basic thrust of the program remained in the South. This was natural, since it was in the South that the real problem existed. This region needed an industrial revival as it tried to move from a predominantly agricultural economy to a balance of agriculture and industry.

One of the first undertakings that used tax-exempt bonds in any volume was a carpet factory in Mississippi in the mid-fifties. A nonmunicipal-bond firm named Gearhardt & Otis was the underwriter. Mr. Edward V. Otis was also an officer of the unofficial newspaper of the municipal-bond industry, the *Daily Bond Buyer.* Mr. Otis' brother, Barron Otis, was the president of the newspaper. The latter was told to have his brother resign, or the bond business would withdraw support for the newspaper. Barron caved in and his brother resigned from the paper.

It is significant that such a minor bond issue could raise such hackles and cause such an upheaval. It turned out that the anger expressed was really that of the people involved on the corporate side of the business. Industrial-revenue bonds were simply not respectable for the major firms. Why?

Recall who controlled the investment-banking business. The corporate-bond partners or officers made all the vital decisions. Most important, they decided that industrial-revenue bonds were a danger to their corporate business, which they correctly regarded as the principal source of revenue for their companies. However, they needed a better, or at least a more acceptable, reason for opposing this type of financing by local areas without directly rejecting them.

The leaders of the investment-banking industry found an issue, good old socialism. Remember that we were in a time when Senator Joe McCarthy found that he could scare as important a man as General Eisenhower as well as the ordinary citizen. The word "socialism" did not mean invoking the spirit of Norman Thomas—it meant communism and all that the Reds stood for. It meant ungodliness, the trampling of rights, and any other horrible affliction that a demagogue could dream up.

What did that have to do with industrial-revenue bonds? Nothing, but it was a handy weapon that could incite everyone. It appealed to the people who worried about increasing government intervention. It seemed to represent the attitude of most of us who feared Big Brother.

The fact that industrial-revenue bonds provided jobs was glossed over. The idea was to believe that the system would provide jobs as it always had. (The opponents of industrial-revenue bonds conveniently overlooked the fact that most of the companies seeking to use these bonds could not have gotten a hearing if they had tried to get corporate financing on Wall Street. In fact, it was a good bet that they could not have gotten past the receptionists to present their cases.)

Therefore as far as the opponents were concerned, the American way was the only way to finance new factories. This meant via corporate bonds. Their opposition was not really based on ideological grounds. They just did not want to lose any business to the municipal upstarts. Furthermore, they did not want to build up the municipal-bond business.

Thus although they acted like knights of the Round Table, they were really barons who wanted to control all they could see. As has happened in other situations, the slogan "the American way" became distorted as it was used to frustrate something that was needed. The industrial-revenue-bond situation was not a shining era in investment banking.

Thus the work of financing these projects went over to the smaller regional firms until well into the sixties. Then, as more states adopted similar laws, larger issues came into the marketplace, and better distribution was demanded. In the interim some investment bankers adopted a constructive attitude on this matter, but the people who were opposed to the idea continued to condemn it by invoking the flag and the American way.

It was around this time that opinion in the bond business began to polarize. The industry's official spokesman, the Investment Bankers Association (now the Security Investment Association) was hardly a true forum. The same people who made the "anti" policy controlled that organization. Their paid employees were expected to write booklets on the danger of industrial-revenue bonds. The votes at the conventions were little more than inside jokes. This pattern continued for a number of years.

In those years it was fashionable to invite a captain of industry to the convention so that he might denounce the practice of using industrial-revenue bonds. One year the featured speaker was an executive vice-president of U. S. Steel. It has never been ascertained whether or not he knew that U. S. Steel had used a variation of this type of financing in a port authority in Texas. This information did not faze the opposition. They went on pouring out even more ludicrous misinformation.

Strangely enough, at the same time there were general-obligation industrial-revenue bond issues which were the responsibility of the community rather than the company for whom the plant was being built. Most of the opposition to this type of financing came from the people who favored industrial-revenue financing. Their opposition was based on the belief that if a company wanted a plant built for its use, it should be able to make the lease payments. The people who opposed industrial-revenue bonds did not oppose general-obligation bonds, which attitude represents some sort of perverse thinking.

Then something began to change. The large corporate clients of the same investment-banking firms that had so vehemently opposed industrial-revenue bonds heard about this type of financing and wondered how it could be used to their advantage. Most of the major firms tried to dissuade their clients, but the companies were being wooed by large committees from local areas, who were roving the country looking for industry to relocate to their states. Some of the results of the entry of the large companies were not reassuring. One example was a $25-million refinery that employed very few people. The big boys had finally gotten into the act, and the consequences were not always pleasant reading.

It might be well to pause here to define what an industrial-revenue bond should not be. The industrial-bond concept was never meant for the huge corporations. Rather, it was meant for the company which was not top-drawer, but was still a good credit risk. Thus the spreading of the concept to the large corporations was a disappointment to the people who had fought for the right of industrial-revenue bonds to survive.

One problem was that most of the large investment firms thrust into the business ("pushed," they claim) knew nothing about how to structure these issues. They learned fast, however, and one of their methods was to lean on the smaller firms for help and advice. They received it because most of the smaller firms wanted to do a favor for a giant of the Street. Soon there were $100 million issued for companies like U. S. Steel. The major investment firms always proclaimed their reluctance, and they protested all the way to the bank.

Late in 1967 some members of Congress, aroused by the fact that their own states had no industrial laws and were losing businesses to others, set about getting rid of industrial-revenue bonds—concept and all. The states made a sorry defense, especially those states that stood to lose the most. They offered little or no resistance to people like Abe Ribicoff of Connecticut (which had no industrial law then, but has one now) and Henry Reuss of Wisconsin (who was still fuming about a company that left Milwaukee a few years before; he would never concede that the real reason they left was that the county of Milwaukee had condemned their property). Most congressmen and senators did not have many thoughts about the controversy, but their aides did. It was a victory for the second echelon, who were convinced that they were destroying some sort of plague.

Actually it was not all that simple. They had strong allies at the U. S. Treasury. Stanley Surrey was an undersecretary of the Treasury devoted to the idea of crushing tax exemption. It was not that Mr. Surrey and his colleagues were actually very disturbed by the concept of industrial-revenue bonds *per se*—just that the issue of industrial-revenue bonds gave Surrey & Co. a chance to jump on their pet peeve, tax-exempt bonds. As December of 1967 came to a close, a giant step had been taken toward destroying the concept of tax exemption.

When the hatchet job was concluded, the Treasury and its allies had gained a law which restricted industrial-revenue bond issues to $1 million. As is usual in such cases, the Congress made exceptions, and some of the exceptions were remarkable. Baseball stadiums, for example, were exempt. Of course that was understandable, because every city needs a stadium for some "poor" baseball-franchise owner. The bill also exempted industrial parks (which may seem the same sort of animal to the uninitiated). The Congress also made an exception for port authorities, because some of them, such as the New York Port Authority (which had opposed industrial bonds), were really closet industrial people who were actually issuing industrial bonds under a different label.

Most of the large investment-banking firms making large profits from pollution bonds do not remember how the exception for pollution bonds came into being. This was suggested by the pro-industrial-bond people to Chairman Wilbur Mills, who carried it through the joint committee conference. The pro-industrial group thought it made sense, and so did Mr. Mills. True to their backgrounds, most of the major firms thought that the exception was exceptional; in other words, that it was their due.

Since then the limitation on industrial-revenue-bond issues has been raised to $5 million. This seemed like a more reasonable figure, although some have been seeking to get Congress to increase it to $10 million. The important thing was that industrial-revenue bonds survived the onslaughts of bias and inertia.

That is the story of what happened in the recent past with industrial-revenue bonds. Now we turn to the problem an investor has concerning these bonds. They should be considered suitable for investment. This does not mean, however, a cursory glance at the bonds, but a good hard look instead at the company for which the project is being built.

It can be said that industrial bonds are similar to corporate bonds. The difference is the tax-exempt exterior of the industrial-revenue bond. The usual basis for deciding whether to buy these bonds depends on whether you like the company or not. This makes it similar to the common stock of a company. We all have companies and groups of industries that we like or dislike.

The basic thing to remember when investing in an industrial-revenue bond is that the company for which the project is being built and which will be responsible for lease payments (which go to paying the principal and interest when due) is your biggest concern. Too many investors worry about the town in which it will be located, but it is the company's health you should be checking. What has the company been doing for the past several years and what is its net worth? This is the most vital statistic, and it can be found in the balance sheet in the prospectus. If there is no balance sheet on the company, forget the bond.

I have developed a formula (which I consider a minimum) that the net worth should be equal at least to the amount of bonds being issued. Although this was considered too permissive ten or fifteen years ago, today many would say that those of us who advocate the one-for-one formula are old hat and possible has-beens.

Some of the more "enlightened" (translated, this means people with bonds to sell that usually cannot meet the one-for-one formula) people argue that the formula rules out proper consideration for sales volume. Nevertheless, old-timers question what could happen if the economy runs into a recession or worse. In that event, net worth will stand up far better than sales subject to the times.

The popular name for industrial-revenue bonds when they are being sold is IDR—Industrial Developing Revenue. It is a type of bond that can be most deceiving because of the mistaken notions many investors have of the guarantees on the bonds. Many investors see that a county or town is sponsoring the issue and think they have a local guarantee, when what is really happening is that the locality is serving as a conduit through which the bonds can be offered. Unfortunately too many communities, in their eagerness to snare industry, forget to do a proper "due diligence" on the company. It hardly profits a community to bring in a poor company that folds and leaves an empty building and many people out of work. Add to this the problem of investors who probably did not show too much due diligence either.

It is shocking to find that many IDR issues around the country are ready to default or have already defaulted. If you check out the companies involved, you will find that most of them have no net worth at all. It makes you wonder about investors, and it proves Barnum right in his observation on suckers. Just as remarkable are the people (such as bankers and merchants) who serve on industrial boards and allow these issues to be sold.

A further look at these issues shows that some of them have been sold to "underwriters" at seventy cents on the dollar, but resold to foolish investors at one hundred. Then when the issue has problems, the irate bondholder looks for the culprits. All who can be found are the board, the bond attorney, and the trustee bank. There are cases where these people are being sued, although the responsibility for the security of the issues did not belong to them. The real culprits are the underwriters and the salespeople who sold the issue to the public. They could have had someone check out the company if they were too busy to do it themselves. The truth is that they were probably dazzled by the high rate of interest.

While pollution bonds are usually issued under IDR regulations, they are also usually issued on behalf of utility companies for the companies with excellent balance sheets. They don't yield as much as the run-of-the-mill industrial-revenue bond. However, they usually represent a concession to the market and can be obtained for better yields. An objective look at pollution-control bonds (again depending on the guarantor) is highly recommended for good investing.

Industrial-revenue bonds are structured in the same way as other revenue issues. There are usually some short-term maturities which we call serials, and the bulk of the bonds are due in twenty, twenty-five, or thirty years. The setting of maturities usually depends on the leasee, because the payments are tailored to the company's needs. The payment that they make to the trustee bank must cover all expenses of the issue—the principal, interest, and other costs such as trustee fees, etc. Remember that the issuing body has no part in any payment; it acts merely as a conduit in having the bonds issued.

This is something that can never be emphasized too much. Bondholders have no recourse, either to the city or the county that issues the bonds. However, I advise that you buy bonds of a city or county in preference to those of an authority. This is because the city and county will make sure that some due diligence has been performed as to whether the company has the ability to pay. Even though they are not themselves liable, most cities and counties would rather not suffer the embarrassment of default if they can prevent it.

The lesson to be learned about industrial-revenue bonds is that they are great investments if approached correctly. However, there are people who could destroy the concept because of the issues that they are sponsoring. Naturally it behooves all local officials to be careful. Investors have to realize that an IDR bond is the easiest type to check out, if they will just look at the balance sheet to see if the bond can meet the one-for-one test. Make sure that the balance sheet is audited by a competent accounting firm. Even the question of whether the bonds are rated becomes secondary to the security.

The history of the industrial-revenue bond has been an interesting as well as a stormy one. The question of whether an investor should buy these bonds, and if so, which ones to buy, is also interesting and challenging. However, following the one-for-one formula takes the mystery out of it. If balance sheets confuse you, however, or if your record of buying common stocks has been bad, then think about general-obligation bonds or tax-free funds. The main thing is to be comfortable.

14

How About
Tax-Free
Funds?

So you are the kind of investor who doesn't want to fool
around with clipping coupons, even tax-free ones. You also
say that you do not want the problem of picking out your
bonds. So I will tell you what I am going to do—I am going
to introduce you to tax-free funds, because they afford you
diversification and convenience, which is what you are talking about.

Over the years I have been very interested in this type of
security. Back in 1952 I investigated it, hoping to use the
established mutual-fund companies as distributors for the
municipal funds. However, they were not ready for such a
move and defeated the proposition by their internal bicker-
ing before it even reached the Congress.

Tax-free funds came into existence because of the dog-
ged persistence of the original sponsors. Any changes that
have been made occurred only after some very difficult
bargaining sessions. This is why all of the funds are identi-
cal in their structure and in what they have to offer. This is
fine for investors because they know that the various funds
are all the same. (However, it is not so good for those who
have had new ideas which became the property of everyone

else after the information was known to the regulatory bodies.)

I believe that the tax-free fund is just what this volume-increasing market has needed. It is a godsend to those investors who just do not want to be bothered with choosing bonds. It is also a great thing for the investor who is mutual-fund-minded but would also like to invest in tax-exempts.

But the greatest benefit of tax-free funds will be the demand they create for bonds that will alleviate the volume that is pounding this market day after day. However, this is no reason for investors to buy. Their only reason should be based on the yield. I believe that this type of security passes these tests, but there have been some criticisms.

Now and then someone will write an article that casts doubt on the security of tax-free funds. The emphasis is always on the portfolio which has been gathered to create the fund. In most cases these portfolios have not contained the very best bonds that could be purchased. However, they were bonds that could be defended and bonds which had enough yield to make them interesting to investors.

One of these articles appeared in an issue of *Barron's* in early 1974, written by a young man who had some limited trading experience. He compared the portfolios of the various funds (the ones being sponsored by Merrill Lynch and cosponsors) to portfolio-type funds run by trust departments of banks and divided among their clients. But he did not mention the yield that a client would get if he or she had picked the low-yield, bank-supervised fund. Most investors would not have been interested in the very skimpy return.

Most of the critical articles about funds concentrate on the load, and there is no doubt that this is an area that must be brought into range. One quote from the *Barron's* article that is worth repeating is, "Motivations for seeking the highest possible return are to cover the load charges and enhance the fund's sales appeal." This is like asking the old joke and pertinent question, "Have you stopped beating your wife?" It is impossible to win. What the author of these articles was hinting at was that the managers of the fund would do most anything in their buying to fill the fund with bonds that would have a satisfactory yield level after the fund was able to take its four or four-and-a-half points load. Some critics have also questioned the rating that Standard & Poor's have given some bond issues, which allowed those bonds to be purchased by the funds. In other words they are saying that these ratings are basically sweetheart ratings.

I would say that this charge is baseless. Where the author of the *Barron's* article made himself a target for criticism was in his denunciation of the bonds of New York City and other urban centers. This was definitely a cop-out on his part, because he was picking on credits that were increasing, rating-wise, at the time.

There is no doubt a load charge of 4 or 4½ percent still charged by some funds does affect the current return that an investor can earn on these funds. One-half percent in the load takes away a negligible amount of your yield. However, there is also a plus point. The load is a one-time situation. These funds do not have annual management fees. There are critics who will say that the low price you get on selling units is actually equal to another load charge. They argue (and rightly so) that if the units have to be resold, the penalty is usually absorbed by the seller of the units.

The Municipal Investment Trust Fund managed by Merrill Lynch has charged a 3½-percent sales charge for some time now. This has to be regarded as a breakthrough in the load area. It will be difficult to get much lower. In fact, most of the MITF competition is still at 4 and 4½ percent. It is difficult to get below 3½ percent because of the expense involved in floating one of these issues. Merrill Lynch has the advantage of being able to underwrite large issues. This brings about a smaller cost per unit and thus a lower sales charge.

It might be a good idea to look at how the purchase price of a unit in tax-free funds is determined. The price is actually determined by the evaluator (Standard & Poor's in most cases). They evaluate the portfolio once each week and the price they arrive at becomes the price of the units for the following week.

There is an element of profit and loss in the gathering of a portfolio that does not affect unit holders. When a sponsor is gathering bonds for a fund, these bonds could go up or down depending on the market. This does not affect the worth. If there is a loss then it is absorbed by the sponsors; it also follows that they receive the profit if the bonds move up in value.

This sometimes disturbs critics of tax-free funds. They seem to want a one-way street. They want the investors to share in the profits but to be free of any losses. Things do not work that way.

Criticisms aside, I think that the two most important attributes of tax-free funds are convenience and diversification. Perhaps I should have listed diversification first, because it might seem as if I am touting an easy way which can be a problem in the end for investors. It is not true in this case and I will show you why.

There is no doubt that diversification can be the greatest attribute that any fund can have. As the markets get lower, there is more diversification as to rating. In July 1974 one prominent fund was advertising that 90 percent of its bonds were rated A or better. In fact, 44 percent of their portfolio was AA and AAA. This means that the fund had taken advantage of the advice that people like myself offer. When the market is lower, upgrade at almost the same price you would have paid for lower-rated bonds previously. This is precisely what the funds do. I would have to defend convenience when that convenience does not hurt what you are doing. The convenience, aside from the gathering of a portfolio in one security, comes in having your bonds evaluated at least once per month, and the fact that your interest is mailed to you sometimes as often as once per month.

Just to prove that something extra can be worked into the tax-free fund market one underwriter recently underwrote an insured fund. This means that the principal and interest on the bonds in the fund are insured, thus guaranteeing payments to the holders. Standard & Poor's has awarded this fund an AA rating even though some of the bonds are rated as low as BBB.

The insured funds that I have seen indicate that the yield to the investor is not too far off the yields of the funds that have no insurance. Is there a catch? No. However, if you want to be technical you would have to say that there is no assurance that the insurance company is going to be able to continue meeting its obligation through the life of the various bonds. But it is a very reliable insurance company and is considered a good risk to meet its obligations if called upon.

There also has been a certain amount of experimentation in funds where all bonds are located in one state, usually to get a tax exemption. There is much to be said about this kind of fund and it should be attractive. However, the reaction of investors has not been overwhelming up to this point and therefore you do not see many funds of this type being marketed.

If you are one of those people who have believed the myth that tax-exempt bonds are hard to sell after original purchase, the tax-free fund makes you a believer in the fact that tax-exempts do make a readily saleable security. The apparatus provides that the sponsor makes bids; but if he does not, then the trustee will buy the units. The result of such an action could be the sale of bonds in the portfolio. Up until June of 1974 this has always been avoided but a group in Los Angeles which was sponsoring a fund of 10,000 ($10 million units) decided that it could not sell any more than about 6,000 (they had begun the selling operation in February), because the market had moved down too far to justify the sales at the prices the sponsor needed.

Thus for the first time (at least to my knowledge) a fund had to sell bonds from its portfolio to redeem the unsold units. This, of course, hurt all the unit holders. It also brought home a lesson in this area. The underwriting of tax-free funds requires that the sponsors be strong capital-wise. It is not an area for companies who only have good ideas, but do not have the capital to sustain necessary losses if they occur.

Here I am championing the large firms over the smaller ones, which is an unusual position for me. However, it cannot be avoided when you consider the liquidity of these funds. (Unfortunately, ingenuity is not the only talent that a tax-free fund manager must possess. The ability to take the consequences of an adverse market is also a prime requisite.)

Another thing to remember about all existing tax-free funds is that they are closed-end funds. This means that they cannot be extended. This also means that if any bonds are called in advance of their maturity, then the fund has to make a distribution to the holders and the fund is reduced by that much. There is no reinvesting of the funds.

Despite my assertion that tax-free funds are good vehicles for investment, each fund must be looked at from the standpoint of what that fund contains. I hope that you do not think that I have written that you should accept any fund because it is diversified and convenient. You must still exercise reasonable judgment as to the portfolio. You must agree with the judgment of the people who have purchased the bonds for the fund. If you do not like just one of the bonds I would tell you to pass it by and wait for the next one.

As I wrote earlier, the lower the market, the better portfolio a sponsor can get. In the higher markets the sponsors are forced to lower-rated situations so as to maintain yield. Therefore it has to be apparent that yield is the most important factor, although it must be yield based on security.

Do not forget that there are always tax-free fund units on sale. There is constant movement in the secondary market which allows you to pick some good bargains. As in the basic tax-free market there is a good chance that your best bargains might be in the secondary market. The factor that works on your behalf is that the evaluator, not the bond dealer, sets the price that you pay for the units in the secondary market. It makes for a very fair way of operating a market.

I have reproduced a glossary for tax-free funds (Appendix 13) which should give you some help in dealing with the principal factors of tax-free funds. I think that potential investors will find it handy when dealing with their first purchase.

Current Return—You usually see bonds computed on a yield basis to maturity. However, since all funds are sold on a dollar basis per $1,000 unit, yield is stated as current return. To figure a current return, you simply divide the net annual income per unit (which is found by dividing the net annual income by the number of units outstanding) by the public offering price that you pay. Of course any change in the net annual income will affect this current return. This is the way a hypothetical fund would look:

Annual Interest Income $68.00
   Per Unit
Less Estimated Annual Expense ....$ 1.50
Net Annual Income Per Unit $66.50
Net Annual Interest Rate Per Unit ... 6.65%
Public Offering Price............ $100.25 per unit
                          [$1002.50]
Current Return 6.63%

15

Some
Definite
No-No's

You may have thought that you had enough or adequate warnings in Chapter 6 (Caveat Emptor), but after watching the evolution of this tax-exempt business for over twenty-five years, I think that you cannot be warned about some things too often.

There are several warnings which need repeating over and over again so people will take the situations seriously. The most important ones involve having loans outstanding when you own tax-exempts, tax swaps, and the evaluations that you are given for your bonds by some bond houses.

Let's take the evaluations first. Too many times false evaluations are given, especially by the firm of origin. This is why it is a good idea to go to someone not connected with the particular bond issue that you bought. Of course there is a certain amount of bad-mouthing that goes on in this business. Therefore you can sometimes call a firm not in the underwriting where your bonds originated, who may make it sound like the worst bond ever issued. You sometimes wonder which is worse—the protective evaluation or the tear-down technique.

However, when you think about evaluations you must

automatically think back to the vice-president who lost his job at the Chase Manhattan Bank in October of 1974 for overvaluing the bank's bond portfolio, which included government bonds, notes, and tax-exempt bonds. Thus when someone asks why you don't get an evaluation, you may wonder whether an evaluation would mean anything.

There is no doubt that bond traders are notorious for hiding bonds or their true prices. Back some years ago a promising bank officer lost his job with a Chicago bank because he was involved in something that they called "the daisy chain." This was a plot to hide the fact that certain bonds had lost quite a bit in value. The scheme was to keep passing the bonds among a group of dealers and dealer banks. Finally the scheme was discovered and several houses almost went out of business, and the vice president of the bank in Chicago went off to another part of the country.

The point of the story is that there is a certain amount of hanky-panky in this area, especially when the dealer has a special interest in the bonds being offered for evaluation.

Now there is an extenuating circumstance in all of this. Many people ask for evaluations when what they really want is a bid. In the language of the business, evaluations, working indications, and bids are three different things. If you are asking for an evaluation, then you are trying to get a bid for the purpose of knowing what your portfolio is worth. A working indication is when you are nearer to selling the bonds, and the bid is something that the dealer making the bid must stand behind.

If you are inclined to think that all of these variations are just too much for an investor to worry about, you are right. You should be able to know what your bond is worth at any time. I know this idea will not be received well in the industry for fear that investors will be coming in looking for bids at all times whether they intend to sell or not.

Of course the absence of any posted market makes some investors nervous. It is not enough to say that they should not be in the market if they are going to be that nervous. That's fine, but show me (and them too) the law that says they cannot ask for bids. This is why we sometimes miss the trappings of an auction market, although in reality the auction market does exist—more so than in other markets.

The expense of going out and getting bids for bonds can be a problem. If one of the computerized brokers is asked to get a bid for a client but it is really only information for the client, he will not be too eager to do it after that. If the request is made almost daily, the dealer handling the account will make the estimate himself.

I believe that all evaluations, whether done for firms or for clients, should be performed by people who have no axes to grind. Too many times have I seen portfolios chopped up by rival firms who recognized the bond of a competitor. This was because the accounting firms used to think that the way to audit a firm was to give out its bond list and let the competitors go to work on it. Being accountants, they did not care about anything except that final number. If I said that a certain bond was worth eighty when it was actually worth ninety, they could not tell.

This is why your own accountant is not the right guy to check out your portfolio. He probably read all he knows about tax-exempt bonds in some meager bulletins issued by his National Group. We need better evaluating than we have. There are several firms who do this work and they have no connection with any bond issues.

There is an excellent system for evaluating bonds. It is a book called *White's Tax Exempt Bond Market Ratings* and it is published by Standard & Poor's. It was invented by one of the greatest characters of the tax-exempt-bond business, Wilson "Pete" White, Jr. It lists most issues and it numbers each issue; there is a yield level that is available each week and which you can key into the numbers assigned the bond issue. The people at Standard & Poor's tell me that this book can be obtained for $180.00.

To be very blunt about it, those who buy bonds and need a day-to-day evaluation should not have bought the bonds in the first place. Bonds are a long-term investment. Those who buy them for a quick profit are in the wrong ball game. Bonds should be purchased for the income—in this case, the tax-exempt income. I am not saying that an investor should not have the right to know what his or her bonds are worth. The truth is that an evaluation (if given honestly) is enough.

Tax swaps are among those very misunderstood situations where the misunderstanding extends to the so-called experts in some of the bucket shops, who do much swapping and make a big deal about it. The truth is that most swaps, if placed under the scrutiny of the IRS, would not stand up. However, it should be said that the IRS asks for a certain amount of this confusion because they set no guidelines. They just make decisions on whether you have been right or wrong. I have been talking (with the IRS and other Treasury people) and writing about this situation for many years, yet no one has ever been able to give guidelines—or perhaps they do not want to do so.

In the meantime there is a group of bond dealers who have set themselves up as experts in the area. They make swaps which my grandchild could tell you were wrong, and yet people fall for them. Many of these swaps are made between customers. This may not sound like a bad idea, but the incestuous action does not make it right when the ingredients are wrong.

A good swap, as I know and understand the procedure, is one where bonds swapped are similar in type, rating, and purpose. For instance, a swap of a city and a state bond of two different ratings would not work or, should I say, should not be done. The maturities should be very similar and the yields used in the exchange should be very close together. I realize that to some people—the so-called experts—this is something from the Dark Ages and does not show any imagination.

I love imagination, but when you are advised to swap New York City (rated A) versus Syracuse (rated Aa), or if the coupons are 4 percent and 5 percent, or if the maturities are about ten years apart, that is not imagination—that is sheer madness. This sort of imagination is an open invitation to the IRS to move in.

You must eventually meet your friend at the IRS and explain what the swap is all about. The "expert" who advised the deal is usually long gone by then.

What this means is that when you are doing a swap you

should consult your accountant and your lawyer, or at least one of them. Let them tell you whether they would do it. If they say no, repeat that *no* loud and clear to the salesman who tried to arrange the swap.

Do not get me wrong—tax swapping in tax-exempts, as in other areas of the business, is a most legitimate situation when it is done right. However, make sure that you are getting the right information from the right people. Also, check on what profit they are trying to make on you. Do not forget that they are not taking a risk on your transactions. Therefore there is no need for them to make a big profit —even if that bright young salesman needs a Mercedes.

We are now back to the first situation—loans that have a relationship to your tax-exempt bonds. People are shocked when the IRS calls them and questions them about mortgaging their house to buy tax-exempt bonds or the fact that they have borrowed money to buy tax-exempt bonds. The problem comes because the taxpayer is trying to get tax deductions too. Now you might ask how the IRS found out about the tax-frees when the interest does not have to be reported. In these days, when the Social Security number is used for all purposes in order to better identify all of us and what we do, it is easy for the IRS to find out this information if they try hard enough.

Not too long ago a man outside of New York wanted to retain me to help him prove that the IRS was wrong in denying him one of the deductions that he was claiming. He was claiming a deduction on a loan for a mortgage yet was also taking his tax-exempt interest. He was certain that I could find precedents among my records showing that the IRS could not tax his tax-exempt bonds. He was most disappointed when I told him that I could not take the case because he was lost before we began.

The record will show that the IRS has won case after case when they can prove that a loan was taken to buy tax-exempts. Therefore it is my advice not to get excited when someone tells you how you can get the government two ways by mortgaging your house and buying tax-exempt bonds. I do not say that you will not get away with it, but I do say that the rate of ripping off the IRS is decreasing all the time. If it is up to the computers there will be no loopholes. Trying to get both sides of the interest deal (getting tax-exempt interest and getting a credit for paying it) is the perfect tax loophole that is being closed and in truth should be. Such deals give tax-exempt bonds a bad press and give some politicians a chance to expound on how evil tax-exempt bonds are. The truth is that there is nothing wrong with the principle except when the unprincipled try to slip through loopholes.

16

What About Those Defaults?

Default is an awful word, whether you are talking about bonds or any other loan. Some of the critics of tax-exempt bonds have taken the several prominent defaults that have occurred and have blown them out of proportion. There have been defaults, but the defaults are very minor when compared to the amount of tax-exempt bonds outstanding.

Let us consider the prominent defaults and analyze why they took place and how could they have been prevented. It may give us some insight and thus help us avoid such issues in the future.

There is no doubt that you will hardly ever find a default in a rated issue although one such issue in the state of Maine (rated AAA by Standard & Poor's) did default several years ago. However, the record will show that very few rated issues have failed since the great Depression. The record will also show that all of those issues that did default have paid off (or are in the process of paying off). Not only have they paid their back interest but most of them have paid interest on interest.

There is an interesting story of how Ed Wright, of St. Petersburg, Florida, started buying bonds in the Depression because he believed they would eventually pay out. He bought such issues as the Treasure Island Causeway near

98

St. Petersburg, and was amply rewarded. He also purchased bonds in Coral Gables, Florida, as well as many others.

Ed Wright became a millionaire. He became a benefactor to the West Coast of Florida where he lived, and he always loved tax-exempt bonds. However, his fame as far as I am concerned is wrapped up in the fact that he won a case in the Supreme Court of the United States and established the principle of interest upon interest.

This happened because of the Coral Gables bonds that he purchased. He believed that he should be compensated for the late payment by being paid interest on interest. He hired a prestigious New York law firm to fight the case. After a long fight he won and established a principle that almost makes defaulted bonds bearable.

This is important to individual investors and you should protect yourself by checking out or having the salesman check out the default section of the indenture of any issue that you may have under consideration. Do not buy an issue where the issuer has the right to deny you interest on interest if and when there is a default. (Since that Supreme Court decision, some issuers have done this. I consider it wrong and foolish of any investor to let them get away with it.)

The principle also works well for investors who buy after the bonds are in default. Many people have made excellent buys in projects that they correctly assessed were at the bottom. They buy the bonds with coupons, which have not been paid, still attached to the bonds. The return can be very generous. Most investors consider this negative investing. It is really not negative at all; in fact, it is fairly positive. What you are doing is making a decision that a certain project is going to be going uphill from then on.

The most famous of all the tax-exempt defaults in the last twenty years was the West Virginia Turnpike. Over the years many plans were put forth for setting the West Virginia issue on its feet. I was one of the people who suggested that the state of West Virginia could do something for the bondholders. The purists chided me and the others who were suggesting that a bail-out for bondholders should take place. We were only interested in helping bondholders, but it seemed that we were wrong.

The argument presented by the purists was that the investors had read, or should have read, the official statements and the feasibility reports, and therefore they were aware of all the facts. They bellowed, "Caveat emptor." However, I did not and still do not believe that the bondholders of some of these issues received the full facts, because I do not believe that many ever read the material. Also, the "art" of disclosure was not something we worried about in the fifties. I do not believe that there was any fraud in the bond presentations but there sure were some big holes. There is doubt (twenty-twenty hindsight, of course) whether the issue should have been sold.

It has been said that the West Virginia issue was sold because some politicians, engineers, contractors, and bond men wanted to make a profit. It was a project that was many years (at least) before its time. The feasibility report was glowing and the bondholder bought. It wasn't long before it became evident that not enough drivers wanted to drive over the road. Over the years there have been many ideas for West Virginia to bail out the project, but the state (like other issuers of like projects) found that its credit rating was not hurt by having a sick child hanging around. Then of course there were the purists who insisted that investors take their medicine when they made a mistake. However, the purists never advocated any punishment for the greedy ones: the contractors, engineers, and some managing underwriters.

The day the city of Chicago's first Calumet issue sold (there were two, and both are in default), it was said that shiny limousines were handed out to the people in Chicago who had the votes to shepherd the project through the Chicago City Council. Of course this could be the usual bad-mouthing of competitors, but in the years ahead there were more and more converts to the rumor as many of the bigwigs behind this ill-fated road were indicted on other charges. The mayor of Chicago has worked hard to get the federal government to take over the skyway. He even succeeded in having amendments attached to important bills in the U. S. Congress. But none of these amendments passed.

The strange thing about the city of Chicago (which received an advance to an AA rating after all of these shenanigans) was its unwillingness to be concerned about the bondholders. The city refused to increase the tolls even though the indenture called for it. It had to be ordered to do so by the courts.

The Chesapeake Bay Bridge and Tunnel Authority was a tremendous issue of $200 million which had its doubters from the start. The issue had a lot going for it: It had Merrill Lynch, Pierce, Fenner & Smith; the First Boston Corporation; and Allen & Co. heading the underwriters. There were all kinds of reserves built into the issue—they funded money for four and a half years of interest payments plus other reserve funds. This enticed a number of underwriters into the deal. They never intended for themselves or their clients to be around for too long a period.

It was not too long before many firms in the Street realized that after the cushion (the reserve fund for interest payments) became deflated there was not much that could be said for the issue. Most of these firms were advising their clients when to sell. Actually, if tax-exempts had been under SEC some of the information might have been considered insider stuff.

The managers indignantly issued denials all over the place, but the record shows that the doubting Thomases were right. They might have been off by a few months but the house of cards known as the Chesapeake Bay Bridge came tumbling down.

Some investors did not know what was going on because the biggest seller, Merrill Lynch, maintained a position in the bonds and tried to hold the market together. Therefore their clients never heard a discouraging word on the bonds. Their ability to assess what was going on was rather bad. In addition, there were people who held out hope that, because this project was an agency of the state of Virginia, the commonwealth would not let the bondholders down. Well, there is always a first time.

Feasibility was again the problem. Wilbur Smith of New

Haven, the traffic engineer, had made no mistakes up until 1960 (the year of the Chesapeake issue) in his previous looks at future revenues of many road projects. The theory was that since he was batting 1.000, he should be given a chance. However, many doubted his reasoning that people would wander over to the Norfolk area and motor down the bleak seashore road to Florida when you could (by then) bypass Baltimore and Washington and zoom (very much more scenically) to Florida. In fact, very few people who made the trip to Florida each year bought the bonds. It was an omen generally disregarded by the underwriters.

Beware of the marginal revenue issue that depends on the report of feasibility and the clout of underwriters. In the Chesapeake issue, many people went into the under-writing because they wanted to make brownie points with the managing underwriters. Most of these people did not retail a bond. They sold their bonds in the Street to other dealers who liked what they read, and who believed that it was not their function to worry about those matters. Unfortunately, intellectuality and responsibility are two qualities lacking in many of these dealers.

The inability to question is dangerous. No investor should allow a dealer to sell him or her bonds without receiving a good explanation of what the bond is all about. There is also the question of whether that dealer really believes in the project and why. It is a sickening feeling to see a bond dealer push a marginal issue on the phone and then bad-mouth the issue at lunch.

The first realization of an impending default brings chills to the market. Panic is the order of the day. Early warnings that a default might be coming are usually only heeded by a minority. However, the word gets around because the lack of revenues is very obvious and figures have a way of being consistent. There is usually no miracle to turn the revenues around.

Again, most of this information has been available, but most dealers do not send out reports. If you buy a bond, make sure that you get all the reports you need. Also ask if the revenues are up to predictions. You should not have to ask, but if you do not get the information, do not hesitate to sever your connections with that firm. The firms that hide their heads like ostriches also hurt their clients.

Despite the record that most issues in the tax-exempt area (and especially those that show increases) usually work out, the first reaction is always very bad. Bonds go down to 25 or so. For instance, in October 1974 West Virginia was at 63½ bid for the 3¾-percent issue. However, this is not bad when you consider the coupon. The Calumet of 3⅜ percent was 42 bid, which is not as good, but again you must consider the low coupon—and also, Calumet had not been struggling as long as West Virginia. Bringing up the rear was the Chesapeake, and here there is mixed reaction. The 32 bid for a 5¾-percent coupon is representative of the fear that it will be a long, long time before this issue works out.

There are all kinds of issues on the defaulted list. (One of the types of issues that used to be prominent on the list but has moved off are the gas-revenue issues.) We have a tramway in Palm Springs, California, which was built by an authority of the state of California (Mt. San Jacinto), but which has not received any help from the state. In fact the state has been hostile to this project, which has added a lot to that area. Also in California we have an automobile speedway sponsored by the city of Ontario. Ontario worked on this project for many years and finally got it financed. Today it is about the sorriest of the defaults.

The record of ski projects and projects like Ontario Speedway has been very bad. If baseball parks and football stadiums were financed on a pure-revenue basis, we would have even more defaults. The inevitable question is, What happened? Invariably the answer lies in the feasibility report. The problem is that people do not always react the way you think they will (see Chapter 8).

However, now that I have described all the bad points, it is time to look at the positive side of some of these issues. True, there are some that will never be revived. However, I have seen some pretty mangled issues come back to life and make their way to liquidity. In fact, if some West Virginia investors had held on they would not have taken the bad losses they did, and would be getting interest on interest today. Of course this is hindsight, but you would be surprised to know how many investors never did sell their bonds.

There are also the investors who join the parade when the bond is down. Many astute investors saw opportunities in West Virginia and Calumet just as Ed Wright did in Florida issues many years ago. The interest-on-interest situation, plus the fact that they are traded flat, which means that you pay no interest when you buy, is attractive. Therefore what the investor buys is unpaid coupons and a chance to be paid the principal when due. (It is at least fourteen years away in West Virginia's case and twenty and twenty-five years in Calumet and Chesapeake.)

These issues that can make it back from the brink of disaster (perhaps that is a little dramatic but that is the way the bondholder feels at that moment) are remarkable in that they are still surviving. They are viable if a bit slow. Traffic increases all the time on these projects and time seems to be on their side. In many gas districts it was a matter of people getting used to natural gas and discarding propane systems that were not as convenient. However, change always creates problems.

When someone like myself discusses defaults, the natural tendency is to make comparisons. I can cite scores of stock issues which have defaulted completely in the weeks previous to this writing and where investors have lost their entire investment. My point is that most tax-exempt investors who happen to be trapped in a defaulted issue usually "live" another day because the issue continues to pay interest, however belatedly. In addition, the principal amount of the issue is usually paid (especially on long term situations) as the problem is cured by time. Even the interest payments that are late earn interest. It is true that some tax-exempt issues have also completely defaulted, but the amount is miniscule. However, a default is not something to be brushed aside as unimportant. Each default is important because it should not happen. Because they are governmental entities, issuers have greater responsibility about the type of issues they authorize. However, the real responsibility lies with the investor and that investor should know the people from whom he or she is buying.

17

The Anatomy
Of a
Bond Issue

Over the years I have written many essays and delivered many lectures about how a bond issue is born. I refer to the area as Hometown, USA, because this represents all cities and towns. Some of the people who have read these essays or listened to me have suggested they were getting a civics lesson. Exactly. This is what municipal bonds are all about. They are the part of Civics I in high school that we never learned.

What happens when a bond issue is authorized in your town or city is civics except that sometimes most of us think of it as politics. Our way of government is being demonstrated. But too many people think that bond issues are just a figment of some politician's imagination, which will possibly enrich that politician.

That is fine for newspaper consumption and the political dialogue that takes place during elections. However, the truth is that most issues are incubated in our minds—yours and mine—because we want, and that *want* is translated into bond issues. We want schools, roads, libraries, hospitals, and you name it, but we want them.

We all do not want the same projects, but somewhere

105

along the line we want something that can only become a reality if bonds are issued.

The first step in organizing a bond issue is getting grass-roots support for that project. It is necessary both to prove the need for the project and to show that it is politically palatable for the elected officials. There is no use pushing a project that cannot be sustained on both counts. What many people forget is that the political motivation is supplied by the voters. Any sign of displeasure by a segment of the voters is enough to kill what you may think is the worthiest project.

We have all sorts of reasons for opposing projects. Some older people oppose new schools because they have no more children to educate. Some people oppose new streets because they do not want any more growth in their area. These reasons may sound selfish but they exist and must be recognized.

Some cities and towns have votes on these matters; others do not. When they are not decided by votes, you can be fairly sure that the elected officials try to determine the feeling of the voters. If they do not, they cannot run for reelection with any hope of making it.

Thus an investor can feel reasonably sure that the issues being financed by Hometown, USA, are not necessarily pork barrels or frivolous issues. This assurance is essential if you are to believe that Hometown, USA, can indeed pay off this obligation.

Okay, where do we start? Suppose you are the chairperson of the drive to build a new library. You organize a committee and finally bring your petitions to the attention of the city council. A friendly councilman or woman introduces a bill committing the city to build a new library. This is the beginning—but only the beginning.

Now the city council must hold hearings. There will be those who do not believe that a new library is necessary because you already have one. However, after a skirmish, sometimes lasting only weeks but sometimes even months or years, the city council says yes, there will be a new library. Its studies show that the library can be erected at a cost of $4 million. It authorizes a bond issue for the project. It decides that the bonds should mature equally—$20,000 bonds per year for twenty years.

If you live in a city that has to have elections on these matters, then an election is set. However, the number of cities and towns that call for referendums on these matters is growing smaller. This is not a matter of curtailing democracy, but a belief that an elected official must stand on his or her record.

Well, whichever way the project is approved, we then move on to the legalities. Notices must be printed. The city attorney and the bond counsel who usually approves the bonds for the city are called in to work out the legal snarls. A date is set for the bond issue by the fiscal officers of the city. In many cases the fiscal officer is aided in his decision by a fiscal consultant who can be either a bond house, a bank, or a consultant who specializes in setting up bond issues.

When the date is decided upon, the notice of sale is printed in the newspapers as the city ordinances require. It is also usually required that the notice be printed in the *Daily Bond Buyer*. The *Daily Bond Buyer* is the tax-exempt bond industry newspaper; it makes sense to have the notice printed here because the various underwriters find the issues they bid on in this paper.

In this notice of sale the terms of the sale are outlined. The prospective bidders are told when the bonds will sell and how the bonds will mature. There is also information about any maximum interest rates (because many states have ceilings on rates) which may restrict the bidders from bidding rates which are too high. It may also contain a restriction on using very high rates in the early maturities. This latter practice is legally correct because it usually falls within the average net-interest cost prescribed by the notice of sales. However, it often puts such a burden on the issuers in the early years that some states and cities have prohibited the practice. The way they do that is to not allow a bidder to have more than a certain percentage between the highest and lowest coupon.

When this notice of sale appears in the *Daily Bond Buyer*, the managing underwriters go to work on structuring their bidding accounts. Actually, most accounts have already been established, although this does not stop an under-writer from forming a new account. However, most un-derwriters stay within the same accounts for many years. In the good markets, firms were always trying to better (add to their commitments) their position, but recently most have stayed with the status quo or dropped out. The issue we are talking about here is a moderately small issue in the context of today's market.

In addition to the manager there may be an average of nine or ten underwriters in each account. The manager and two other firms may commit for $500,000 each; five other firms or banks might be in for $400,000; while two smaller firms may have $250,000 each. As this is a general-obligation of Hometown, USA, banks can bid on the issue. In fact, there probably will be many bids made.

The next thing the city and its financial advisors have to do is to visit the rating agencies. The rating agencies want to see the latest figures. After they decide what the bonds should be rated, they publish their findings. The city pays for this service and the costs are charged to the bond issue. Let's assume that both Moody's and Standard & Poor's have rated the bonds A.

Then everyone waits for the day of the sale. The sale is by sealed bids. The notice of sale contains a bidding form or at least the form to be followed. Hometown, USA, might be a thousand miles from some of the bidders and therefore the account managers arrange to have local banks or bond dealers cover the sale. There is one other important item: A certified check in the amount of 2 percent (or in this issue, $80,000 must accompany the bid), or the bid is not ac-cepted.

Before the bid can be made, an underwriter must gather his fellow underwriters and decide on what to bid the issue. The process is one of comparison. They begin with what other comparable A-rated bonds are selling for and they go on from there. They decide the coupons and the yields for each maturity and they decide on the amount of profit per bond. In an issue like this the profit might be a little less or a little more than $10 per $1,000 bond, which is not much. Profits vary. In strong markets they are low and in weak markets they are higher. What a profit margin basically reflects is the down-side risk. Simply put, if the bonds cannot be sold at the yields decided, then the profit margin becomes the cushion. It usually isn't enough if you are wrong.

Now we are at city hall in Hometown and the bids are being handed in. If the notice of sale calls for the bids to be in at twelve noon they had better be there or they are not accepted, even if the late bid is a better one than all the rest. The bids are opened and the tabulations are examined —many times a bid may be figured wrong. After all the bids are checked the city announces the winning bid. This may take an hour or more.

However, back on Wall Street and in other financial districts they are already checking out each other, and the results are known about one minute after twelve noon. Of course, every once in a while there is a bid that is not known, and that one may win the bonds. In the meantime, the people who thought they won were already offering bonds. This does not happen too often, but it has happened a few times and sometimes in some large issues.

Let us say that ABC Bank has bought the bonds. The job of selling starts immediately. The managing underwriter sets an order period of an hour or two and all members must enter their orders in that period and cannot confirm bonds to clients until they are confirmed by the managers.

Group-account orders have priorities. These are orders where all members of the underwriting account share in the profit and they usually cover several maturities. For instance, a bank (perhaps the manager in this case) will take all the bonds through ten years, which is half the issue. If you had asked for $5,000 of those bonds you would not get them. This annoys many investors but it is not a legitimate complaint.

Your salesperson's firm may not be in the issue but they can still get bonds because a dealer's concession is allowable to them and represents their profit for selling the bonds to you. On new issues and most other tax-exempt situations the price to you is a net price with no commission added. Make sure that you never pay a commission on a tax-exempt unless your broker is acting as an agent, and then the charge should be about $2.50 per bond.

There are other things that the managing underwriter must do. They will have to arrange for an ad (hopefully not like many that I decry in Chapter 9). The city must arrange for the printing of the bonds and the bond counsel must begin his job of deciding whether the bonds are legal. You have about thirty days before the bonds are delivered, and this takes us to the next chapter.

18

The Mechanics
Of a
Bond Delivery

In Chapter 17 we went as far as the selling of the bond issue for Hometown, USA. We were ready for the procedure that is necessary to deliver those bonds to institutions and you. Let us suppose that you have purchased $5,000 of the bonds due in 1989. You have received your confirmation that the bonds have been sold to you on a when-as-and-if-received-by-us basis. This means that the dealer or bank who sold you the bonds will deliver the bonds to you if he gets them.

Why wouldn't he get them? There are many reasons why a delivery might not go through, although most of them do. The attorneys might find some problems with the issue. A group of taxpayers might go into court to have the issue restrained. The only problem that you should not have is the failure of the underwriters to pick up the bonds and deliver your bonds to you.

This is because the majority of underwriters are able to pick up an issue when it is ready. The words "pick up" in this instance refer to the ability of the underwriters to pay for the issue before they have received the money from the investors. In Chapter 6, I warned that you should not necessarily help your dealer pay for the bonds. The bond business is a risk business and dealers should be able to pick up their bonds without help from their customers.

In the hypothetical issue that I set up in Chapter 17 we were up to the delivery stage. However, before picking up and redelivering the bonds there is a lot of paper work and printing to be done. For instance, the printing of the bonds. A tax-exempt bond is a very complicated item. It has to have coupons attached for the life of the bond. This of course means different sets of coupons for each maturity. There is a great deal of documentation on a bond, plus the printed legal opinion (in most cases) of the bond counsel. The bond counsel is the one responsible for getting the bonds printed in that he must provide the wording that goes with the bond. He must also check out bond number one to see if it is correctly printed. Every once in a while a bond gets printed incorrectly and there are a lot of red faces, but this does not happen too often.

During this period the bond counsel is checking out the issue completely to see if there is anything illegal about its sale. Actually, he usually does this prior to a sale, but he has to check out court decisions in order to be prepared to render his opinion that the issue is legal.

During this period, if the bonds are all sold, the underwriters wait as do the investors. You, the investor, have not paid any money as yet and the underwriters have paid only 2 percent of their bid. Often the underwriters are still struggling to sell the bonds up to the time the bonds are delivered. In fact, they may be forced to sell bonds at lower prices than they sold to you. What does this mean to you? Nothing. It comes under the heading of winning a few and in this case losing a few. It also points up the hazards of buying new issues.

There has been much debate over the years as to why the time lag between sale and delivery is so long. I was on an *ad hoc* committee about fifteen years ago which looked at the problem and tried to shorten the delivery period, but it is still a long, drawn-out situation.

One of the problems is that some citizens, perhaps your

next-door neighbors, are thinking about challenging a bond issue. These cases are usually governed by certain state laws. If a litigant can file suit against a bond issue and just have his or her own costs to worry about, then there would be more suits. However, if, as in many states, the losing litigant has to pay all costs, then it is a different deal. They hesitate before they file nuisance suits. Without disparaging the right of a citizen to file a suit, I must say that most of these cases that I have seen over the years have been nuisance suits.

As the time of delivery draws near, the city or home town and the managing underwriters set a date for the delivery. This gives the underwriters a chance to bill the clients for the bonds.

In this case let us assume that the bonds were dated July 1 and the delivery to the underwriters will take place on July 15. This means that the redelivery of bonds might take place on July 16 or 17. In the days of tight money, when it is costly to carry bonds, the dealers or the banks try to get the bonds delivered as fast as possible.

When this redelivery date is set, the bonds are confirmed to the institutional and individual customers. If July 17 has been set as the date, you will receive a bill from the bank or dealer you purchased them from with the price of the bonds figured to that date plus sixteen days of interest (as the bonds were dated July 1). Of course you receive tax-exempt interest from July 1 because when you turn in the first coupon it will be a six-month coupon. Occasionally there is a short coupon because of dating problems. For instance, if the bonds were dated October 1 and the issuers wanted all their bonds due January and July, then they would attach a three-month coupon to the bond. If that issue were delivered in mid-October you would still be entitled to a three-month coupon on January 1.

Thus if July 17 is the delivery date, you must have the funds to your bank or dealer on or before that date. As you can see there is a two-day lag before the bonds are delivered. However, the managing underwriter obtains a loan for the entire account for the purpose of carrying the bonds until delivery. The way they do it is to have each of the underwriters deliver his funds to the bank on the day of delivery, thus satisfying the loan.

You can see why it is so important for the managing underwriter to have solvent companies in the issue. The failure of an underwriter to pick up his bonds would force all the others to do it in proportion to their commitments in the overall underwriting. Thus if company B failed to pick up 200 bonds, that amount of bonds would have to be split among the other underwriters in proportion to their over-all part of the underwriting account. This has not happened often, but it has happened—especially in these days of very tight money.

Now let's concentrate on how that small purchase (but so important to you) works out. Your dealer (who may or may not be a member of the underwriting group) has sent you a confirmation. The numbers may seem like Greek to you, but you can check as to whether the number of days and the interest is okay. In Chapter 20, I will show you how to figure that interest easily.

You should have someone pick up your bonds as quickly as possible. There is no excuse for long delays. I would recommend that the bonds be in your safe-deposit box and not in any vault unless your seller is a bank. You should make arrangements to have the bonds delivered to your bank. Of course if you handle your own bonds you can go to the underwriters' office and pick up the bonds yourself. Make sure that whoever picks up the bonds inspects them to see that they are the right ones (in your case it will be one $5,000 piece) as to maturity and that all the coupons are there.

Make sure that the legal opinion is either printed on the bond or that you have a copy of it. Also see to it, if the issue is a revenue-bond issue (the Hometown issue was not), that you receive a final copy of the official statement, because in a revenue-bond issue the delivery is not complete without this statement.

You should also have a copy of the official statement even for a general-obligation issue. File it with the bonds so that you know the circumstances of the issue, in case you want to sell the bonds. I would also recommend that you make a card with the pertinent data on it for your information. Write the name of the issue as it appears on the bond, and the coupon and the maturity day plus the date of the issue. Also place on this card the name of the trustee bank and the paying-agent bank so that you can decide which is more convenient when you want to cash in your coupons. This will give you a record to look at when you are attempting to get a bid or an evaluation on the bonds, without having to go to the vault.

This is a good time to warn you that you will probably have a bearer bond. This means that if you lose it or allow it to be stolen (if you leave it around you could be allowing it to be stolen), the thief could cash in the coupons, although he might have trouble if the reported theft is given publicity. However, why have any problems at all? Place your bonds in a safety box and enjoy the tax-exempt interest.

This means that you must tear off a coupon every six months. Do not tear off coupons in advance because if for some reason you have to sell the bonds, the delivery could be flawed because of the detached coupon. If your bonds are at your bank they may tear the coupons for you and claim the interest in your behalf.

This is how bonds are delivered. In large issues it is a gigantic task, but it is all part of this business and there are people working every day, with the help of computers, trying to make the process easier and more efficient. However, you still have to know what is going on so that you can know that you are getting the right bonds.

19

All About
Bond Insurance,
Discounts,
Calls,
Tenders, Etc.

In this particular chapter I am going to be writing about some of the situations that bond holders will face from time to time. Many of these situations deserve a chapter of their own. However, I am going to condense my discussions and try to explain them in abbreviated sections.

Bond insurance—This is a growing field in which several insurance companies are now insuring various facets of a bond issue. In the general-obligation area the insurance company will insure that the principal and interest are paid by the issuing bodies over the life of the issue. When this insurance is issued, Standard & Poor's will give either a AA or AAA rating (depending on the insurance company issuing the policy) on the bonds insured even though the bond issue without insurance might only deserve a BBB rating.

In the lease type of revenue bonds (generally industrial-revenues) there are other companies who will guarantee the lease payments, which of course lead to the payment of

116

the principal and interest on the bonds. I have already covered the type of insurance that is given on tax-free funds in Chapter 14.

Now the sixty-four-dollar questions: (1) Does this insurance help marketability? and (2) How dependable are the companies? I am not sure that the insurance has made that much of an impression up to now but this could be because many investors do not understand it. I know that I have been disappointed in the small number of insured issues. How dependable are the companies? I do not think that Standard & Poor's would base its rating of AA or AAA on a company's guarantee if they did not think that company was in good shape. However, the ultimate decision of whether you think a certain company has the ability to meet its commitments is a personal one. You can get help from your accountant or attorney on this question. Take a look at their balance sheets and their record. Treat them the same as you would a bond issue.

Calls—Call or redemption features bother many investors. Over the years I have met many investors who refuse to buy any bonds that have call features. However, this is increasingly hard to do except in relatively short-term general-obligation issues. Most revenue issues have call features.

What is the function of the call? It is merely a device whereby the issuer gets a chance to call in your bonds by paying you a premium (which is stipulated when you buy the bonds) and can thereby retire the bonds or refinance the project. The latter case usually prevails when the project has been doing well revenuewise and there is a chance of refinancing at lower rates.

When all the bonds of an issue or a maturity are not called they are usually call bonds in inverse order. This is why some people try to get the highest-numbered bonds in a maturity.

How do investors fare in the matter of calls? I think they do well because as long as the call price is high enough you are protected. However, it is important that you take a good look at the call schedule and how it works. Read my explanation in an official statement in Appendix 11.

Discount bonds—There is good news and bad news about discount bonds, but it can all be good if you use some discretion when buying them. I know of no better way to invest, especially in a high-interest-rate market, because the bargains are there. In my opinion, there is no better way to invest for a college education than via discount bonds.

Remember—if you do not receive the right amount of yield you could be in trouble. If you hold the bonds until maturity (which is usually the aim) then you *must pay a capital-gains tax.* Let us assume that you were to buy a 3½-percent bond due in five years at 7.3 percent. If you were to figure in a 25-percent capital-gains tax, then the effective yield would be 6.6 percent, which would be in line with other current coupon issues in that maturity range. The way to figure what the effective yield would be is explained in the next chapter.

If after figuring what your effective yield would be after capital gains you find that the yield is considerably lower than the yields being offered in the market, pass it by and look for another offering.

Be very careful of a discount bond that is called a fractional. It is another get-rich-quick scheme. Fractionals are the bonds with very low coupons—one-quarter and one-half of 1 percent—which sell for very low prices. The rationale for this type of bond was that some insurance companies can use them in their portfolios. However, I do not consider them suitable for individual investors. Do not be misled by some hot-shot salesman that you can make a lot of money on this type of investment. Ask your accountant how you will fare taxwise if you buy them.

Interest dates—Sometimes an investor gets bowled over by a salesperson who says the bonds are J&J or A&O. What he or she means is that the interest is due January and July or April and October in the latter case. Why is this important to know? Well, it lets you know when your bonds are due for interest payment, which is what this investing is all about. In the previous chapter I discussed how interest dates are set and what the date of the issue means.

It is sufficient to remember that there are only the follow-

ing interest-date combinations, and they can either be one
or fifteen, which means the first day of the month or the
fifteenth day.

> J&J—January and July
> F&A—February and August
> M&S—March and September
> A&O—April and October
> M&N—May and November
> J&D—June and December

Tenders—A tender offer is usually made by a city or an
authority that has money in the bank and wants to buy
outstanding bonds so as to lower its interest-cost requirements. Tenders usually abound in bad markets. This means
that the issuer will usually be able to buy back bonds at
considerably less than the price at which they were issued.

When a tender is advertised, the issuers usually agree to
buy a certain amount of bonds at the lowest prices ten-
dered. This means you are in a contest and you will find out
how badly someone wants to sell his or her bonds.

Actually, the process is similar to that used by companies
that went public and now want to buy back their stock.
But those companies usually put a price on the stock; this
is different from the bond tender. I am not sure which
is fairer. The best thing about either situation is that it is
optional on the part of the holders.

How does the investor find out about these tenders?
Many of them are printed in the *Wall Street Journal* in the
form of ads in or near the bond section. Of course this is
another service that you can expect of the person who
handles your bond-buying. He or she should bring this to
your attention, and should also help you with the pricing
and file the form for you. This all comes under the heading
of service.

Sinking-fund operations—Most revenue issues have sinking
funds. Some of them are mandatory but some of them are
not—they may have accumulated funds since they do not
wish to call bonds at premiums when the bonds are selling at

deep discount if the bonds came out at a time when interest rates were low.

These sinking funds are managed by the trustee bank. They operate very quietly because they are under no obligation to act publicly except when they ask for tenders. But there are many bond dealers who follow these situations very closely. It is difficult work and needs a lot of research. In some cases there are "sweetheart" situations where a trustee will favor one dealer over others, but you are going to find this kind of thing in all phases of business life.

So where do you come in as an individual investor? It is difficult for an individual to operate in this market without the cooperation of the person who sells you bonds. They can tell you about these situations if they know about them, but they usually do not. The information is usually known only to the traders, who are not famous for worrying about investors. They usually have enough problems worrying about their positions and making a profit. The problem for the individual investor is not to be picked off. If you hold a bond that could be a candidate for a call and you get a bid for the bond, ask a lot of questions. Just do not let some trader make a big profit on you.

Advance-refunded issues—These are not as important as they used to be because the Treasury has revised its regulations on the arbitrage of tax-exempt issues. Here is how it worked: An issuer would see that because its credit had improved, its bonds could be refunded at lower rates. However, there may have been bonds outstanding that were not callable. In other words, these particular bonds would have to remain outstanding until their maturity date. In an advance refunding, these bonds in effect are escrowed because cash or U. S. Treasury Bonds are put up with the trustee to cover their interest and redemption price. Thus the bonds become AAA. Most individual investors sell the bonds to banks at a good profit. These issues are very few and far between unless the credit of the issue moves very much higher. This is because the Treasury sets a limit on the coupons that can be set in the refunding. While it was easy to do these refundings, there were many of them. The

Treasury caught on to the fact that there were sometimes two issues outstanding representing one project. One was the refunded bonds in escrow but still outstanding, and the other was the new issue. However, it was fun while it lasted. If it did not prove anything else, it proved that tax-exempt-bond people are great mathematicians.

20

Tax=Exempt Bond
Math
Made Easy

Some investors are bothered quite a bit about all the high-sounding math of yields, percentages, and so forth, in bonds. They are impressed by their confirmations, which show the price carried out to many places. Many common-stock buyers found that the arithmetic involved there was quite simple. In fact they even found that doing a price/earnings ratio was not difficult. If you mention bond math, however, they recoil in horror.

This reaction is unfounded because when you strip away all the fancy frills and the sophisticated calculators, it is just simple arithmetic. Now if you love gadgets, you can—if you haven't already done so—buy one of the new computers that will do everything. It seems that they are used for everything including totaling the grocery list.

I am not telling you not to buy a calculator, only that a pencil and paper and some of that old-time math are sufficient. I find doodling with yields very stimulating.

This chapter will cover the situations that require whatever math you need for bonds. Of course, there is a lot more math in bonds than this—figuring out amortization schedules, for example—but what follows is all you will need.

1 ● Formulas for figuring out what the tax exemption means for you in your tax bracket.
2 ● How to figure interest.
3 ● How to figure yields—including current, to maturity, and discount yields.

I first started using the formula method for figuring tax equivalents years ago, when I found that many people do not like to disclose their tax brackets. I therefore let them sit with the pencil and paper and told them how to work the formula. It always worked well for them—I hope it does for you.

This formula works two ways. You can find the tax equivalent of either a tax-exempt bond or a taxable security. In either case the formula begins with ascertaining your tax bracket and then finding the differential:

$$\begin{array}{r} 100 \text{ percent} \\ \text{Less} \quad \underline{?? \text{ (your tax bracket)}} \\ ?? \text{ (the differential)} \end{array}$$

Let's assume that you are in the 32-percent tax bracket. You have been offered a tax-exempt bond with an 8-percent yield. You want to know what the taxable equivalent is without looking at the chart which you probably would not carry everywhere. Well, the differential is 68 percent, and you divide this into the 8 percent:

$$\frac{11.76\%}{68 \overline{/\ 8.00}}$$

Thus you have found that the equivalent taxable yield is 11.76 percent. Now suppose you were seeking to find what you must earn in a tax-exempt bond to equal an interest rate of 10.5 percent (taxable) being offered to you. Once again you use the differential, but this time you multiply as follows:

$$\begin{array}{r} 10.50 \\ \times \quad .68 \\ \hline 7.14 \end{array}$$

So you see that you require a 7.14-percent tax-exempt yield to equal the offering of the taxable security.

Knowing how to figure interest is a skill you can use in many endeavors, not only bonds.

First of all, remember that tax-exempt bonds are figured on a 360-day year, while U. S. Treasury Bonds and other transactions such as mortgages are figured on a 365-day basis. If you would like to check the interest on your confirmation, or if you would like to find out how much tax-exempt interest you made in a certain period, just follow this example. If you buy $5,000 of 7 percent bonds you would earn $350.00 per year. The bonds are due January 1, 1975, and you are having them delivered to you March 14. This means that you must pay two months, thirteen days interest (you always figure up to the day before delivery). One day equals approximately $.9723. Multiply that by seventy-three days and your answer should be $70.98. You should be able to come within a penny or two of the figures on the confirmation. Actually, if you were to look at an interest table you would find the official figure is $70.97. Close enough? Remember, the table was prepared with computers and figures were carried out to many, many places.

There is another area where figuring yields can be very illuminating. Remember that the interest you earn and the discount or the premium you pay determine what yield you earn. All examples being used assume a $1,000 bond, even though most bonds are in denominations of $5,000.

One thing that confuses tax-exempt investors is that bond dealers do all their transactions in either dollars or yield to maturity. As I have pointed out before, most investors do not expect to be alive as long as some of their very long-term investments, which might mature as late as 2015. The yield most of them are interested in is the current return. You hardly ever see current return shown in an ad for bonds. However, many dealers show it in their offering sheets. You can see this in the Lebenthal offering sheet reproduced as Appendix 4 in this book.

Current return has to do only with the interest that you earn. You need two factors. Let's say that you have purchased a 7-percent bond at 102—how do you determine the current return? It is simple. You divide the coupon by the amount paid as follows:

$$
\begin{array}{r}
6.86\% \\
1020\,\overline{)7.000} \\
\underline{6\,120} \\
8800 \\
\underline{8160} \\
640 \\
\underline{612}
\end{array}
$$

Thus 6.86 percent is what you are earning.

Since yield to maturity is the way bond dealers and banks express yields in ads, let us find out how this is arrived at. Let's assume that this is a bond with a 6.5-percent coupon due in ten years, and you purchased it at 105. What is the yield to maturity?

First you find the current return, which is:

$$
\begin{array}{r}
6.19\% \\
105\,\overline{)6.50} \\
\underline{6\,30} \\
200 \\
\underline{105} \\
950 \\
945
\end{array}
$$

Then you divide that 5-percent premium you paid by ten years, and you find that this reduces your yield (5.0 percent ÷ 10 years) by .5 percent per year. Subtract this and you find

$$
\begin{array}{r}
6.19\% \text{ (current yield)} \\
-\ \underline{.50\%} \\
5.69\% \text{ (yield to maturity)}
\end{array}
$$

Now if the bond was a discount bond at 6.5 percent for twenty years and you purchased it for ninety, you have two situations. You want to find the yield to maturity, but you also have to take into account that Uncle Sam demands a 25-percent capital-gains tax from you if you do hold those bonds for twenty years (which is possible). Again you find the current return:

$$
\begin{array}{r}
7.22\% \\
90\,/\overline{6.50} \\
\underline{6\,30} \\
200 \\
\underline{180} \\
200
\end{array}
$$

Taking the ten-point discount over the twenty years, you find that it is again worth .5 percent (10 percent ÷ 20 years), but this time, since it represents a discount, you add it to the current yield.

$$
\begin{array}{r}
7.22 \\
+\ \ .50 \\
\hline
7.72\%
\end{array}
$$

This is the yield to maturity, but this is not the yield you will earn, because you will have to pay that 25-percent capital-gains tax. Thus all you will have gained from that 10-percent discount ($100) after the capital-gains tax of 25 percent will be $75, or an effective discount of 7.5 percent instead of 10 percent. Therefore the factor becomes .375 (7.5 percent ÷ 20) rather than .5, and this is the true yield to you:

$$
\begin{array}{r}
7.220 \\
+\ \ .375 \\
\hline
7.595\%
\end{array}
$$

Some of the above calculations may seem bothersome, but I maintain that in addition to being a good mental exercise, it gives you a better look at bonds in the tax-exempt market. It also removes much of the mystery when you find out that these things can be figured out so easily and so quickly.

How to Become A Bond Expert By Reading The Papers

I am not talking about all of the technical problems of setting up bond issues or the expertise of being able to judge how bonds should be rated. What I am talking about is being a good judge of what lies ahead in the market. I think that I have given you enough ideas to help guide you in your choice of investment. However, timing is another matter and can, when all is said and done, be the most important one of all.

All you really need to do is read the *Wall Street Journal* daily. Aside from its financial content, I find that its other features are also very interesting.

If you have the time, there is also excellent information in *U. S. News & World Report* and in *Business Week*. I might also recommend my own column in the *OTC Market Chronicle*, a weekly publication.

However, the *Wall Street Journal* on a daily basis gives you a rundown of the various sales of new issues, including tax-exempts, corporates, and governments. Do not forget that all bonds are related because they all go to make up a major section of what we consider the money market.

Aside from the statistical information it contains, the *Journal* has some interesting people writing on its editorial pages, with many points of view from economists such as Walter Heller and Paul McCracken. I find the editorials in the *Journal* very interesting and I use them, even though I rarely agree with them. You might say that I lean more toward Walter Heller than toward Milton Friedman.

This is how I use the *Wall Street Journal* editorials: In the monetary crisis of 1974, the editorialists at the *Journal* became almost hysterical when rates were starting to move down. They implored Dr. Arthur Burns, the Federal Reserve chairman, to hold the line and keep rates up.

Whether I agreed with the editorials was not important. I took this to mean that the rates were indeed going to go down, and the *Journal,* as the publication that stands for the old-time religion (as regards finance), was making a last stand. In the next few weeks, the prime rate did move down substantially.

Now this does not sound too scientific, but I am not sure that economics is very scientific. I am not sure how some of the so-called experts arrive at their predictions, but I can assure you that a majority of them just have gut feelings. This is also the basis of the *Wall Street Journal* editorial viewpoints. My favorite nasty crack is to suggest to the financial people that they start using an astrologer.

There are other ways to gauge the markets ahead without using the gut-feeling approach, although I recommend that a little of it be kept in your thinking mechanism. Here are some of the things you will find in the *Wall Street Journal* that will give you clues to what may happen:

1 ● Each Monday they print a tax-exempt index. Now, the *Bond Buyer Index* (published by the *Daily Bond Buyer*) is thought to be the official one in the industry, but no individual investor can afford $732 a year for a subscription to the *Bond Buyer*. To be truthful, the *WSJ* index runs fairly close to the *Bond Buyer* average. The fact is that most indices use the same bonds as the bases for their index. The *OTC Market Chronicle* also runs one each week that I compile. These various indices indicate the direction of the market. They run inversely—in other words, if the market im-

proves, the yield goes down; and if the market worsens, the yield goes up.

2 • The *Wall Street Journal* covers the important sales in all of the markets and gives reports on how they do. Years ago the tax-exempt-bond people never gave out balances, but everything eventually changes. This also gives you an idea of what is going on as to yield levels and reception.

3 • The *Journal* gives you capsule comments on what various bond dealers and buyers for institutions are saying. Over the years this part of their coverage has improved.

4 • Of course the reports on the prime rate are important as well as those on the cost of federal funds. They are usually found on the bond page.

5 • Each Friday there is a story on the Federal Reserve Bank weekly report. This should be studied. The total amount of loans is most important to the money market, and the money market controls the bond market. If loans are going up, then we are in for tighter money; and if they are going down, this is an indication of easier money being ahead.

If you take a few minutes each day to read these various articles, you should know what lies ahead for the bond market. In this way, you can either go ahead with an investment or hold back. It seemed to me that when we reached the 12-percent-rate mark in 1974, there was not much further to go. That, therefore, represented the low of the market. Conversely, as the prime rate tumbles, you know that rates are going to be lower.

The record of the past several years shows that the time spans of up markets (when yields are low) tend to be much shorter than down markets (when yields are high). Therefore the wait until yields start to move up again usually has not been very long. Of course this could change. I think it is indicative of the times we live in with the inflationary aspect and demand for capital.

I always recommend that bond investors be aware of political trends. In the past fifty years the Republican party has stood for "hard money," while the Democrats have usually been supporters of "easy money." Therefore you should keep an eye on politics. If you see a Republican trend, then you know that the old-time religion might be dominant again. If you see the Democrats moving ahead, then you might expect that money will be easier. However, nothing is certain, and these roles might even shift. They may even make the money market nonpolitical. Anything is possible.

Unemployment has a lot to do with what happens in a bond market. It is strange but the bond business depends on economic disasters to do better—you will find that yields go down when unemployment rises. It is the old theory that bonds offer a better investment shelter in bad times than anything else. This could be true, but I feel that bonds are an investment for all seasons.

Inflation is the hated word of institutional buyers. Each time the rate of inflation goes up they cringe and wonder whether they can afford bonds because of the fixed rates. While I am not an advocate of inflation, I do not get as paranoid about it as some of the people I see writing in (or being quoted in) the *Wall Street Journal.* I recommend that you do not, either. I agree with Dr. Milton Friedman on his idea of indexing bonds. This would mean a variable rate, and it has been used with many corporate bonds.

The problem is whether it can be used in tax-exempt general-obligations. I do not think it can, because most officeholders like to know the rate of interest. A rate that could float up would scare them. It can be used in tax-exempt-revenue situations, and I think that it might be a larger part of the bond scene in the years ahead.

One thing to keep in mind when you are looking at the bond market is that your outlook is not the same as the bond dealer's. To the bond dealer it is a good market when the yields are going down and the prices are going up. This is not to your advantage unless you want to sell some bonds that you bought in a lower market.

Your goal is to find the right time to buy. You also have to keep your funds active. Keeping them in a checking account will not help. When you are waiting, you should look for some short-term situations like tax-exempt anticipation notes.

Let us plot a hypothetical case. The yields in the market have been going down for several weeks. In fact the *Wall*

Street Journal tax-exempt index is about as low as it has been all year. You have read that some bankers are talking about large increases in loans. Times are good, but there is a hint of renewed inflation. It just happens that you have funds available at this time, and you think that you might want to buy some tax-exempt bonds. The signs are clear: *Wait.*

Okay, you agree that you should wait, but then what should you do? You look around for some short-term notes (tax-exempt, if possible, but straight U. S. Government bills for ninety days could work too) if the wait seems short. Of course, if you think that the up market has wended its course and a change is imminent, you might hold the cash and wait a bit longer. You could, however, also take the attitude that the down market has a long time to run. Then you could invest in a three-months note. The worst that can happen is that you sell out the short-term notes before they mature to get into longer-term bonds. There may be a slight loss, but in the long run it might be worth it.

In this book I have written about the short and the long term as far as investing. In this chapter I am referring to short and long term as they pertain to your investment thinking. You may read what a variety of economists have to say, and you will find that it is usually long-term. Actually it is easy to make long-term predictions. However, people who underwrite and trade bonds daily do not have the luxury of thinking for the long term. They must come up with the short-term approach because gut decisions have to be made.

You, as an investor, must work your ideas somewhere in between. You do not have to make gut decisions. Therefore you can be longer term and yet you cannot be an out-and-out long termer, or else you might do nothing. You would sit with your funds in the savings bank with little earnings, while you wait for your long-term hopes to come true.

I am convinced that most bond investors have more ability than they realize. I know that most of you can do as well as the salesman who is calling you and trying to sell you some bonds that his firm owns. If you are generally aware of what is going on in the market, then you are in a good position to deal with any salesperson. Establish the fact that you know what's going on—then you do not have to be following anyone. Accept the suggestions that I have given in this chapter, and you will really be informed—it is not necessary to know everything.

Let what happens in your investing be your idea, and not some salesperson's. This does not mean that you should not accept suggestions; but if you are informed, then you can deal with those suggestions in an intelligent manner.

What About the Future of Tax-Exempt Bonds?

Many people fear that the tax-exemption privilege will be eliminated and they will be stuck with bonds that no longer have the exemption.

Your only risk in buying a tax-exempt is the market, not the possibility of having your tax exemption taken away. Now, having made this statement, I will justify it.

Perhaps the idea that our local areas have the right to issue tax-exempt bonds does not impress many people. However, when you consider that the city of Hometown, USA, can issue bonds without getting the approval of some bureaucrat in Washington, as our friends in England, Italy, and France must, it is quite a deal.

The right to issue our own bonds is perhaps more important as a part of our local government than we realize. I am not discussing whether some of the officials in local government are everything they should be, but then that is our fault and our responsibility to cure the problem via the voting booth. The fact that we have the right to issue bonds is important. The reciprocity (no federal tax on local bonds, no state tax on federal bonds) that has existed since Justice John Marshall's decision has to be considered a plus be-

133

cause of what it has accomplished. Our schools, hospitals, roads, and other projects are monuments to this system.

It seems that every time tax exemption is threatened as it is "indicted" for being one among a bunch of so-called tax loopholes, the people who count always stand up and speak out. There is no doubt that when some people see rich individuals buying tax-exempt bonds, they think, "What an abuse." But is it?

Just so that you will understand what the alternative is, I am going to discuss what the Treasury would like to see. They would like all bonds to be taxable. They claim that this would save them money. They do not seem to realize that pension funds and mutual life insurance companies, which pay no taxes and buy more than $20 billion in bonds per year, would probably turn away from Treasury to local bonds. The drain on the Treasury would be that much greater.

There has been a debate raging for many years as to whether the matter of tax exemption is a constitutional problem or not. This means that the final decision could end up in the Supreme Court. I have always thought that the courts were reluctant to get into this situation. A decision to bring all bonds under federal control would be a difficult one.

The Congress does not want any part of the problem because of the pressure from the local areas.

I would not want to state that tax exemption will never be eliminated. Remember what I said above: There is no risk that *your* bonds may become taxable.

The one thing that I am absolutely certain about is that even if future tax-exempt bonds are banned, the existing bonds would continue to bear tax exemption. In fact, if the Treasury is successful in banning future issues, the bonds that you hold would become much more valuable.

They would, in effect, become museum pieces. This would mean that you would be holding a bond that could not be replaced by other tax-exempt bonds. There is ample precedent on situations like this. The U. S. Treasury had some bonds that were tax-exempt, but after 1941 all bonds and notes issued by the Treasury and the various agencies of government became taxable. However, the issues outstanding retained their tax exemption.

There is another reason why I am so convinced that the investor who buys a tax-exempt bond will not be stuck with a taxable security (which could bring on financial disaster for some people). This is my conviction that we have an almost sacred regard for contracts in this country.

When you buy a tax-exempt bond (just as with any type of bond) you make a contract to lend money. The other party makes an agreement to repay you a certain amount of interest every six months and to redeem that bond from you at a stated future date. In a tax-exempt bond, the local issuing body also covenants that the interest that you will receive will be tax-free. That is your contract, and you have the right to see that it is carried out.

I cannot see any Congress, administration, or court that would deny the validity of your contract. If they did, it would be a national disaster that could affect anyone with a debt contract, which is why it will not happen.

I can see where the federal government could conceivably pay off your bonds at 100 to remove them from the market. They might even replace them with fully taxable bonds at a higher rate of interest, although I think that is not likely to happen. All I am trying to point out is that you will not be stuck. That is the basic fear that most bondholders and would-be holders have.

Therefore I can see no reason why all investors who can gain from tax exemption should not be holders of tax-exempt bonds. Remember, most of the myths about tax-exempt bonds are just that: myths. If you accept my reasoning as set forth in this chapter that you will not lose your tax exemption, and if you accept the evidence that I have set forth in this book that tax-exempt bonds are marketable, I wonder why you are waiting to invest in tax-exempt securities.

However, I would like to remind you just one more time that you should not buy tax-exempt bonds without due thought and discussion with the people who give you financial advice. Tax-exempt bonds are a boon for this nation and they can be a boon for you, but you must do your part in performing due diligence. You must take time to consider just what type of bond you need. Make sure that you know what that bond is all about. Just as it is your (and my) responsibility to make the administration of our local areas better through electing qualified and honest officials, it is your responsibility to buy bonds with your eyes wide open. If you will, you can help eliminate the bucket-shop operators who would sell unsuspecting people defaulted bonds or other undesirable issues.

Tax-exempt bonds and funds are a splendid way to invest. They have weathered depressions and other economic disasters. If you have been on the point of buying but have had some apprehensions, I hope that I have cleared them up. Even though I have written a lot about the pitfalls, I think that so long as you recognize and avoid them, you will thoroughly enjoy your tax-exempt investments.

APPENDIX 1

TAX-EXEMPT-BOND VOLUME FOR THE PAST FIFTY YEARS
(The figures are in millions)

1925	$1,405	1950	$3,694
1926	1,362	1951	3,278
1927	1,478	1952	4,401
1928	1,390	1953	5,558
1929	1,442	1954	6,969
1930	1,383	1955	5,977
1931	1,252	1956	5,446
1932	937	1957	6,958
1933	1,128	1958	7,449
1934	1,175	1959	7,681
1935	1,196	1960	7,230
1936	1,156	1961	8,360
1937	984	1962	8,558
1938	1,229	1963	10,106
1939	1,099	1964	10,544
1940	1,498	1965	11,084
1941	1,229	1966	11,089
1942	576	1967	14,288
1943	508	1968	16,374
1944	712	1969	11,460
1945	819	1970	17,761
1946	1,204	1971	24,331
1947	2,354	1972	22,940
1948	2,990	1973	22,735
1949	2,995	1974	22,725

APPENDIX 2

WHO OWNS THE OUTSTANDING TAX-EXEMPT BONDS?

There are over $190 billion in tax-exempt bonds outstanding. The following table reflects the various groupings of investors who hold these bonds:

		% of Total
Commercial banks	$95,661,000,000	50.3
Insurance companies	33,807,000,000	17.8
Individuals*	50,524,000,000	26.6
State and local government, various funds	3,957,000,000	2.2
Savings banks	921,000,000	.5
Corporations	4,038,000,000	2.2
Brokers	1,130,000,000	.6
TOTAL	$190,038,000,000	

* This grouping includes bonds purchased by trust departments of banks for clients or held in estates.

APPENDIX 3

THE TAX-EXEMPT BOND GLOSSARY

This glossary for the most part was compiled by John M. Nash for his booklet "Tax-Exempt Municipal Bond Guide." However, I have added some definitions which I think are appropriate.

This is not a list to memorize, but it is handy to have around when you read an article or a prospectus and the words do not seem to be those that you use in everyday conversation.

Accrued interest—Interest earned on a bond since the last coupon payment or since the dated date, whichever is later.

Ad Valorem tax—A tax based on the assessed value of property.

Amortization—Special periodic payments which pay off a debt.

Assessed valuation—The valuation placed on property for purposes of taxation.

Basis book—A book of mathematical tables used to convert yield percentages to equivalent dollar prices.

Basis price—The price expressed in yield or net return on the investment.

Bearer bond—A bond which has no identification as to owner. It is, therefore, presumed to be owned by the bearer, or the person who holds it. A bearer bond is said to be in bearer form.

Blue list—This is a publication printed daily which lists offerings being made by dealers and dealer banks. The publication can only be subscribed to by dealers and dealer banks. No investor, whether institutional or individual, can buy a subscription. However, your sales organization can use it when seeking bonds for you.

Bond—An interest-bearing promise to pay with a specific maturity.

Broker—The word broker when used in connection with tax-exempt bonds, means a firm which acts as an agent for dealers and dealer banks. They have no transactions with investors either institutional or retail. They act for a stipulated rate per bond and do not take a position in any bonds.

Bucket shop—A bucket shop is a bucket shop whether it be in stocks or bonds. This is the kind of firm whose integrity is questionable because its selling practices are that way.

Businessman's risk—This is a title given to certain high-yielding bonds because they usually represent some sort of risk or have speculative aspects.

Callable bond—A bond which is subject to redemption prior to maturity at the option of the issuer.

Closed lien—A pledge made solely to one issue which prohibits pledging of the resource.

Coupon—That part of a bond which evidences interest due. Coupons are detached from bonds by the holders—usually semiannually—and presented for payment to the issuer's designated paying agent, or deposited in his own bank for collection.

Coverage—This is a term usually connected with revenue bonds. It indicates the margin of safety for payment of debt service, reflecting the number of times or percentages by which earnings for a period of time exceed debt service payable in such period.

Current yield—A relation stated as a percentage of the annual interest to the actual market price of the bond—same procedure as computing a stock yield.

Dealer—This is the title for firms or banks who underwrite and trade tax-exempt bonds.

Debt limit—The statutory or constitutional maximum debt-incurring power of a municipality.

Debt ratio—The ratio of the issuer's debt to a measure of value, such as assessed valuation, real value, etc.

Debt service—Required payments for interest on and retirement of principal amount of a debt.

Default—Failure to pay principal or interest promptly when due.

Denomination—The amount or par value of a bond which the issuer promises to pay on the bond's maturity date.

Discount—The amount, if any, by which the principal amount of a bond exceeds the cost price.

Dollar bond—A bond which is quoted and traded in dollars rather than in yield.

Double-barrelled bonds—A bond secured by a pledge of two or more sources of payment, *e.g.*, special assessments and unlimited taxing power of the issuer.

Feasibility study—A study made by an engineering or CPA firm as to whether a revenue project is feasible and whether the principal and interest of the issue can be paid when due.

Federal funds—The rate paid by banks for overnight interbank loans.

General-obligation—A bond secured by pledge of the issuer's full faith and credit and taxing power.

Gross debt—The sum total of a debtor's obligation.

Guarantor—This usually refers to a company that is guaranteeing the debt service on an industrial revenue bond issue. It can also be the issuing authority in some cases.

Index—An index in tax-exempt bonds is usually the average yield for an A-rated bond in twenty years, although there are indices with other maturities. The most prominent indices are the Bond Buyer Twenty-Bond Index and the Dow Jones Municipal Index.

Industrial-revenue bond—A bond issued to construct a plant or factory for a private comany. The bonds are tax-exempt because they are issued by a governmental unit, although that entity is usually not responsible for the repayment of the principal and interest on the bonds.

IDR bonds—This is a nickname for the above bonds brought into usage by sales people in the business.

Interest—Compensation paid or to be paid for the use of money.

Interest dates—The dates on which interest is payable to the holders of the bonds, usually set at semiannual intervals on the first or the fifteenth of the month.

Interest rate—The interest payable each year, expressed as a percentage of the principal.

Investment banker—A firm which underwrites stock and bond issues.

Issuer—A municipal unit which borrows money through sale of bonds.

Legal opinion—An opinion concerning the legality of a bond issue by a recognized firm of municipal-bond attorneys specializing in the approval of public borrowings.

Limited-tax bond—A bond secured by the pledge of a tax which is limited as to rate or amount.

Marketability—The measure of the ease with which a bond can be sold in the secondary market.

Maturity—The date upon which the principal of a bond becomes due and payable.

Moral obligation—This is the description of revenue bonds which do not carry a direct obligation of the issuing body but which are felt to be moral obligations of that government body if sufficient revenues are not generated.

Museum piece—The name given to a bond that is rarely seen in the market and which usually has great attraction for investors.

NASD—The abbreviation for the self-governing National Association of Security Dealers.

Net debt—Gross debt less sinking-fund accumulations, and all self-supporting debt.

New-housing-authority bonds—A bond issued by a local public-housing authority to finance public housing. It is backed by the solemn pledge of the U. S. Government to see that payment is made in full.

New-issue market—Market for new issues of municipal bonds.

Official statement (commonly called a Prospectus)—An official document prepared by the investment banker or the issuer which gives in detail the security and financial information relating to the issue.

Overlapping debt—That portion of the debt of other governmental units for which residents of a particular municipality are responsible.

Over-the-counter market—A securities market conducted by dealers throughout the country through negotiation rather than through the use of an auction system as represented by a stock exchange.

Par value—The face amount of a bond—$1,000 or $5,000.

Paying agent—Place where the principal and interest is payable. Usually a designated bank or the treasurer's office of the issuer.

Premium—The amount, if any, by which the price exceeds the principal amount of a bond.

Prime rate—This is the preferential rate that banks give to their top clients. It is the rate that is commonly used by the market to determine the level of interest rates.

Principal—The face amount of a bond, exclusive of accrued interest.

Public purpose—In tax-exempt bonds, public purpose means that the issue being sold has been created to serve the needs of the public. Public purpose is the most critical criterion of a bond issue.

Ratings—Designations used by investors' services to give relative indications of quality. See Appendix 12 for ratings.

Refunding—A system by which a bond issue is redeemed from the proceeds of a new bond issue at conditions generally more favorable to the issuer.

Registered bond—A bond whose ownership is registered with the issuer or its agents, either as to both principal and interest or as to principal only.

Revenue bond—A bond payable from revenues secured from a project which pays its way by charging rentals to the users, such as toll bridges or toll highways, or from revenues from another source which is used for a public purpose.

Scale—Re-offering terms to the public of a serial issue showing price or yields for each maturity.

SEC—The abbreviation for the Securities and Exchange Commission.

Secondary market—Market for issues previously offered or sold.

Security—When the word security is used in connection with tax-exempt bonds, it indicates the backing for bonds upon which an investor depends, whether it be the general taxing power of the community or revenues to be collected in a project.

Self-supporting debt—Debt incurred for a project or enterprise requiring no tax support other than the specific revenue earmarked for the purpose.

Serial bond—A bond of an issue which has maturities scheduled annually or semiannually over a period of years.

Sinking fund—A reserve fund accumulated over a period of time for retirement of a debt.

Special-tax bond—A bond secured by a special tax, such as a gasoline tax.

Subdivision—A unit of government such as a county, town, city, or village.

Syndicate—A group of investment bankers who buy (underwrite), wholesale, a new bond issue from the issuing authority and offer it for resale to the general public.

Tax base—The total resources available for taxation.

Tax-exempt bond—A bond, the interest on which is exempt from federal income tax.

Tax-exempt bond fund—Registered unit-investment trusts, the assets of which are invested in a diversified portfolio of interest-bearing municipal bonds issued by the states, cities, counties, and other political subdivisions.

Tenders—The method issuers use to buy bonds when they have accumulated excess funds. The tenders are usually sought when the bonds are selling at prices below their issuance or call prices.

Term bond—A bond of an issue which has a single maturity.

Trading market—The secondary market for issued bonds.

Trustee—A bank designated as the custodian of funds and official representative of bondholders.

Unlimited-tax bond—A bond secured by pledge of taxes which may be levied in unlimited rate or amount.

Yield—The net annual percentage of income from an investment. The yield of a bond reflects interest rate, length of time to maturity, and write-off of premium or discounts.

Lebenthal's latest tax-free bonds.

We own and offer, subject to prior sale and/or change in price.

MOODY'S RATING	PAR AMOUNT	SECURITY	COUPON RATE	MATURITY	YIELD TO MATURITY / CURRENT YIELD	YIELD AFTER 25% CAPITAL GAINS TAX	OUR BID PRICE AS OF PUBLICATION DATE / APPROXIMATE OFFERING PRICE

MUNICIPALITIES IN NEW YORK STATE
Coupon interest is exempt from all present New York State and New York City as well as Federal Income Taxes

NEW YORK CITY

Rating	Par	Security	Coupon	Maturity	YTM	Current	After tax	Bid	Offering
A	450,000	NEW YORK CITY	7.00%	8/1/76	6.50%	6.94%	--	101	MARKET
A	425,000	NEW YORK CITY (WHEN IS'D)	8.00%	4/15/77	6.70%	7.77%	--	103	MARKET
A	550,000	NEW YORK CITY " "	8.00%	4/15/78	6.90%	7.74%	--	103 3/8	MARKET
A	470,000	NEW YORK CITY " "	8.00%	4/15/83	7.15%	7.59%	--	105 3/8	MARKET
A	450,000	NEW YORK CITY " "	8.00%	4/15/85	7.25%	7.59%	--	105 1/2	MARKET
A	1,000,000	NEW YORK CITY " "	8.00%	4/15/86	7.30%	7.59%	--	105 1/2	MARKET
A	1,000,000	NEW YORK CITY " "	8.00%	4/15/87	7.35%	7.60%	--	105 3/8	MARKET
A	1,000,000	NEW YORK CITY " "	8.00%	4/15/88	7.40%	7.61%	--	105 1/4	MARKET
A	1,000,000	NEW YORK CITY " "	8.00%	4/15/89	7.45%	7.63%	--	105	MARKET
A	1,000,000	NEW YORK CITY (WHEN IS'D)	7.75%	4/15/86	7.30%	7.49%	--	103 1/2	MARKET
A	1,000,000	NEW YORK CITY " "	7.75%	4/15/87	7.35%	7.50%	--	103 3/8	MARKET
A	1,000,000	NEW YORK CITY " "	7.75%	4/15/88	7.40%	7.52%	--	103	MARKET
A	1,000,000	NEW YORK CITY " "	7.75%	4/15/89	7.45%	7.55%	--	102 3/4	MARKET
A	530,000	NEW YORK CITY " "	7.75%	4/15/90	7.50%	7.57%	--	102 3/8	MARKET
A	1,000,000	NEW YORK CITY " "	7.75%	4/15/91	7.50%	7.57%	--	102 1/2	MARKET
A	1,000,000	NEW YORK CITY " "	7.75%	4/15/92	7.55%	7.60%	--	102	MARKET
A	1,000,000	NEW YORK CITY " "	7.75%	4/15/93	7.55%	7.60%	--	102	MARKET
A	1,000,000	NEW YORK CITY " "	7.75%	4/15/94	7.60%	7.63%	--	101 5/8	MARKET
A	1,000,000	NEW YORK CITY " "	7.75%	4/15/95	7.60%	7.63%	--	101 5/8	MARKET
A	55,000	NEW YORK CITY " "	7.75%	4/15/96	7.65%	7.67%	--	101 1/4	MARKET
A	335,000	NEW YORK CITY	3.50%	10/01/80	7.85%	4.39%	7.05%	79 3/4	77 3/4
A	5,000	NEW YORK CITY	4.00%	10/01/80	7.70%	4.84%	7.03%	82 3/4	79 3/4
A	5,000	NEW YORK CITY	3.75%	5/15/82	7.80%	4.85%	7.12%	77 3/8	75
A	60,000	NEW YORK CITY	3.50%	1/01/83	8.00%	4.77%	7.27%	77 5/8	75
A	20,000	NEW YORK CITY	3.75%	7/15/88	8.00%	5.34%	7.43%	61	59
A	5,000	NEW YORK CITY	3.75%	1/01/89	8.00%	5.83%	7.52%	64 1/2	62

OTHER OFFERINGS IN NEW YORK STATE

Rating	Par	Security	Coupon	Maturity	YTM	Current	After tax	Bid	Offering
Baa	10,000	HEMPSTEAD UFSD#10 (NASS.)	4.00%	12/01/75	7.00%	4.13%	6.29%	97	95 3/8
A	25,000	BUFFALO (ERIE)	2.90%	12/1/76	7.00%	3.14%	6.06%	92 3/8	90 1/2
A	25,000	BUSTI ELLICOTT CSD#1 (CHA)	2.50%	1/01/78	7.25%	2.88%	6.20%	86 7/8	84 3/4
A	15,000	GREENE COUNTY, N.Y.	6.60%	11/15/76	5.30%	6.43%	--	102 5/8	MARKET
A	15,000	(Optional 1984 @ 105)	6.60%	11/15/78	5.30%	6.30%	--	104 7/8	MARKET
A	5,000		6.60%	11/15/79	5.30%	6.24%	--	105 7/8	MARKET
A	35,000		6.60%	11/15/87	6.15%	6.34%	--	104 1/8	MARKET
A	50,000		6.60%	11/15/88	6.25%	6.39%	--	103 3/8	MARKET
A	5,000		6.60%	11/15/91	6.50%	6.53%	--	101 1/8	MARKET
A	10,000		6.60%	11/15/93	6.60%		--	100	MARKET
Baa	10,000	HEMPSTEAD UFSD#14 (NASS.)	4.00%	7/01/78	7.00%	4.42%	6.38%	90 1/2	88 5/8
Baa	20,000	HEMPSTEAD UFSD#5 (NASSAU)	4.30%	5/01/80	6.90%	4.87%	6.41%	88 3/8	86
Baa	20,000	BROOKHAVEN CSD#1 (SUFF.)	3.40%	2/15/83	7.45%	4.52%	6.78%	75 3/8	72 1/2
AA	100,000	N.Y.S. PORT COMM. CAR, GTD	6.00%	6/01/83	5.10%	5.70%	--	105 1/4	103 1/2
		(PR. TO CALL 1979 @ 102)							
Baa/1	5,000	ELLERY CSD#1 (CHAT'QUA)	2.40%	7/01/83	7.80%	3.61%	6.88%	66 5/8	64
Aa	140,000	NEW YORK STATE	7.00%	8/01/88	5.50%	6.12%	--	114 1/2	111 1/2
A	5,000	COEYMANS (ALBANY)	6.60%	1/15/90	6.60%	6.56%	6.59%	99 1/4	97
A	30,000	NEW YORK STATE	6.00%	8/01/90	5.65%	5.19%	--	103 3/4	101

LISTINGS OF MUNICIPALITIES IN STATES OTHER THAN NEW YORK

Rating	Par	Security	Coupon	Maturity	YTM	Current	After tax	Bid	Offering
A/1	10,000	BALTIMORE CO., MD.	2.75%	6/01/80	7.50%	3.49%	6.57%	78 3/4	76 5/8
Baa	10,000	PASSAIC, NEW JERSEY	2.70%	11/01/81	7.90%	3.73%	6.96%	72 1/2	69 3/4
Baa/1	5,000	PHILADELPHIA, PA.	3.75%	7/01/83	8.50%	5.26%	7.77%	71 1/2	68 7/8
Baa/1	3,000	PHILADELPHIA, PA.	3.20%	7/01/86	8.60%	5.26%	7.88%	61	57 7/8
A	5,000	NORTH BRANFORD, CONN.	4.50%	11/15/86	7.30%	5.79%	6.95%	77 7/8	74
Baa/1	50,000	PHILADELPHIA, PA.	3.25%	7/01/87	8.60%	5.49%	7.94%	59 1/4	57
	10,000	MASSACHUSETTS COM'WLTH	3.00%	11/01/89	7.15%	4.82%	6.65%	62 3/8	59 1/8
Baa/1	20,000	PHILADELPHIA, PENN.	6.75%	1/01/97	8.15%	7.87%	8.08%	85 7/8	82 1/4

To help you find the bond you're looking for, we give each of the bonds on our list a symbol that stands for a basic, major investment need.

 For the most current tax-free income here and now, and every time you clip a coupon, look for high coupon bonds marked with the rising sun.

 If you don't need income now, but are building up a fund for the future—look for low coupon rates at deep discounts marked with an acorn.

 If you want to make money both ways—appreciation at maturity and a good current yield right along—look for the combination of good coupon and good discount marked with a bee.

 If you have just $1000 or so to invest at a time and want to get started in municipals now, look for "odd lots" or blocks we'll sell in $1000 pieces, marked with the ear of corn.

 For a gift within the $3000 tax-free allowance, look for $5000 blocks selling for 50 to 60 cents on the dollar, marked with the diploma.

Buy these bonds by calling (212) 425-6116. For regular mailings, write Lebenthal & Co., Inc., One State Street Plaza, New York, N.Y. 10004.

We want to be your Heroes.

A SAMPLE PAGE FROM THE BLUE LIST

This publication, which is available only to dealers and dealer banks, lists the amount on the left side (10 means $10,000), the name of the issue, the coupon (*i.e.*, 3.55%), the maturity date, the yield, and the dealer offering the bonds.

WASHINGTON—CONTINUED

Amt	Issue		Coupon	Maturity			Yield	Dealer
10	METRO.SEATTLE SWR.RV		3.55	1/ 1/89			7.25	ALEX BROWN(BALTIMORE)
10	METRO.SEATTLE SWR.RV		3.40	1/ 1/91			7.40	EDWARDS & HANLY
15	METRO.SEATTLE SWR.RV		4.375	1/ 1/93		*	7.20	WEEDEN & CC.,INC.
5	METRO. SEATTLE SWR.RV		3.70	1/ 1/95			6.75	BAKER,WATTS & CO.
25	METRO.SEATTLE SWR.RV		4	1/ 1/00			7.00	JOHN J.RYAN&CO.(NWK)
85	N.E. LAKE SWR.DIST.	P/R 102 1/2	8.25	8/ 1/00	/85		6.40	SEATTLE NORTHWEST
10	PEND OREILLE	P.U.D. #1	3.20	8/ 1/05	C		60	STERN,LAUER & CO.
10	PORT ANGELES WTR.REV.		4.40	1/ 1/80			7.00	DEAN WITTER & CO.INC
25	PORT OF SEATTLE REV.		6.50	5/ 1/76			6.25	HIB.O*CON,WK(HOUSTON)
5	PORT OF SEATTLE REV.		4.40	11/ 1/81			7.00	MERRILL LYNCH(NY)
20	PORT OF SEATTLE	.	5.20	4/ 1/89			6.40	THE NORTHERN TR. CO.
70	PORT OF SEATTLE	P/R P/C 102	6.60	2/ 1/94	/88		6.30	MERRILL LYNCH(NY)
500	PT.OF SEATTLE RV P/R 102 (M-100)		6.70	6/ 1/97	/88		6.30	L.F. ROTHSCHILD&CO.
5	PORT OF SEATTLE REV.	P/R 102	6.70	6/ 1/97	/88		6.65	BLYTH EASTMAN DILLON
10	PORT OF SEATTLE REV.	P/R 102	6.75	2/ 1/98	/88		6.40	BLYTH EASTMAN DILLON
100	PORT OF SEATTLE	P/R P/C#101	6.90	4/ 1/00	/88		6.30	MERRILL LYNCH(NY)
100	PORT OF TACOMA	G.O.	6.10	6/ 1/92			6.10	MARSHALL & MEYER,INC
20	PORT OF TACOMA	G.O.	6.30	6/ 1/96			7.00	SEATTLE NORTHWEST
70	PORT OF TACOMA	G.O.	6.50	6/ 1/01			7.05	SEATTLE NORTHWEST
85	PORT OF TACOMA		6.50	6/ 1/02			7.05	SEATTLE NORTHWEST
10	PORT OF TACOMA		6.60	6/ 1/04			7.05	SEATTLE NORTHWEST
25	SEATTLE		4.80	10/ 1/96			6.50	WEEDEN & CC.,INC.
50	SEATTLE	G.O.	5.40	9/ 1/00			6.75	FOSTER & MARSHALL
500(	SEATTLE		5.50		3		6.75)(	WEEDEN & CC.,INC. (BEAR,STEARNS & CO.
170(	SEATTLE (PRE-REFUNDED	11/1/85 1C2	6.50	11/ 1/09	/85		6.20)(	L.F. ROTHSCHILD&CO.)
155(	SEATTLE (PRE-REFUNDED	11/1/85 102	6.50	11/ 1/10	/85	*	6.30)(	L.F. ROTHSCHILD&CO.)
11	SEATTLE LT.+PWR.REV.		3.50	3/ 1/84			7.00	ALEX BROWN(BALTIMORE)
25	SEATTLE LT.+PWR.REV.		3.50	3/ 1/84			7.00	DEAN WITTER & CO.INC
25	SEATTLE LT.+PWR.REV.		3.50	3/ 1/86			7.15	BROWN BROS.HAR.(BOS.)
10	SEATTLE LT.+PWR.REV.		3.50	8/ 1/90			7.20	BLYTH EASTMAN DILLON
10	SEATTLE LT.+PWR.REV.		5.15	12/15/97			6.45	SPENCER TRASK & CO.
50	SEATTLE SWR. REV.		5.25	11/ 1/98		*	7.00	SEATTLE NORTHWEST
25	SEATTLE WTR. REV.		3.75	1/ 1/80			7.25	WEEDEN & CC.,INC.
20	SKAGIT CO.P.U.D.=1	WTR.REV.	3.20	10/ 1/83			7.50	HANIFEN,IMHOFF(NY)
25	SNOHOMISH COUNTY	S.D. 311	5.35	1/ 1/89			7.00	SEATTLE NORTHWEST
10	SPOKANE CO.S.D.=81		2.90	1/ 1/90			6.50	ADAMS,MCENTEE & CO.
25(			6.20	6/ 1/87			6.15)	
15(	SUNNYSIDE S.D. # 201	G.C.	6.20	6/ 1/89			100)(	SEATTLE-FIRST NAT.BK
15(	YAKIMA CO. C 6/1/84 AT 100	hI	6.40	6/ 1/93			100)(	KIDDER,PEABODY & CO.
50(			6.40	6/ 1/94			100)	
50	TACOMA		4.80	2/ 1/83			6.50	THOMSON,MCKINN,AUCH.
15	TACOMA LT.+PWR.REV.		3.50	1/ 1/92			7.25	CHESTER HARRIS & CO.
20	TACOMA LT.+PWR.REV.		4.10	1/ 1/97			7.50	MERRILL LYNCH(NY)
100	TACOMA LT.+PWR.REV.		3.90	1/ 1/02		*	59 1/2	AMERICAN SEC. CORP.
55	THURSTON COUNTY	W.I.+2	7.50	6/ 1/77		*	5.75	THE NORTHERN TR. CO.
80	THURSTON COUNTY	W.I.+2	7.50	6/ 1/78		*	5.75	THE NORTHERN TR. CO.
75	THURSTON COUNTY	H	7.50	6/ 1/79		*	5.75	THE NORTHERN TR. CO.
90	THURSTON COUNTY	W.I.+2	7.50	6/ 1/80		*	5.80	THE NORTHERN TR. CO.
95	THURSTON COUNTY	W.I.+2	7.50	6/ 1/81		*	5.85	THE NORTHERN TR. CO.
100	THURSTON COUNTY	W.I.+2	7.50	6/ 1/82		*	5.90	THE NORTHERN TR. CO.
105	THURSTON COUNTY	W.I.+2	7.50	6/ 1/83		*	6.00	THE NORTHERN TR. CO.
15	THURSTON COUNTY	W.I.+2	7.50	6/ 1/84		*	6.00	THE NORTHERN TR. CO.
20	THURSTON COUNTY	WI+2P/C 100	6.875	6/ 1/85	/84	*	6.00	THE NORTHERN TR. CO.
75	THURSTON COUNTY	WI+2 P/C100	5.85	6/ 1/86	/84	*	6.15	THE NORTHERN TR. CO.
105	THURSTON COUNTY	hI+2 P/C 100	5.90	6/ 1/87	/84	*	6.25	THE NORTHERN TR. CO.
30	THURSTON COUNTY	h.I.	6.10	6/ 1/91		*	7.00	HAYDEN,STONE,INC.
75	THURSTON CO.L.T.	C/100 h.I.	6.10	6/ 1/92	/84		7.00	SEATTLE-FIRST NAT.BK
85	THURSTON COUNTY	W.I.	6.20	6/ 1/93			7.00	SEATTLE NORTHWEST
85	THURSTON COUNTY	W.I.	6.20	6/ 1/94		*	7.00	HAYDEN,STONE,INC.
55	THURSTON COUNTY	W.I.	6.50	6/ 1/99			7.00	SEATTLE NORTHWEST
345	THURSTON CO.(OLYMPIA)	WI(265,80)	6.50	6/ 1/00-01	*		7.10-7.10	JOHN NUVEEN & CO,INC
610	THURSTON CO.(OLYMPIA)	WI(295,315)	6.50	6/ 1/02-03	*		7.10-7.10	JOHN NUVEEN & CO,INC
330	THURSTON CO.(OLYMPIA	OLYMPIA WI	6.50	6/ 1/04	*		7.10	JOHN NUVEEN & CO,INC
15	TACOMA LT.+PWR.REV.		4.50	7/ 1/78			6.50	SPENCER TRASK & CO.
100	U.WASH.TUIT.FEE REV	SER C	4.125	5/ 1/83	C		6.50	SEATTLE-FIRST NAT.BK
5	UNIV. OF WASH.		5.20	10/ 1/84			5.50	FIRST OF MICHIGAN
50	VAL VUE SWR.DIST.		6.75	7/ 1/81			100	SEATTLE NORTHWEST

THE BLUE LIST RETRIEVAL SYSTEM

An investor has asked for a certain type of tax-exempt bond from his broker, and this is what the Blue List Retrieval System has reported back to the broker in a matter of minutes.

As shown below, 21 items met this customer's needs. You will note they were also sorted out by price, yield, and maturity for his further convenience.

Screening Parameters

Yield of 6.25% or better after 48% tax   General obligation bonds   Maturities between 1984 and
Current yield 6% or better   Quality rating of BBB or B

```
BLUELIST RETRIEVAL        30APR74


ENTER 4-CHARACTER PASSWORD

BLUELIST FUNCTION?
screen cy:6 48aft:6.25 type:go m:1984-1989 r:bbb+
     21 LINES IN REPORT
DO YOU WANT IT PRINTED?
yes twor sort:p,y,m
  ST  AMT       SECURITY        RATE    MAT     YLD-PRC OFFERED BY
  TN   15 MAURY CO.            5.000 01SEP89    7.000 SYNDICATE
          CY  6.145 48AFT  6.604 PRC TO MTY  81.370 S&P      A    MDY    A
  TN   15 MAURY CO.            5.000 01SEP88    7.000 SYNDICATE
          CY  6.092 48AFT  6.580 PRC TO MTY  82.070 S&P      A    MDY    A
  TN   30 LAKE COUNTY          7.000 01JAN85   96.000 SYNDICATE
          CY  7.292 7.426 YLD TO MTY            7.551 S&P          MDY    BAA
  TN   40 LAKE COUNTY          7.250 01JAN88   96.000 SYNDICATE
          CY  7.552 48AFT  7.643 YLD TO MTY     7.727 S&P          MDY    BAA
  PA  120 PHILADELPHIA S.D.    6.000 01MAR86C   6.400 EDWARDS & HANLY
          CY  6.205 48AFT  6.307 PRC TO MTY  96.700 S&P      BBB MDY    BAA
  PA   25 BEAVER COUNTY        6.250 01A0R84    6.500 LOEB,RHOADES & CO.
          CY  6.365 48AFT  6.435 PRC TO MTY  98.190 S&P      A    MDY    A
  PR  100 P.R. MUN.FIN. AG     6.250 01JUL87  100.000 BANCO CREDITO NY
          CY  6.250 48AFT  6.250 YLD TO MTY     6.250 S&P      A    MDY    A
  PR  225 P.R. MUN. FIN. AG    6.250 01JUL87  100.000 FIRST BOSTON CORP.
          CY  6.250 48AFT  6.250 YLD TO MTY     6.250 S&P      A    MDY    A
  PR  250 P.R. MUN. FIN. AG    6.250 01JUL87  100.000 KUHN,LOEB & CO.
          CY  6.250 48AFT  6.250 YLD TO MTY     6.250 S&P      A    MDY    A
  PR  100 P.R. MUN. FIN. AG    6.300 01JUL88  100.000 BANCO CREDITO NY
          CY  6.300 48AFT  6.300 YLD TO MTY     6.300 S&P      A    MDY    A
  PR 1045 P.R. MUN. FIN. AG    6.300 01JUL88  100.000 SYNDICATE
          CY  6.300 48AFT  6.300 YLD TO MTY     6.300 S&P      A    MDY    A
  PR 2505 P.R. MUN. FIN. AG    6.300 01JUL89  100.000 SYNDICATE
          CY  6.300 48AFT  6.300 YLD TO MTY     6.300 S&P      A    MDY    A
  NY  500 NEW YORK CITY        6.300 01SEP89 *100.000 FIRST NATL CITY BK
          CY  6.300 48AFT  6.300 YLD TO MTY     6.300 S&P      A    MDY    A
 +PA   10 PHILADELOHIA S.D.    6.700 01NOV85    6.500 BACHE & CO PHILA.
          CY  6.594 48AFT  6.546 PRC TO MTY 101.600 S&P      BBB MDY    BAA
 +NY   70 NEW YORK CITY        7.000 01FEB85    6.100 L.F. ROTHSCHILD&CO
          CY  6.541 48AFT  6.314 PRC TO MTY 107.010 S&P      A    MDY    A
 +NY   50 NEW YORK CITY        7.000 01FEB86    6.150 L.F. ROTHSCHILD&CO
          CY  6.541 48AFT  6.330 PRC TO MTY 107.020 S&P      A    MDY    A
 +NY    5 NEW YORK CITY        7.000 01JUL87    6.150 MERRILL LYNCH NY
          CY  6.507 48AFT  6.323 PRC TO MTY 107.580 S&P      A    MDY    A
  NY  100 NEW YORK CITY        7.000 01OCT87    6.100 ABRAHAM & CO.INC.
          CY  6.472 48AFT  6.281 PRC TO MTY 108.160 S&P      A    MDY    A
  PA   25 PHILADELPHIA         7.500 01JUL85    6.250 CHAS.W.WOODS INVES
          CY  6.823 48AFT  6.529 PRC TO MTY 109.930 S&P      BBB MDY    BAA
 +NY   30 NEW YORK CITY        7.400 15APR85    6.100 L.F. ROTHSCHILD&CO
          CY  6.711 48AFT  6.300 PRC TO MTY 110.270 S&P      A    MDY    A
  NY   50 NEW YORK CITY        7.400 15AUG84    6.000 ABRAHAM & CO.INC.
          CY  6.690 48AFT  6.337 PRC TO MTY 110.620 S&P      A    MDY    A
```

APPENDIX 7

THE MECHANICS OF GETTING A BID

In this example of how your bonds are handled in the secondary market, we are using an example of how a trade is handled at J. J. Kenny & Co., Inc. The Kenny organization has over 400 dealers on their private wire system. Your broker or dealer bank will contact the Kenny organization and tell them that you (of course they do not mention your name) have $20,000 New Jersey bonds of 3¼ percent due in 1982 for a bid.

Within minutes your bonds are flashed over the Kenny system. The bids come in all day long. The high bid will not be decided until about 3 P.M. so that everyone interested in bidding has a chance to bid. This, of course, gives you every chance of getting the best bid. However, it also leads some people to think that there is something wrong with the secondary market mechanism. There is not. You are getting the best bid possible and because of the market, it just takes a little longer. I can tell you that it is worth the wait.

In this case, eighteen separate bids are received for your bonds. The high and low bids of this particular transaction were forty basis points apart, which in this maturity amounted to $22.50 per thousand-dollar bond.

Kenny's service did not cost you anything. Of course, you have to pay your broker a commission. The buyer pays the Kenny commission, which was only $1.25 per bond or the magnificent sum of $25.00 for the entire transaction. Your broker made at least double that amount as a charge to you. Despite inflation the brokerage rate charged by Kenny and other brokers has remained at $1.25 per bond over the years in most trades. It is one of the few services that has defied inflation.

147

THE PRINCIPAL DOLLAR BONDS IN THE TAX-EXEMPT MARKET

DESCRIPTION	COUPON	MATURITY	DESCRIPTION	COUPON	MATUF
Chelan County, Washington P.U.D. #1	5	7/1/13	New Jersey Turnpike Authority	5 3/4	1/1/C
Chelan County, Washington P.U.D. #1	5 1/8	7/1/23	New Jersey Turnpike Authority	5 7/8	1/1/C
Chicago O'Hare International Airport	4 3/4	1/1/99	New Jersey Turnpike Authority	7	1/1/●
Chicago O'Hare International Airport	6.80	1/1/99	New York State Mortgage Agency	5.70	10/1/9
Columbia Power Storage Exchange	3 7/8	4/1/03	New York State Power Authority	3.20	1/1/9
Connecticut	5.25	7/1/02	New York State Power Authority	3 3/4	1/1/●
Consumer Public Power District Nuclear	5.10	1/1/03	New York State Power Authority	4 1/8	1/1/C
Consumer Public Power District Electric	5.10	1/1/03	New York State Power Authority	4.20	1/1/●
Dallas-Fort Worth Regional Airport	6 3/4	11/1/00,01	New York State Power Authority	4 3/8	1/1/●
Delaware River & Bay Authority	3 3/4	1/1/04	New York State Power Authority	5 5/8	1/1/)
Delaware Turnpike Authority	4 1/8	1/1/02	New York State Power Authority	5 7/8	1/1/)
Delaware River Port Authority	5 5/8	1/15/09	New York State Power Authority	6 7/8	1/1/)
Douglas County, Washington P.U.D. #1	4	9/1/18	New York State Thruway Authority	3.10	7/1/●
City of Eugene, Oregon (Trojan Nuclear)	6 3/4	9/1/09	New York State Urban Development	6.60	1/1/)
Florida Turnpike Authority	4 3/4	11/1/01	New York State Urban Development	6 3/8	10/1/)
Florida Dept. of Trans. (Turnpike)	7.10	11/1/10	Ohio Turnpike Authority	3 1/4	6/1/●
Grant County, Washington P.U.D. #2 Refund	3.80	4/1/98	Oklahoma Turnpike Authority Series A	4.70	1/1/●
Grant County, Washington P.U.D. #2 Refund	3.85	4/1/09	Oklahoma Turnpike Authority Series C	6	1/1/9
Grant County, Washington P.U.D. #2 Refund	3 7/8	11/1/05	Oklahoma Turnpike Authority Series C	6 1/4	1/1/●
Greater N.O. Expressway Comm. Series A	4.90	11/1/06	Oroville-Wyandotte Irrigation California	4 1/4	7/1/'
City of Henderson, Kty. Elec. Lt. & Pwr	6 3/4	3/1/03	Pennsylvania Turnpike Commission	3.10	6/1/●
Illinois State Toll Highway Commission	3 3/4	1/1/95	Port of New York Authority	3 1/4	4/1/●
Illinois State Toll Highway Commission	4 3/4	1/1/98	Port of New York Authority	3 3/8	5/1/●
Illinois State Toll Highway Commission	6 3/4	1/1/10	Port of New York Authority	3 3/8	121/●
Indiana Toll Road Commission	3 1/2	1/1/94	Port of New York Authority	3 3/8	5/1/●
Jacksonville Expressway Authority	4	10/1/92	Port of New York Authority	3 3/8	12/1/●
Jacksonville Expressway Authority	4.10	10/1/03	Port of New York Authority	3 3/8	2/1/
Kansas Turnpike Authority	3 3/8	10/1/94	Port of New York Authority	3.40	9/1/●
Kentucky Turnpike Authority	4 3/4	7/1/06	Port of New York Authority	3.40	2/1/●
Kentucky Turnpike Authority	4.85	7/1/00	Port of New York Authority	3.40	10/1/●
Kentucky Turnpike Authority	5 7/8	7/1/08	Port of New York Authority	3 1/2	11/1/●
Kentucky Turnpike Authority	6.20	7/1/11	Port of New York Authority	3 1/2	10/1/●
Kentucky Turnpike Authority	6 1/2	7/1/10	Port of New York Authority	3 1/2	5/1/●
Kentucky Turnpike Authority	7.20	7/1/10	Port of New York Authority	3 1/2	6/1/
Kentucky Turnpike Authority	7 3/8	7/1/10	Port of New York Authority	3 5/8	2/1/●
Maine Turnpike Authority	4	1/1/89	Port of New York Authority	3 5/8	10/1/
Maryland Bridge & Tunnel	5.20	10/1/08	Port of New York Authority	4	3/1/●
Massachusetts Port Authority	3.80	7/1/04	Port of New York Authority	4 3/4	7/15/●
Massachusetts Port Authority	5 7/8	7/1/08	Port of New York Authority	5	2/1/
Massachusetts Port Authority	6	7/1/11	Port of New York Authority	5 3/8	11/1/●
Massachusetts Port Authority	3.30	5/1/94	Port of New York Authority	5 1/2	12/1/●
Nebraska Pub. Power Dist. (Nuclear)	6.60	1/1/04	Port of New York Authority	6	2/1/
Nebraska Pub. Pwr. Dist. (Electric)	6.60	1/1/04	Port of New York Authority	6.40	11/1/
Nebraska Public Power District	5.80	1/1/13	Port of New York Authority	6 5/8	8/1/
New Jersey Highway Authority	6 1/2	1/1/11	Port of N.Y. & N.J. Authority Rev	6	6/1/
New Jersey Turnpike Authority	4 3/4	1/1/06	Richmond Met. Authority (Expressway)	7	1/15/
New Jersey Turnpike Authority	5 1/8	1/1/08	South Carolina Public Service Authority	6 3/8	7/1/
New Jersey Turnpike Authority	5.20	1/1/08	Yuba City, Water Ag. California	4	3/1/

A TYPICAL LEGAL OPINION

REED, MᶜCARTHY & GIORDANO

(REED, HOYT, WASHBURN & MᶜCARTHY)

ATTORNEYS AND COUNSELORS AT LAW

LEO A. McCARTHY
GERARD GIORDANO, JR.
HARVEY A. NAPIER

JAMES A. LAPENN
JAMES A. MOYER

60 WALL TOWER

(70 PINE STREET)

NEW YORK 10005

TELEPHONE
AREA CODE 212
H NOVER 2-1931

May 2, 1974

Borough Council of the
Borough of Woodcliff Lake,
County of Bergen,
New Jersey.

Gentlemen:

We have examined a certified copy of the record
of proceedings and other papers submitted to us relating to the issuance of $4,050,000 Sewer Bonds of
THE BOROUGH OF WOODCLIFF LAKE (herein referred to as
"Borough") a municipal corporation of the State of
New Jersey, located in the County of Bergen. The
bonds are coupon bonds registrable as to principal
only or both principal and interest and consist of
eight hundred ten bonds of the denomination of
$5,000 each, numbered from 1 to 810 inclusive, in
the order of their maturity, dated May 1, 1974 and
constituting an issue of bonds payable in annual
installments on May 1 in each year as follows:viz:

$100,000 in the year 1975,
$105,000 in the year 1976,
$110,000 in the year 1977,
$115,000 in the year 1978,
$120,000 in the year 1979,
$125,000 in the year 1980,
$130,000 in the year 1981,
$135,000 in the year 1982,
$140,000 in the year 1983,
$145,000 in the year 1984,
$150,000 in the year 1985,
$155,000 in the year 1986,
$160,000 in the year 1987,
$165,000 in the year 1988,
$170,000 in the year 1989,
$175,000 in the year 1990,
$180,000 in the year 1991,
$185,000 in the year 1992,
$190,000 in the year 1993,
$195,000 in the year 1994,
$200,000 in the year 1995,
to 1999, inclusive, and
$100,000 in the year 2000.

The bonds bear interest from their date at the rate

(continued)

Borough Council of the
Borough of Woodcliff Lake,
County of Bergen,
New Jersey.

                              -2-

of 5.60% per annum and such interest is payable on
May 1, 1975 and thereafter semi-annually on November
1 and May 1. The bonds are issued pursuant to the
Local Bond Law (Chapter 2 of Title 40A of the New
Jersey Statutes as amended) and three bond ordinances
duly adopted by the Borough Council on August 10,
1970, September 13, 1971 and June 14, 1973. We have
not examined any of the bonds other than the executed
bond numbered 1.

        In our opinion the bonds are valid and legally
binding obligations of the Borough, and the Borough
is authorized and required by law to levy on all
real property taxable by the Borough such ad valorem
taxes as may be necessary to pay the bonds and the
interest thereon without limitation as to rate or
amount, and the interest on the bonds is exempt from
Federal income taxes under existing statutes and
court decisions.

                              Very truly yours,

TYPICAL NEW-ISSUE ADS

The following four ads are reproduced so that you have an idea what to expect from new-issue ads:

1 ● This is a new type of approach to investors. It gives you an idea of what the issue is about and offers to send you a preliminary official statement. These ads are well worth answering.

2 ● This is an ad that gives the investor much of what he or she wants to know for a preliminary look, including ratings, security, and price. This is what a new-issue ad should look like.

3 ● This is an issue that is secured by bond insurance, which becomes the credit involved.

4 ● This ad is reproduced because it gives a great deal of information about the issue. It fails in only one area—no ratings.

How to Obtain

Fully Tax-Free Interest Income by Investing in Puerto Rico's Electric System

The Puerto Rico Water Resources Authority, the Commonwealth of Puerto Rico's electric utility, plans to issue Power Revenue Bonds in December for additional construction and for expansion of its power system. The Authority was established in 1947 and has been a prime factor in the industrial, commercial and residential growth of the Commonwealth.

The interest on the Power Revenue Bonds offered will be **exempt from Federal, State, and local taxes** in the opinion of bond counsel. While no interest rate has been determined as yet, rates will be competitive with the high yields presently being offered by comparably secured tax-exempt bonds.

The issue will consist of $100,000,000 of Power Revenue Bonds, with serial bonds maturing in 1976 through 1989 and term bonds maturing on July 1, 1999 and July 1, 2014.

The Power Revenue Bonds are payable solely from the net revenues of the Authority's electric power system deposited to the credit of the Renewal and Replacement Fund, after the required deposits have been made to the Puerto Rico Water Resources Authority Electric Revenue Bonds Sinking Fund and the General Reserve Fund under an earlier indenture. Neither the credit of the Commonwealth of Puerto Rico nor that of any of its political subdivisions is pledged for the payment of the bonds.

(continued)

The offering of Power Revenue Bonds is made solely by the Official Statement of the Puerto Rico Water Resources Authority. For a free copy of the preliminary Official Statement, contact your local securities dealer or mail the coupon to the Municipal Bond Department of any of the firms listed below.

The First Boston Corporation
Municipal Bond Department
20 Exchange Place
New York, New York 10005

Blyth Eastman Dillon & Co.
Incorporated
Municipal Bond Department
14 Wall Street
New York, New York 10005

Merrill Lynch, Pierce, Fenner & Smith
Incorporated
Municipal Bond Department
One Liberty Plaza, 165 Broadway
New York, New York 10006

Kidder, Peabody & Co.
Incorporated
Municipal Bond Department
10 Hanover Square
New York, New York 10005

Smith, Barney & Co.
Incorporated
Municipal Bond Department
20 Broad Street
New York, New York 10005

Please send me a free copy of the preliminary Official Statement of the Puerto Rico Water Resources Authority.

Name _____

Street _____ City _____ State _____ Zip _____

Telephone _____
(business)   (residence)

In the opinion of Messrs. Chapman and Cutler, Chicago, Illinois, Bond Counsel, interest on the Series A Bonds is exempt from all present Federal income taxes under existing statutes, regulations, court decisions and rulings, except that such exemption is not applicable with respect to any Series A Bonds for any period during which they are held by a person who is a substantial user of the Initial Project Facilities or any person considered to be related to such person within the meaning of Section 103(c)(6)(C) of the Internal Revenue Code of 1954, as amended.

NEW ISSUE

RATINGS:
Moody's: Aaa
Standard & Poor's: AA

$35,000,000

Illinois Industrial Pollution Control Financing Authority
Pollution Control Revenue Bonds, 1974 Series A
(Commonwealth Edison Company Project)

The Series A Bonds, issued to provide funds for water pollution control facilities (the "Initial Project Facilities"), are limited obligations of Illinois Industrial Pollution Control Financing Authority and, except to the extent payable from Bond proceeds, are payable solely from the revenues to be derived from the sale of the Initial Project Facilities to Commonwealth Edison Company (the "Company") pursuant to a Pollution Control Facilities Agreement of Sale. The obligation of the Company to pay the purchase price will be provided for by the delivery to the Trustee of First Mortgage Bonds of

Commonwealth Edison Company

Dated July 1, 1974   Due as shown below

The Series A Bonds will be issuable as coupon Bonds in the denomination of $5,000 each, registrable as to principal only, and as fully registered Bonds in the denomination of $5,000 or any multiple thereof. Coupon Bonds and fully registered Bonds are interchangeable. Principal and semi-annual interest (January 1 and July 1, first payment January 1, 1975) are payable at the principal corporate trust office of The First National Bank of Chicago, Trustee and Paying Agent. The Series A Bonds are subject to mandatory and optional redemption prior to maturity as more fully described in the Official Statement.

$10,000,000 5.80% Bonds due July 1, 1986 — Price 100%
$25,000,000 6⅞% Bonds due July 1, 2004 — Price 100%

(plus accrued interest)

The Series A Bonds are offered when, as and if issued and received by the Underwriters and subject to the approval of legality by Messrs. Chapman and Cutler, Chicago, Illinois, Bond Counsel and certain other conditions. It is expected that the Series A Bonds in definitive form will be available for delivery in New York, New York on or about July 11, 1974.

The First Boston Corporation

Bacon, Whipple & Co.	A. G. Becker & Co. *Incorporated*	William Blair & Company	Blunt Ellis & Simmons *Incorporated*
Blyth Eastman Dillon & Co. *Incorporated*		Goldman, Sachs & Co.	Halsey, Stuart & Co. Inc. *Affiliate of Bache & Co. Incorporated*
Hayden Stone Inc.	Hornblower & Weeks-Hemphill, Noyes *Incorporated*		Hutchinson, Shockey, Erley & Co.
E. F. Hutton & Company Inc.	Kidder, Peabody & Co. *Incorporated*		Lehman Brothers *Incorporated*
McMaster Hutchinson & Co.	Merrill Lynch, Pierce, Fenner & Smith *Incorporated*		John Nuveen & Co. *Incorporated*
Reynolds Securities Inc.	L. F. Rothschild & Co.		Salomon Brothers
Shearson, Hammill & Co. *Incorporated*	Van Kampen Wauterlek & Brown, Inc.		Dean Witter & Co. *Incorporated*

American Securities Corporation   Edwards & Hanly   Fahnestock & Co.   First of Michigan Corporation

Harris, Upham & Co. *Incorporated*   W. E. Hutton & Co.   Bonniwell & Co. *Incorporated*   Channer Newman Securities Company

The Chicago Corporation   Howe, Barnes & Johnson, Inc.   The Illinois Company *Incorporated*   Loewi & Co. *Incorporated*

McCormick & Co. *Incorporated*   Mesirow & Company   Mullaney, Wells & Company   Rodman & Renshaw, Inc.

Stifel, Nicolaus & Company *Incorporated*   M. B. Vick & Company, Inc.

June 21, 1974

Interest is Exempt, in the opinion of
Bond Counsel, from all present
Federal Income Taxes.

Standard & Poor's Rating: AAA

<u>NEW ISSUE</u>

$8,655,000

City of Carbondale, Jackson County, Illinois

Water and Sewer Revenue Refunding
Bonds, Series 1974—A and B

Payable at the American National Bank and
Trust Company of Chicago, Chicago, Illinois.

The City has secured a commitment from
the Municipal Bond Insurance Association
to guarantee unconditionally and
irrevocably the full and prompt payment
of the bond principal and interest to the
Paying Agent.

Amounts, Coupon Rates,
Maturities and Yields or Prices

(dated May 1, 1974)
(due May 1, as shown below)

Amount	Coupon	Maturity	Yield/Price
$125,000	7%	1979	5.50%
135,000	7	1980	5.50
145,000	7	1981	5.50
155,000	7	1982	5.60
165,000	7	1983	5.70
175,000	7	1984	5.75
190,000	7	*1985	5.80
200,000	7	*1986	5.85
215,000	7	*1987	5.90
230,000	7	*1988	5.95†
245,000	7	*1989	6.00†
265,000	7	*1990	6.10†
285,000	7	*1991	6.20†
305,000	6¾	*1992	6.25††
325,000	6¾	*1993	6.30††
345,000	6¾	*1994	6.40††
370,000	6½	*1995	6.45††
395,000	6½	*1996	100
420,000	6.60	*1997	6.55††
445,000	6.60	*1998	100
475,000	6.70	*1999	6.65††
505,000	6.70	*2000	100
540,000	6¾	*2001	100
575,000	6¾	*2002	100
615,000	6¾	*2003	100
810,000	6¾	*2004	100

*Callable in accordance with the
Optional Provisions as set forth in the
Official Statement.
†Priced to 5/1/84 call @ 103
††Priced to 5/1/90 par call

This announcement is not an offer to sell nor a solicitation of an
offer to buy these securities. Offering is made only by means of
the Circular, copies of which may be obtained from the undersigned.

John Nuveen & Co.   UMIC, Inc.
Incorporated

May 28, 1974

APPENDIX 11

UNDERSTANDING THE OFFICIAL STATEMENT
(OR PROSPECTUS, IF YOU INSIST)

I have picked the following official statement because it is a very complete one and covers many aspects of a revenue bond, including a feasibility report. This very complete document is the kind of official statement that you should get when you receive an official statement. Of course, general-obligation issues do not have as much detail. It is in the revenue issues where this information is necessary for you to make a judgment. It gives me great pleasure to reproduce this particular official statement. As you can see, it is not new, but it is a successful project. The official statement was prepared by the managing underwriters whose names are listed on the cover page. However, the document is the property of the Montefiore Hospital and is attested to by their chairman. We thank them for the right to reproduce this official statement. One of the underwriters is Herbert J. Sims, the chairman of Herbert J. Sims & Co., Inc. He has done more for hospital and health-care financing than any other man in the securities industry, and that takes in a lot of ground.

I am going to give you a list of important sections to look at, which should be the same in most issues except that all underwriters differ in approach. The principal thing to worry about is that you receive all the information that you or your investment advisors need to make an intelligent decision.

Cover page—The cover page gives you quite a bit of information on the issue. It gives you the dated date, which is the date of issue, and the due dates and when the interest is payable. A preliminary official statement may not mention the name of the trustee bank, but if you buy the bonds you will be provided with a final official statement. In this case we are dealing with a final official statement.

There is also a statement as to who has issued the legal opinion. In other words, the cover page tries to give as much information about the issue as possible. Do not forget that this issue was sold in 1973, and therefore the rates are a bit out of date. I like the idea of putting the ratings on the cover page. Too many underwriters do not, but I think that it is an integral part of any official statement. You as an investor are entitled to know these ratings without having to make calls about them.

One of the most important sections of the cover page is the paragraph that tells you who is responsible for paying these bonds out. In this case the investors can only look to the Montefiore Hospital, and not the U. S. Government, the state of Pennsylvania, or even the county of Allegheny. In this particular issue, the hospital can handle the responsibility fine.

156

However, in other revenue issues be sure to know who is responsible for the payment of that all-important interest and principal.

The cover page has a brief description of the redemption and mandatory redemption features. For a more complete rundown as to what it means, the investor would turn to pages 30 and 31 where the redemptions are discussed and where the Sinking Fund is shown. A Sinking Fund makes a mandatory redemption possible. Mandatory means just what you think it does. The issuer must redeem a certain amount of bonds per year. This in effect makes it a much shorter issue for some investors. The bonds are usually redeemed in inverse order basically making it last in, first out. However, in some issues, the Trustee will pick the bonds to be redeemed by lot.

The following page contains a short statement. This is an attempt to capsulize the entire issue. However, it is not a substitute for reading the entire official statement.

The official statement actually begins on page 1. Page 1 through part of page 20 is devoted to information about the hospital. The best part about this section is that it is interesting. You can learn everything that you should know about this hospital from its history and programs to its personnel. The service area of the hospital is also covered, plus the capital-development program.

In reading over the latter, you will find that if you had been an investor in this issue, you and your fellow bondholders would not have been carrying the whole load. You will find that the U. S. Government is involved, as well as the concerned people of the area through donations. The latter is important. It is a most important plus point and it is something to look for when you look at an issue such as this. This does not mean that there is anything wrong with 100-percent financing (which means that the bond issue takes care of everything), but there is something reassuring when you know that you have partners either by government subsidy or the donation of concerned people.

On page 20 you get the details of a mortgage loan which is being paid off. Page 21 gives you a rundown on other indebtedness, plus how the money provided by the bond investors will be used. Never buy a bond if the official statement does not give you a complete breakdown like this one.

Pages 22 through 25 give you the figures that count and tell you whether the hospital is making money or not. In this case you can see that they have been doing very well. If this were a new project, we would be looking for a feasibility report. A feasibility report is usually prepared by a hospital consultant, many of whom are part of major accounting firms. There is one problem with the usual feasibility report that appears in many of the newer projects. Most of them are very vague as to whether they believe the project to be feasible or not. Many of these people are fearful of being sued if the project does not work out. However, if the feasibility report does not say yes or no, but just maybe, then you as an investor are not getting the guidance with established situations such as the Montefiore Hospital.

Pages 26 through 33 cover the lease and trust indenture by giving summaries of these documents. I do not recommend that you read the original documents unless you have a legal, accounting, or securities background. The summaries that are provided here are ample for your needs. Especially important is the redemption section on page 30, which gives you the schedule for retiring bonds. On page 31 you are also given the sinking-fund schedule. These payments are mandatory and go to redeem those $8,265,000 bonds due in 2003.

You might say that pages 32 and 33 cover the ground rules that the issuer must follow. The rules are set out for investment policy, stating whether or not additional bonds can be issued. You can also have the covenants of the authority plus the remedies in case of a default (an awful word you cannot avoid if you want to be realistic), which does not seem likely in this project. Under the heading of Modifications, on page 33, you find out the procedures under which the issuer can change the indenture. While it may look like an escape hatch, it is really there for your benefit so that an issue that is having trouble can remedy the problems.

Page 34 has statements on the tax exemption of the bonds, and again the legal opinions. This is where the Allegheny County Hospital Development Authority, through which the bonds have been issued, signs the official statement. It is countersigned by the president of the Montefiore Hospital Association of Western Pennsylvania, Milton Porter. All of this means that this official statement has been authorized by the governmental entity (the Allegheny County Hospital Development Authority) and the hospital, Montefiore. It is not merely the concoction of a bond underwriter (although one helped to prepare it). Make sure that any official statement of a revenue issue is signed by the authority. Otherwise you are not getting the proper representations.

Pages 35 through 50 are not technically part of the official statement, but they contain three important sections. There is a listing of the staff and a summary of the services in 1963–1968 and 1973 (page 42). The accountants take over from pages 43 through 50, and your own accountant could have a field day on this section. Again, there are very interesting facts to be learned from the footnotes of a balance sheet. Try reading one—you may even like it.

The same goes for an official statement. Do not avoid them. Skip some of the detail, but look for the important aspects such as I have pointed out here. Here too you may find that official statements can be interesting. If they are not, just pass up the issue. It seems to me that issuers and underwriters owe it to investors to present this type of information in a way that the average investor can understand and even enjoy.

NEW ISSUE

In the opinion of counsel, interest on the bonds, under existing statutes and decisions, is not subject to present Federal income taxes. Tax free in the Commonwealth of Pennsylvania under existing laws except for inheritance, estate, succession or gift or any other tax not levied directly on the bonds, their transfer or income derived therefrom.

$11,630,000
ALLEGHENY COUNTY HOSPITAL DEVELOPMENT AUTHORITY
ALLEGHENY COUNTY, PENNSYLVANIA

Hospital Gross Revenue Bonds—Series C, 1973
(The Montefiore Hospital Association of Western Pennsylvania, Sublessee)

Dated: October 1, 1973   **Due: October 1, as shown below**

Principal and semi-annual interest (October 1 and April 1, first coupon April 1, 1974) payable at Mellon Bank N.A., Pittsburgh, Pennsylvania, Trustee; coupon Bonds of $5,000 denomination registrable as to principal only.

The Bonds are subject to redemption prior to maturity on thirty days' notice at the option of the Authority, as follows: Bonds maturing after October 1, 1983 are subject to redemption in whole or in part at any time on and after October 1, 1983, at 101% plus accrued interest and at reducing prices thereafter. Bonds maturing after October 1, 1978 are subject to redemption in part on any interest payment date on or after October 1, 1978, at 101% plus accrued interest and at reducing prices thereafter, but only out of moneys in the Bond Redemption and Improvement Fund.

The Bonds due October 1, 2003 are subject to mandatory redemption from the 1973 Series C Bond Sinking Fund at 100% commencing October 1, 1989.

The proceeds of the sale of the Bonds will be used to repay the Connecticut General Life Insurance Company first mortgage balance of $5,542,128, the Union National Bank loan of $4,100,000, and $400,000 due to contractors for construction. Also from the bond proceeds, $500,000 will be provided for hospital equipment, $807,000 will be deposited in the Debt Service Reserve Fund and the expenses related to the issuance of the Bonds will be paid.

The Bonds are being issued pursuant to a Trust Indenture dated as of October 1, 1973, under which Mellon Bank N.A., Pittsburgh, Pennsylvania, is Trustee, and are secured by a pledge of the receipts and revenues of the Authority to be derived from the subleasing of the Hospital Premises, as herein defined to The Montefiore Hospital Association of Western Pennsylvania, (the "Hospital"), a Pennsylvania non-profit corporation.

AMOUNTS, MATURITIES AND COUPONS

Amount	Due October 1	Coupon	Amount	Due October 1	Coupon
$155,000	1974	4.75%	$230,000	1982	5.10%
165,000	1975	4.75	240,000	1983	5.15
170,000	1976	4.80	255,000	1984	5.15
180,000	1977	4.85	265,000	1985	5.20
190,000	1978	4.90	280,000	1986	5.20
200,000	1979	4.95	295,000	1987	5.25
210,000	1980	5.00	310,000	1988	5.25
220,000	1981	5.05			
			8,265,000	2003	5.80

Price: 100%
(Accrued Interest to be added)

Butcher & Singer
Salomon Brothers
Blyth Eastman Dillon & Co.
Incorporated
Merrill Lynch, Pierce, Fenner & Smith
Incorporated
Herbert J. Sims & Co., Inc.

The Bonds are offered when, as and if issued, subject to the approving legal opinion of Co-Bond Counsel Messrs. Berkman Ruslander Pohl Lieber & Engel, Pittsburgh, Pennsylvania, and Beck, McGinnis & Jarvis, Pittsburgh, Pennsylvania.

Date of Official Statement October 3, 1973

SHORT STATEMENT

(Subject in all respects to more complete information in this Official Statement)

ALLEGHENY COUNTY, the site of Montefiore Hospital, is located in Western Pennsylvania. The Coun is an industrial and corporate headquarters center with a 1970 population of 1,605,016. The Hospital is locat in the Oakland section of the City of Pittsburgh.

ALLEGHENY COUNTY HOSPITAL DEVELOPMENT AUTHORITY was created pursuant to a resol tion of the Board of Commissioners of Allegheny County and is the issuer of the Hospital Gross Revenue Bon The Authority will enter into a thirty year lease and sublease with the Hsopital to be dated October 1, 1973.

THE MONTEFIORE HOSPITAL ASSOCIATION of Western Pennsylvania is a voluntary, non-pro non-sectarian, University affiliated teaching hospital incorporated in 1905. The Hospital is a short term, ac care, general medical-surgical hospital with 490 beds and a medical staff of 288 physicians and dentists.

In July 1973, the Hospital completed a $22,900,000 capital development program which increased the b capacity from 321 beds to 490 beds and increased the gross square feet space of the Hospital from 228,000 602,000 square feet. This program included the construction of an eleven story $19,000,000 Frank Wing, reno tion of the B level of the Katz Pavilion, development of the Leo Lehman Research Wing and construction o 42 unit house staff residence.

BOND PROCEEDS will be applied as follows: $5,542,128 to repay the Connecticut General Life Insura Company mortgage, $4,100,000 to repay the Union National Bank loan, $400,000 due contractors, $500,C for hospital equipment, $807,000 for Debt Service Reserve Fund and the balance will be used to pay the expen of this bond issue.

THE SUBLEASE provides for the payment of rentals by the Hospital from the gross revenues of the Hosp sufficient to pay principal, interest, Authority expenses and maintain reserves as specified in the Trust Indentu The Hospital covenants that it will charge and collect rates, fees and charges sufficient to provide net reven equal to at least 120% of average annual debt service requirements on all outstanding bonds.

THE HOSPITAL is an affiliate of the United Jewish Federation of Pittsburgh and in the past ten years I received financial support in the amount of $2,331,773 from the Federation.

COVERAGE: Historical net income available for debt service for fiscal 1972 and 1973, calculated before United Jewish Federation annual appropriation and adjusted to eliminate interest and depreciation, amoun to 1.53 and 1.62 times the Hospital's projected net rental payment for this Bond issue. Net income projected by Hospital will cover the Hospital's annual net rental payments 2.49 times in fiscal 1974 and 2.52 times in fiscal 19

THIRD PARTY PAYMENTS provided 99% of total patient revenues in fiscal 1973 as follows:

Blue Cross	33%
Medicare	43%
Medicaid	9%
Commercial Insurance	14%
Total Third Party Payments	99%
Private Pay	1%
Total Patient Revenue	100%

This Official Statement does not constitute an offer to sell Bonds in any jurisdiction to any person to whom it is unlawful to make such offer in such jurisdiction. No dealer, salesman or any other person has been authorized to give any information or make any representation, other than those contained herein, in connection with the offering of the Bonds, and if given or made, such information or representation must not be relied upon. Neither the delivery of this Official Statement nor the sale of any Bonds implies that there has been no change in the matters described herein since the date hereof.

TABLE OF CONTENTS

	PAGE
Plan of Financing	1
The Authority	1
History and Organization	3
United Jewish Federation Of Pittsburgh	5
Existing Facilities	6
Medical Staff	7
Administrative and Professional Officers	9
Service Area	10
Patient Care Programs	12
Medical Education	13
Research	14
University Health Center of Pittsburgh	16
Capital Development Program	18
Mortgage and Other Indebtedness	20
Uses of Bond Proceeds	21
Statement of Historical and Projected Operations—Coverage	22
Bond Amortization Schedule	24
Third Party Payments	25
Lease and Sublease	26
Indenture	29

EXHIBITS:

A. Medical Staff	36
B. Summary of Services	42
C. Accountants' Report and Financial Statements	43

OFFICIAL STATEMENT OF

ALLEGHENY COUNTY HOSPITAL DEVELOPMENT AUTHORITY
ALLEGHENY COUNTY, PENNSYLVANIA

relating to its
Hospital Gross Revenue Bonds—Series C, 1973
(The Montefiore Hospital Association of Western Pennsylvania, Sublessee)

This Official Statement, including the cover page and Exhibits, is furnished in connection with the offering of $11,630,000 principal amount of Hospital Gross Revenue Bonds—Series C, 1973 (the "Bonds"), of Allegheny County Hospital Development Authority (the "Authority") being issued pursuant to a Trust Indenture dated October 1, 1973 (the "Indenture"), under which Mellon Bank N.A., Pittsburgh, Pennsylvania, is Trustee.

The Authority has no power to pledge the credit or taxing power of the Commonwealth of Pennsylvania or any political subdivision, nor shall the Bonds be deemed to be obligations of the Commonwealth or any of its political subdivisions, nor shall the Commonwealth or any political subdivision thereof be liable for the payment of principal of, premiums, if any, or interest on the Bonds, nor are the members, officers or employees of the Authority personally liable on its obligations.

PLAN OF FINANCING

The Montefiore Hospital Association of Western Pennsylvania (the "Hospital"), has leased certain hospital facilities to the Authority under the terms of an Agreement of Lease dated October 1, 1973, (the "Lease"), and the Authority has leased such facilities (the "Hospital Premises") back to the Hospital under the terms of an Agreement of Sublease, dated October 1, 1973 (the "Sublease"). Rental payments due and payable to the Authority by the Hospital under the Sublease are in amounts sufficient to cover debt service requirements, annual Authority expenses, and to maintain a Debt Service Reserve Fund. Pursuant to the Sublease, the Hospital has pledged the gross receipts, derived from the Hospital Premises other than the first two thousand ($2,000) dollars received monthly from the ownership or operation of its pharmacy and grants, gifts, bequests, contributions and other donations specifically restricted by the donor or grantor, (the "Gross Receipts") to the extent required for the monthly payment of rent.

THE AUTHORITY

The Authority is a body corporate and politic created pursuant to a resolution of the Board of Commissioners of the County of Allegheny (the "County"), under the Act of the General Assembly of the Commonwealth of Pennsylvania approved May 2, 1945, P.L. 382, as amended and supplemented, known as the Municipality Authorities Act of 1945. The Authority may acquire, hold, construct, improve, maintain, own, operate and lease in the capacity of either lessor or lessee, hospitals and related facilities, and other projects acquired, constructed or improved for hospital purposes. A Certificate of Incorporation, dated June 17, 1971 has been issued to the Authority by the Secretary of the Commonwealth of Pennsylvania. The Authority's existence will continue 50 years from that date.

The governing body of the Authority is a Board consisting of seven members appointed by the County Commissioners of Allegheny County. Members of the Authority Board are appointed for staggered five-year terms and may be reappointed, but they may not be County Commissioners. Present members of the Authority Board are:

Member	Office	Position
John M. Arthur	Chairman	Chairman of the Board, Duquesne Light Company
Erroll B. Davis	Vice Chairman	Advertising & Public Relations Consultant, Davis-Lavelle & Associates
Guy V. Mendola	Treasurer	President GVM Pontiac Inc.
Phyllis T. Kernick	Secretary	Treasurer, Penn Hills Township
Wilbur D. Clark	Assistant Secretary-Treasurer	Editor, North Hills News Record
Elliott G. Falk	Board Member	Vice President Robert Morris College
John P. Hester	Board Member	Judge, Allegheny County Common Pleas Court

Professional Advisors

Hospital Architects	Donald Ritchie Associates Chestnut Hill, Massachusetts
Hospital Auditor	Touche Ross & Co. Pittsburgh, Pennsylvania
Hospital Counsel	Berkman Ruslander Pohl Lieber & Engel Pittsburgh, Pennsylvania
Co-Bond Counsel	Berkman Ruslander Pohl Lieber & Engel Pittsburgh, Pennsylvania Beck, McGinnis & Jarvis Pittsburgh, Pennsylvania
Trustee	Mellon Bank N.A. Pittsburgh, Pennsylvania
Managing Underwriters	Butcher & Singer Salomon Brothers Blyth Eastman Dillon & Co., Incorporated Merrill Lynch, Pierce, Fenner & Smith, Incorporated Herbert J. Sims & Co., Inc.

2

HISTORY AND ORGANIZATION

The Montefiore Hospital Association of Western Pennsylvania is a voluntary, non-profit, non-sectarian University affiliated teaching hospital incorporated in March, 1905,

. . . to conduct and operate the hospital and dispensaries in connection therewith, and to carry on such educational, philanthropic, scientific and research activities as are incidental to modern hospital work without discrimination as to race, color or creed.

Any person may become a voting member of the Hospital upon application and payment of $25.00 annually or by becoming a voting member of the United Jewish Federation of Pittsburgh. The business of the Hospital is conducted by a Board of Trustees of 27, of whom one-third are elected at the annual meeting of the Association, 9 life trustees, i.e. trustees with 12 or more years of service, 1 honorary trustee, and 4 ex officio members, the President and Executive Director of the United Jewish Federation of Pittsburgh, the President of the Ladies Hospital Aid Society and the Executive Director of the Hospital. The Board of Trustees is responsible for the management of the property, business, funds and affairs of the Hospital. The members are:

3

The firm of Berkman Ruslander Pohl Lieber & Engel, one of the Co-Bond Counsel, is also General Counsel to the Hospital. Two partners in the firm, Allen H. Berkman and Marvin S. Lieber, are members of the Hospital's Board of Trustees.

The responsibilities entrusted to the Board of Trustees are fulfilled between regular meetings of the Board by an Executive Management Committee consisting of 10 members. An auxiliary, the Ladies Hospital Aid Society, consisting of 3,000 members, was organized in 1898, and presently has as its primary objective the support of the Hospital and its programs. During the past 10 years the Ladies Hospital Aid Society has raised more than $1 million through a variety of charitable functions to support the Hospital's capital and operating programs.

4

UNITED JEWISH FEDERATION OF PITTSBURGH

Although dedicated to the provision of health services on a non-sectarian basis since its founding, the Hospital was established through the efforts of Pittsburgh's Jewish community and continues to be a Jewish sponsored institution. The Hospital became an affiliate of the Federation of Jewish Philanthropies, the Jewish community's social planning and budgeting, and central fund raising agency, when that agency was organized in 1912. The Hospital received its first Federation financial support at that time. During the past ten years the United Jewish Federation of Pittsburgh, the Federation of Jewish Philanthropies successor agency, has raised almost $35 million of which $2.3 million has been allocated to Montefiore Hospital, the largest amount provided to a local agency.

FEDERATION SUPPORT OF MONTEFIORE HOSPITAL

Year	Support Received
1963-64	$ 196,094
1964-65	196,094
1965-66	215,310
1966-67	231,534
1967-68	244,941
1968-69	249,402
1969-70	251,462
1970-71	248,985
1971-72	248,981
1972-73	248,970
TOTAL	$2,331,773

Montefiore Hospital actively participates in the Federation's social planning activities. The President and Executive Director of the United Jewish Federation serve as ex officio members of the Hospital's governing board and voting members of the United Jewish Federation are voting members of the Hospital. Many hospital trustees serve as active members of the Federation's Board of Trustees and committees. The President of the Hospital serves as an ex officio member of the United Jewish Federation's Board of Trustees, as do the Presidents of the other Federation beneficiary agencies.

ACCREDITATION, APPROVALS, AND MEMBERSHIPS

Accreditation

Montefiore Hospital is accredited by the Joint Commission on Accreditation of Hospitals, which is made up of the American College of Physicians, the American College of Surgeons, the American Hospital Association, and the American Medical Association.

Approvals

American Medical Association for Intern Training and for Residencies in Medicine, Surgery, Anesthesiology, Ophthalmology, and Pathology

American Dental Association for Dental Intern Training and Oral Surgery Residency

American College of Surgeons for a Cancer Registry Program

Liliane S. Kaufmann School of Nursing is approved by the Pennsylvania State Board of Nursing Examiners and accredited by the National League for Nursing

School of Radiologic Technology is approved by the American Medical Association and the Joint Review Committee on Education in Radiologic Technology

Memberships

> Council of Teaching Hospitals, Association of American Medical Colleges
>
> American Hospital Association
>
> Hospital Association of Pennsylvania
>
> Hospital Council of Western Pennsylvania
>
> Blue Cross of Western Pennsylvania
>
> Health and Welfare Association of Allegheny County

Medicare Certification

Montefiore Hospital is a participating hospital and home health agency for health insurance under the Social Security Program.

EXISTING FACILITIES

Montefiore Hospital is a short term, acute care, general medical-surgical hospital which provides a full range of services and at present operates a total of 490 beds consisting of 434 acute care beds, 24 intensive care beds, 12 cardiac care beds, and 20 self care beds. Originally located on Centre Avenue in the Hill District of Pittsburgh, the Hospital was moved in 1929 to its present location on Fifth Avenue at Darragh Street in the Oakland section, the City's education and cultural center. Within this area are located the University of Pittsburgh, Carnegie-Mellon University, Carlow College, Chatham College, Carnegie Museum, Phipps Conservatory, Frick Museum and Schenley Park. The Hospital's 6.8 acre site is physically within a two block area which encompasses the University of Pittsburgh Medical School, Presbyterian-University Hospital, Children's Hospital of Pittsburgh, Eye and Ear Hospital of Pittsburgh, Magee-Womens Hospital, Western Psychiatric Institute and Clinic and the Oakland Veteran's Administration Hospital. This site contains the Hospital's entire physical plant.

The Katz Pavilion, which opened in 1929, is a 13 story structure containing 262 acute care beds, 24 intensive care beds, 12 cardiac care beds, 20 self care beds, supportive services, and ambulatory care facilities in 143,000 square feet of space. The renovation and modernization of the B level of the Katz Pavilion to provide modern intensive and cardiac care facilities was completed in June, 1973, at a cost of $1.5 million.

In 1953, the Hospital opened the 13 story, 85,000 square foot Liliane S. Kaufmann School of Nursing and residence facility. This building was constructed at a cost of $1.9 million and privately financed.

A seven story, 42 unit, 29,000 square foot House Staff Residence Building was completed in 1963. The building, which provides housing for interns, residents and fellows participating in the Hospital's education programs, was constructed at a cost of $900,000 and is financed through Federal Housing and Home Finance Agency bonds. This building is not included within the definition of "Hospital Premises" as that term is defined in the indenture, lease, and sublease and as used herein. The revenues from this building have not been pledged by the Hospital for the payment of rentals due under the sublease.

Construction of the 11 story, 325,000 square foot Frank Wing, 20,000 square foot Leo Lehman Research Wing, and 125,000 square foot 434 car integral parking garage was completed in June, 1973, at a total cost of $20.5 million. The Frank Wing contains 172 medical-surgical beds, a 250 seat auditorium, operating rooms, emergency rooms, laboratories, x-ray and rehabilitation suites and other supportive facilities. The Leo Lehman Research Wing contains three floors of medical and surgical research laboratories, a vivarium and supportive facilities.

6

MEDICAL STAFF

The organization and quality of medical care at Montefiore Hospital is the delegated responsibility of the chiefs-of-service and Medical Staff. The Medical Staff is organized for the purposes of:

- insuring that all patients admitted to the Hospital or treated in the Outpatient Department receive the best possible care
- initiating and maintaining self governance
- serving in an advisory capacity to the governing board and administration
- providing education and maintaining educational standards
- stimulating the interest of the staff in the pursuit of clinical investigation and scientific research as they relate to the promotion of patient care and the highest possible professional standards of practicing physicians

The Medical Staff is made up of 288 physicians and dentists holding admitting or consultation privileges at Montefiore Hospital.* One hundred and ninety-four members of the Medical Staff hold faculty appointments at the University of Pittsburgh Schools of Medicine and Dental Medicine.

DISTRIBUTION OF MEDICAL STAFF BY SPECIALTY

Specialty	Number of Physicians
Allergy	6
Anesthesiology	4
Cardiology	13
Clinical Immunology	1
Dentistry & Oral Surgery	42
Dermatology	1
Endocrinology	8
Gastroenterology	7
General Medicine	28
General Surgery	13
Hematology	5
Industrial Medicine	1
Infectious Disease	3
Internal Medicine	25
Nephrology	3
Neurology	5
Neurosurgery	7
Nuclear Medicine	2
Obstetrics-Gynecology	10
Oncology	2
Ophthalmology	17
Orthopedic Surgery	8
Otorhinolaryngology	7
Pathology	7
Pediatrics	6
Peripheral Vascular	1
Physical Medicine & Rehab	1
Plastic Surgery	1
Podiatry	7
Proctology	2
Psychiatry	6
Pulmonary Disease	4
Radiology	9
Respiratory Disease	3
Rheumatology	9
Thoracic Surgery	8
Urologic Surgery	6
TOTAL	**288**

*See Exhibit A for full listing of Medical Staff

7

The activities of the Medical Staff are carried out by a Medical Executive Committee comprised of the President and Vice President of the Medical Staff, Physician-in-Chief, Surgeon-in-Chief, Pathologist-in-Chief, Radiologist-in-Chief, Anesthesiologist-in-Chief, and three at-large members of the Medical Staff. The operations and management of the Hospital are the responsibility of the Executive Director—Chief Executive Officer, who is responsible to the institution's governing board. Assisting the Executive Director, in addition to the Chiefs-of-Service, are an Associate Director for Planning, Assistant Directors for Nursing, Personnel, Fiscal, and Administrative Services, two Administrative Assistants, a Public Relations Director and a Director of Management Engineering Services. The Hospital's organization, in addition to the clinical services, is subdivided into 21 operating departments: dietary, laundry, security, housekeeping, social service, rehabilitation, fiscal, purchasing, medical library, home care, medical records, pharmacy, volunteer services, nursing, planning, public relations, personnel, maintenance, central escort and messenger service, ambulatory care services, central supply and inhalation therapy.

EMPLOYEE COMPLEMENT

Department	Number of Employees
Ambulatory Care Services	30
Administration	8
Anesthesiology	16
Central Escort	29
Central Supply	14
Department of Medicine	104
Department of Surgery	33
Dietary	138
Fiscal Services	91
Home Care	5
Housekeeping	83
Inhalation Therapy	6
Laundry	23
Long Range Planning	2
Maintenance	37
Medical Library	3
Medical Records	30
Nursing	578
Pathology	82
Personnel Services	6
Pharmacy	13
Public Relations	3
Purchasing	14
Radiology	46
Rehabilitation	14
Security	16
Social Service	15
Volunteer Services	2
TOTAL	1,441

8

ADMINISTRATIVE AND PROFESSIONAL OFFICERS

Irwin Goldberg, Executive Director of the Hospital, received a Bachelor of Science degree in Business Administration from the University of Pittsburgh in 1949. Mr. Goldberg joined the Hospital in 1951 as Controller and subsequently served as Assistant Director before becoming Executive Director in 1961. Mr. Goldberg is a member of the American Institute of Certified Public Accountants, and a Fellow of the American Public Health Association, American College of Hospital Administrators and Hospital Financial Management Association. Mr. Goldberg recently served as Chairman of the Ad Hoc Medical Assistance Evaluation Committee by appointment of the Secretary of Public Welfare of the Commonwealth of Pennsylvania, and is a member of the Health Manpower Task Force of the State Advisory Council for Comprehensive Health Planning.

Daniel Kane, Associate Director for Planning at Montefiore Hospital, received a Bachelor of Business Administration from the City College of New York in 1960; a Master of Science in Hospital Administration from Columbia University in 1964; and the degree of Doctor of Public Health from the University of Pittsburgh in 1973. Prior to becoming affiliated with Montefiore in 1969, Mr. Kane served as Assistant Vice President at the Roosevelt Hospital, New York. He is a Fellow of the American Public Health Association and a member of the American College of Hospital Administrators. Mr. Kane serves as an Assistant Professor in the Department of Public Health and Preventive Dentistry at the University of Pittsburgh School of Dental Medicine and is a frequent contributor to the health administration literature.

James Steinkirchner, Assistant Director for Fiscal Services of Montefiore Hospital, received his Bachelor of Business Administration from the University of Pittsburgh in 1961. Prior to coming to Montefiore as an Assistant Director, Mr. Steinkirchner was the Controller of the Richmond Memorial Hospital, Richmond, Virginia. He is a Fellow of the Hospital Financial Management Association.

Philip Troen, M.D., Physician-in-Chief, received his A.B. degree magna cum laude from Harvard College in 1944 and his M.D. from Harvard Medical School in 1948, and is a member of Phi Beta Kappa. Dr. Troen received his internship and residency training at Boston City Hospital and Beth Israel Hospital in Boston, and served on the staff of Beth Israel and the Harvard Medical School before joining Montefiore Hospital in 1964. In addition to his position at Montefiore, Dr. Troen serves as Professor of Medicine and Associate Chairman of the Department of Medicine at the University of Pittsburgh School of Medicine. Dr. Troen is a diplomate of the American Board of Internal Medicine. Dr. Troen was a recipient of six (6) post-doctoral fellowships including a Guggenheim Fellowship, in such well known institutions as Beth Israel Hospital, the Mayo Clinic, and the Karolinska Hospital in Stockholm. He received a commendation award with medal pendant for meritorious achievement as a Captain in the Army Medical Corps. Dr. Troen is a member of numerous professional societies including the American Society for Clinical Investigation, American Society of Biological Chemists, and the Endocrine Society, and has published more than thirty (30) original research papers in the medical literature.

Mark M. Ravitch, M.D., Surgeon-in-Chief, received his A.B. degree from the University of Oklahoma in 1930 and M.D. from the Johns Hopkins University School of Medicine in 1934. Dr. Ravitch is a member of Phi Beta Kappa, Phi Eta Sigma, Phi Sigma and Alpha Omega Alpha. He received his internship and residency training at Johns Hopkins Hospital and served as a Major in the U.S. Army Medical Corps. Before joining Montefiore Hospital in 1969, Dr. Ravitch served as Professor of Pediatric Surgery, Professor of Surgery and Head of the Division of Pediatric Surgery at the University of Chicago. Prior to that he had been Surgeon-in-Chief at the Baltimore City Hospital and at Mt. Sinai Hospital, New York City; and Professor of Surgery at the Johns Hopkins University and Columbia University. In addition to his responsibilities at Montefiore Hospital, Dr. Ravitch is Professor of Surgery at the University of Pittsburgh School of Medicine. Dr. Ravitch is a diplomate of the American Board of Surgery and the Board of Thoracic Surgery. He has held many special appointments including consultant in surgery to the Veteran's Administration and member of the Surgery Study Section of the National Institutes of Health and has held editorial positions on such major medical journals as *Surgery*, *Pediatrics* and the *Journal of Surgical Oncology*, and is Editor-in-Chief of *Current Problems in Surgery*. Dr. Ravitch is a member of numerous professional organizations including the American Surgical Association, the Society of University Surgeons, the Southern Surgical Association, the Society for Vascular Surgery and the American

Association for Thoracic Surgery. He has been the recipient of major honors and awards including Honorary Fellowship in the Royal College of Physicians and Surgeons, Glasgow, Scotland; Ladd Medal Recipient of the American Academy of Pediatrics; Vishnevskiy Institute Medal, Moscow, U.S.S.R., and has served as visiting lecturer and professor at such institutions as Duke University, University of Malaysia, the University of Brisbane and the Korean National Medical School. Dr. Ravitch is the author and/or co-author of eight (8) books, forty-two (42) chapters in major publications, and more than 240 papers in the professional literature.

Harvey Mendelow, M.D., Pathologist-in-Chief, received his A.B. degree from the Brooklyn College in 1947 and M.D. from the State University of New York College of Medicine in 1951. He received his medical training at Mt. Sinai Hospital, New York and served in the U.S. Army as a Research Chemist, Manhattan Atomic Bomb Project. Before joining Montefiore Hospital in 1958, Dr. Mendelow served as Assistant Attending Pathologist at Mt. Sinai Hospital. In addition to his position at Montefiore, Dr. Mendelow serves as Clinical Professor of Pathology, University of Pittsburgh School of Medicine. Dr. Mendelow is a diplomate of the National Board of Medical Examiners. He is a Fellow of the American Society of Clinical Pathology, and the College of American Pathologists as well as numerous professional societies, and has published more than sixteen (16) papers in the medical literature.

Stephen Finestone, M.D., Anesthesiologist-in-Chief, received his B.A. degree cum laude from Hobart College in 1952, and his M.D. from the New York University College of Medicine in 1956. He received his internship and residency training at the Mt. Sinai Hospital, New York City. Dr. Finestone served as a Captain with the U.S. Army in Korea. Before becoming Montefiore's Anesthesiologist-in-Chief in 1964, Dr. Finestone served on the staff of Mt. Sinai Hospital in New York City and subsequently as Assistant Attending Anesthesiologist at Montefiore Hospital. Dr. Finestone is a diplomate of the National Board of Medical Examiners and the American Board of Anesthesiology. He is a Fellow of the American College of Anesthesiologists, holds membership in numerous professional societies, and is a member of the Board of Directors, Chairman of the Membership Committee and Alternate Director of the Pennsylvania Society of Anesthesiologists. In addition to his position at Montefiore Hospital, Dr. Finestone serves as Associate Professor of Clinical Anesthesiology at the University of Pittsburgh School of Medicine, and Medical Director of the Health Center School of Anesthesia for Nurses. Dr. Finestone has authored and/or co-authored a number of publications which have appeared in the medical literature.

Harford W. Friedman, M.D., Radiologist-in-Chief, received his B.A. from the University of Michigan School of Literature and Science in 1937, and his M.D. from the University of Michigan School of Medicine in 1941. He received his internship and residency training at Cleveland City Hospital and the University of Michigan Medical Center, respectively. He joined Montefiore Hospital's staff after his residency training in 1945 and became Montefiore's Radiologist-in-Chief in 1956. Dr. Friedman is a diplomate of the American Board of Radiology and holds membership in the American College of Radiology and the Radiological Society of North America. In addition to his work at Montefiore Hospital, Dr. Friedman holds the position of Clinical Associate Professor of Radiology at the University of Pittsburgh School of Medicine.

SERVICE AREA

In the fiscal year ending June 30, 1973, 12,287 individuals were admitted to Montefiore Hospital as inpatients, accounting for 140,748 patient days. More than 59 percent of these individuals reside in the City of Pittsburgh, while almost 27 percent live in other communities within Allegheny County. More than 14 percent of total admissions were accounted for by individuals living in other counties within the Commonwealth of Pennsylvania and other states, primarily Ohio and West Virginia.

During the same period more than 38 percent of the Hospital's total admissions and almost 65 percent of those admissions from the City of Pittsburgh emanated from Montefiore's primary service area, i.e. four communities geographically contiguous to the Hospital. Because of its long standing relationship with these communities, i.e. the Hill District, Oakland, Squirrel Hill and Hazelwood, the Hospital has undertaken a commitment to work with their residents to plan for and implement comprehensive health services programs. The implementation of the Comprehensive Dental Care Program in the Hill District and Oakland, and the Hazelwood Health Center in the Hazelwood community are examples of health programs which arose out of planning efforts in which community representatives and hospital officials participated and out of which community health priorities were identified.

Primary Service Area

Community	1970 Population	% Admissions	% Days
Hill District—5th Ward	21,688	7.1	9.8
Oakland—4th Ward	21,233	8.6	8.8
Squirrel Hill—14th Ward	44,337	18.5	16.2
Hazelwood—15th Ward	23,782	3.8	4.1
TOTAL PRIMARY SERVICE AREA	111.040	38.0	38.9

General Service Area

Pittsburgh (excluding primary service area)	409,071	21.3	26.5
Allegheny County (excluding Pittsburgh)	1,084,899	26.5	21.2
All Other		14.2	13.4
TOTAL GENERAL SERVICE AREA		62.00	61.1
TOTAL SERVICE AREA		100.0	100.0

EMPLOYERS OF INDIVIDUALS UTILIZING MONTEFIORE HOSPITAL*

Allegheny Ludlum Steel Company
Aluminum Company of America
American Bridge Division—United States
  Steel Corporation
Atlantic & Pacific Tea Company
Baltimore & Ohio Railroad
Bell Telephone Company of Pennsylvania
Blaw Knox Company (Division of
  White Consolidated Industries, Inc.)
The Board of Public Education of
  Pittsburgh Schools
Calig Steel Drum Company
Carnegie-Mellon University
Dravo Corporation
Duquesne Light Company
Gimbel Brothers Department Stores
Greater Pgh. Dairy Industry Association
Gulf Oil Corporation
H. J. Heinz Company

Jones & Laughlin Steel Company
Joseph Horne Company
Kaufmann's Department Store
Levinson Steel Company
Mellon Bank, N.A.
Mesta Machine Company
National Record Mart, Inc.
Penn Central Transportation Co.
Pittsburgh Athletic Association
Pittsburgh Plate Glass Company
Pittsburgh Steel Company
Republic Steel Corporation
United Mine Workers
United States Steel Corporation
Webster Hall Hotel
Weirton Steel Company
Western Electric Co., Inc.
Westinghouse Electric Corporation
Wheeling Pittsburgh Steel Corp.

As can be seen from these data, Montefiore Hospital's general service area encompasses a large number of communities with disparate social, economic, and cultural characteristics. The use of the Hospital by individuals from such a wide geographic area is for the most part explained by the Hospital's role as a University affiliated teaching hospital providing secondary and tertiary referral care services for the Western Pennsylvania region.

*Between 1965 and 1969 more than 20 percent of the Hospital's patients were employed by the corporations listed.

PATIENT CARE PROGRAMS

Because of its role as an advanced teaching hospital and tertiary care resource, the Hospital offers a full spectrum of comprehensive medical and surgical services. Among the diagnostic services provided are biochemical profiles, including iso-enzyme studies, hematologic studies, serologic studies including fluorescent antibody procedures, renal pathology, histologic studies, endoscopy, esophagoscopy, gastroscopy, duodenoscopy, sigmoidoscopy, liver biopsy, intestinal motility studies, intestinal biopsy, protein hormone assay, adrenal studies, thyroid studies, fertility studies, cellular kinetic studies, red cell metabolic studies, electrocardiography, phonocardiography, cardiac catherterization, electroencephalography, angiography, echocardiography, tread mill stress testing, electromyography, isotope studies, pulmonary function examinations, blood gas analysis, radioimmunoassay, immuno-electrophoresis, diagnostic radiologic studies, thermography, neuroradiography, mammography, renal biopsy, cytogenetics and audiology.

Special treatment units at the Hospital include an emergency room suite, operating room suite, post-operative recovery room, intensive care unit, coronary care unit, neurosurgical intensive care unit, self-care unit, day surgery program, activities of daily living unit, dental and oral surgical suite, rehabilitation unit, and radiation therapy unit. Among the special treatment services available are peritoneal dialysis, cardioversion, pacemaker implantation, cardiac monitoring, intensive care monitoring, neurosurgical monitoring, isotope therapy, telecobalt therapy, interstitial and intracavitary irradiation therapy, orthovoltage, superficial therapy, direct catheter chemotherapy, nerve block therapy, inhalation therapy, anesthesia, photocoagulation therapy, intravenous therapy, entero-stomal therapy, infection surveillance, physical therapy, speech therapy, recreational therapy and stroke therapy.

The Hospital has made great strides in implementing the progressive patient care concept. Progressive patient care refers to the concentration of resources on a patient and his or her medical problems in the quantity and scope most appropriate at a particular time. Progressive patient care emphasizes prevention, treatment and rehabilitation. Inherent in the provision of progressive patient care is the organization of care on several different levels, i.e. ambulatory care, emergency care, intensive care, intermediate (acute) care, self care, and home care.

The Hospital operates an outpatient department with 27 divisions or clinics including general medicine and the medical specialties, general surgery, plastic surgery, otolaryngology, ophthalmology, gynecology, neurosurgery, orthopedics, proctology, neurology, podiatry, and dentistry and oral surgery. More than 33,500 visits were made to the outpatient department during the fiscal year ending June 30, 1973. In addition, almost 35,000 visits were made by private outpatients. The Hospital also operates a day surgery program for patients whose surgical problems can be adequately treated on an ambulatory basis at significant savings to patients and the public. In addition to its hospital based outpatient services, Montefiore Hospital has operating responsibility for the Hazelwood Health Center, a neighborhood health center located in Pittsburgh's 15th ward. The Hazelwood Health Center, which recorded more than 5,000 visits in the year ending June 30, 1973, enables residents in a community which previously had meager medical resources, to obtain comprehensive health services. Montefiore also operates, in cooperation with the Pittsburgh Model Cities Program, a Comprehensive Dental Care Program for residents of the two communities in the Model Cities area. More than 14,000 visits were made to the dental program in 1973, which in addition to its base unit at the Hospital, is operated through two satellites in the community.

The Hospital's emergency room is staffed 24 hours a day for the evaluation and treatment of acute medical and surgical emergencies. The facility, in which 20,964 individuals were treated in fiscal year ended June 30, 1973, also has a 10 bed holding unit for individuals requiring observation for a short period of time but for whom inpatient hospital care is either not indicated or questioned. The intensive care unit, a new 24 bed facility, is oriented to the needs of patients with life threatening medical and surgical problems requiring concentrated evaluation, monitoring and treatment. The 12 bed cardiac care unit and 6 bed neurosurgical intensive care unit, like the intensive care unit, also provide specialized monitoring, evaluation and treatment for patients with life threatening cardiac and neurosurgical problems, respectively. The Hospital is unique in having all of its acute care facilities on one floor of the Hospital which contains 70,000 square feet of space. This enables the Hospital to concentrate a full spectrum of highly sophisticated diagnostic and treatment modalities on the patient's medical needs without the necessity of vertically transporting the patient between floors.

The Hospital's intermediate or acute care facilities, encompassing most of the institution's inpatient beds, are organized around the needs of patients requiring medical, nursing, and other supportive services but not in the concentration required for patients in the special care units previously described. The cooperative or self care unit is organized around the needs of patients admitted to the Hospital for special diagnostic or treatment services whose needs do not require the concentration of resources found in intermediate care units, and patients who, while originally admitted to an intensive and/or intermediate care units, no longer require concentrated services and can satisfactorily progress in an environment more closely paralleling that at home and stressing semi-independence from institutional routine at significant less cost. The Hospital's home care program, the first one established in the Commonwealth of Pennsylvania, provides medical, nursing, rehabilitation and social service for patients in their homes. Patients admitted to the home care program would otherwise require inpatient hospital or extended care services. The Hospital's efforts in rehabilitation are supported by the maintenance of a representative of Pennsylvania's Bureau of Vocational Rehabilitation within the Hospital's rehabilitation unit and cooperative agreements with the Western Restoration Center, Jewish Home and Hospital for the Aged, and other rehabilitation oriented agencies.

Jewish Home and Hospital for the Aged

Through a group practice program jointly operated by Montefiore Hospital and the Jewish Home and Hospital for the Aged (the "Home"), the Hospital has accepted responsibility for the provision of medical and health services to the residents of the Home, which is located in the Squirrel Hill section of Pittsburgh. The Medical Director of the Home is a full-time physician in the Hospital's Department of Medicine, and together with five members of the Hospital's attending Medical Staff constitute Geriatric Associates, the group of primary care physicians providing medical services to the Home's residents. More than 5,800 primary care visits were made to the Home's residents during calendar year 1972. In addition, 139 residents of the Home have been hospitalized for inpatient care at the Hospital. This program is entirely financed through third party reimbursement programs.

MEDICAL EDUCATION

As an advanced teaching Hospital, Montefiore Hospital has a major commitment to health sciences education at the post-secondary, undergraduate, and post-graduate levels. The Hospital is a primary resource for the University of Pittsburgh Schools of Medicine and Dental Medicine. During the fiscal year ending June 30, 1973, 211 second, third and fourth year medical students, and 131 third year dental students received part of their undergraduate education at Montefiore Hospital. During the same period, 90 interns, residents and fellows participated in graduate medical education programs in medicine, surgery, anesthesiology, pathology, radiology, dentistry and oral surgery, and ophthalmology, in programs approved by their respective specialty boards. The availability of highly qualified medical and dental staffs, of which 194 members hold faculty appointments at the University of Pittsburgh, and modern, fully equipped facilities at Montefiore Hospital have contributed to the ability of the Schools of Medicine and Dental Medicine to expand their entering classes in response to national need.

Through its affiliation with the University of Pittsburgh Schools of Pharmacy, Health Related Professions, Social Work and Graduate School of Public Health, 155 students obtained clinical experience in the disciplines encompassed within each of these schools. In addition, 28 students were enrolled in the University Health Center of Pittsburgh's School of Nurse Anesthetists, of which the Hospital's Anesthesiologist-in-Chief is Director, 196 students in the Hospital's Liliane S. Kaufmann School of Nursing, and 22 in its School of Radiologic Technology. Finally, 37 students in the Carlow College baccalaureate nursing program and 110 students in the Pittsburgh Board of Education sponsored practical nurse, and nurse aide-orderly programs received their clinical education at the Hospital. Interaction between the senior health professionals on the Hospital's staff of 1,441 employees and 288 physicians and large number of students participating in educational programs at the Hospital adds immeasurably to the high quality environment for patient care which exists at Montefiore, in addition to insuring a continuing supply of well trained health professionals for the Hospital, the University Health Center of Pittsburgh and the tri-state area.

13

University of Pittsburgh School of Medicine (2nd, 3rd & 4th year).....................	211*
University of Pittsburgh School of Dental Medicine (3rd year).........................	135
University of Pittsburgh Graduate School of Public Health (Administrative Resident)......	2
University of Pittsburgh School of Social Work....................................	4
University of Pittsburgh School of Health-Related Professions	
Department of Medical Technology......................................	40
Department of Physical Therapy...	85
University of Pittsburgh School of Pharmacy.......................................	24
University Health Center of Pittsburgh School of Nurse Anesthetists..................	28
Montefiore Hospital Liliane S. Kaufmann School of Nursing..........................	196
Montefiore Hospital School of Radiologic Technology..............................	22
Montefiore and Pittsburgh Board of Education sponsored programs for training of:	
Practical Nurses...	30
Nurse Aides and Orderlies...	80
Carlow College School of Nursing..	37
TOTAL STUDENTS...	894

*Department of Medicine.........	150
Department of Surgery..........	45
Department of Anesthesiology....	16
	211

RESEARCH

Biomedical research is a natural adjunct to patient care and medical education and has been carried out in specialized facilities at Montefiore Hospital since 1951. Members of Montefiore's Medical Staff are involved in major research projects in the basic and clinical sciences. Current research projects are supported by extramural grants totaling $220,000. Among the areas of investigation are:

Medicine

Renal Disease

- The effect of intracellular acid base balance on the metabolism of cells.
- Clinical investigation in the treatment of chronic renal disease with immuno-suppressive agents.
- Investigation into the effect of inadequate oxygen supply on function of the kidney to aid in the understanding of kidney function in both health and disease.

Gastroenterology and Nutrition

- Investigation of the intestinal absorption of protein and carbohydrates in normal subjects and in patients with intestinal and pancreatic disorders.
- Investigation into the absorption of amino acids from the gastrointestinal tract and study of the effect of amino acid metabolism on nutrition.

Hematology

- Investigations aimed at defining the mechanism responsible for the control of normal and leukemic white blood cell production.
- Investigation of platelet function.

Cardiology

- Investigation of the use of specific cardiac iso-enzymes in the diagnosis of small myocardial infarctions.
- Investigation of ventricular wall motion in angina pectoris using the echocardiogram.

Infectious Disease
- Investigation into the immune response to infections caused by H influenza, the most common cause of meningitis in children (a cooperative project with Children's Hospital).
- Investigation into the treatment of experimental osteomyelitis, a chronic infectious disease of the bone, using an animal model which the investigator has developed.
- Investigation of the use of influenza vaccine and the immunology of influenza.
- Investigation into the effect of a new antibiotic on immune functions in man.

Immunology
- Investigation into the activities of lymphocytes and their involvement in immune responses of the body.

Endocrinology
- Investigation into kidney and endocrine interrelationships in the development of hypertension.
- Investigation in human reproductive endocrinology and the diagnosis and treatment of male infertility and the normal physiology of development and reproduction.
- Investigation of the biosynthesis and metabolism of steroid hormones.

Nuclear Medicine
- Investigation of nuclear medicine techniques for the study of organ function in health and disease.

Surgery

General Surgery
- A study of surgically induced ischemia in the mammalian fetus.
- Investigation in the healing of intestinal anastomosis.
- A study of the development and use of automatic stapling instruments.
- Investigation into the interaction of lidocaine and thiamylal in the rhesus monkey. (A cooperative project with Magee-Womens Hospital.)
- A study into the development and use of the bioautofuel cell to obtain electricity from body fluids via direct energy conversion.

Neurosurgery
- A study of the gastric barrier in hydrocephalics.
- Clinical evaluation of preferential cerebral hypothermic perfusion as a method to achieve bloodless neurosurgery.
- Investigation into the creation of chemothermal gradients for the treatment of malignant brain tumors.

Anesthesiology

- Evaluation of haldol for treatment of post-anesthesia nausea and vomiting in the recovery room.
- Investigation into sensory disturbances following ketamine anesthesia.
- Efficacy of librium in controlling post-ketamine delirium.
- Use of ketamine in carotid endarterectomies.

Pathology

- Use of the electron microscope to study pathology of the urinary and gastrointestinal tracts, and nerve tissue.
- Investigation of the microcirculation of the heart through use of microradio-angiography.
- Study of acalculus cholecystitis.
- Investigation into the interstitial cells of the kidneys to study peroxiditive and phagocytic function.
- Use of autoradiographic technique to study proliferative glomerule nephritis.
- Investigation into shistosomal nephropathy.
- A study of pathogenetic mechanisms of immune complex nephritis.
- Investigation into the pathology of lesions produced by percutaneous radiofrequency cervical cordotomy.
- Study of the development and use of techniques for the fractionization of isoenzymes.

Radiology

- Investigation into the ovarian vein syndrome.
- A study of the use of the percutaneous balloon catheter technique for the treatment of intracraneal aneurysms.
- Investigation into the collection of cholecystographic contrast media in a large ulcerating leiomyoma of the stomach.

UNIVERSITY HEALTH CENTER OF PITTSBURGH

Montefiore Hospital is a member of the University Health Center of Pittsburgh, a corporation, the members of which are the University of Pittsburgh and the major affiliated teaching hospitals. The other hospital members of the University Health Center of Pittsburgh are Presbyterian-University Hospital, Eye and Ear Hospital of Pittsburgh, Children's Hospital of Pittsburgh, Magee-Womens Hospital, and the Western Psychiatric Institute and Clinic. The University of Pittsburgh's interest is largely centered in its Schools of Medicine, Dental Medicine, Pharmacy, Nursing, Health Related Professions and Public Health. The University Health Center of Pittsburgh is the only academic health center in Western Pennsylvania and in addition serves a major part of Ohio and West Virginia. The University Health Center of Pittsburgh was organized for the purposes of establishing "a mechanism for the coordination and implementation of policies and programs for the common benefit of its member institutions" and for the promotion of "the operation and growth of the Health Center as an efficient, well rounded, and effective community and regional health resource." More specifically, the Health Center is now engaged in a major ambulatory care planning effort designed to coordinate the academic and clinical programs in ambulatory care in the member institutions and to develop and obtain experience with new models of health care delivery. The Health Center is planning a major program in cancer detection and therapy in cooperation with the National Cancer Institute and the American Cancer Society. The Center operates major programs in neuro-sciences, nephrology, pediatrics, neonatology, obstetrics, psychiatry, ophthalmology, otolaryngology and other specialized areas of medicine and surgery. The Health Center institutions have a combined operating budget of $90 million and a combined capital investment of $200 million. In addition, the Health Center operates a Land Bank which is capitalized at $4.3 million. The University Health Center of Pittsburgh is a major producer of health manpower for the tri-state area. In 1973, the University's six schools of the Health Professions trained more than 3,000 students.

The University Health Center of Pittsburgh is governed by a Board of Trustees composed of two representatives from each of the member institutions. The trustees are:

The University of Pittsburgh's Vice Chancellor for Health Professions serves as President and Chief Executive Officer of the Center.

In 1972, 610,143 inpatient days of care were provided in the Health Center Hospitals, representing 24 percent of the inpatient days provided in Allegheny County's 29 hospitals.

Beds as of June 30, 1973

Children's Hospital of Pittsburgh	225
Presbyterian-University Hospital	565
Western Psychiatric Institute and Clinic	120
Eye and Ear Hospital	172
Montefiore Hospital	490
Magee-Womens Hospital	335*
Veteran's Administration Hospital	749**
TOTAL	2,656

.*Does not include 185 bassinets
**Associated with the Health Center

In addition, there were more than 85,000 visits to the Health Center ambulatory care programs. The University Health Center of Pittsburgh operates for the benefit of its member institutions central clinical chemistry, hematology, data processing, laundry, and pharmacy services. These centralized programs had combined operating budgets of almost $10 million in the fiscal year ending June 30, 1973. Operating activities at the member institutions are periodically reviewed for the purpose of identifying programs and services which could be made more efficient and effective through a centralized or coordinated approach.

The trustees, professional staff, and administrative staff of Montefiore Hospital actively participate in Health Center governance and management. A Montefiore Hospital trustee serves as Treasurer of the University Health Center of Pittsburgh and Montefiore trustees are represented on the Executive, Land Bank, and Ambulatory Care Committees of the Health Center governing board. A member of the Hospital's governing board also serves as a trustee of the University of Pittsburgh and as a member of that board's health professions subcommittee. Montefiore's chiefs-of-service hold faculty appointments within the University of Pittsburgh School of Medicine and are actively involved in Health Center activities. The Hospital's Physician-in-Chief serves as Associate Chairman of the School of Medicine's Department of Medicine, and as a member of the Health Center Medical Staff Committee and subcommittees thereof. Montefiore's Surgeon-in-Chief serves as Professor of Surgery in the School of Medicine, as a member of the Executive Committee of the Department of Surgery, and as a member of the Health Center Medical Staff Committee. The Hospital's Anesthesiologist-in-Chief holds the appointment of Associate Professor of Clinical Anesthesiology, in addition to serving as a member of the Executive Committee of the Department of Anesthesiology and Medical Director of the Health Center School of Nurse Anesthesia. The Hospital's Pathologist-in-Chief serves as Professor of Clinical Pathology, and is a member of the Executive Committee of the School of Medicine's Department of Pathology. Montefiore's Radiologist-in-Chief holds an appointment as Clinical Associate Professor of Radiology at the School of Medicine. In addition, 194 physicians and dentists on Montefiore's Medical Staff hold faculty appointments in the Schools of Medicine and Dental Medicine.

Montefiore Hospital's Executive Director serves as a member of the University Health Center Administrators Committee, Council of Deans and Administrators, and as Administrative Representative to the Health Center Public Relations Committee. Administrative and management personnel now serve or have served as Chairmen of various Health Center committees including Nursing Service Administrators, Public Relations, Controllers, Medical Records and Personnel.

CAPITAL DEVELOPMENT PROGRAM

Program

In July, 1973, Montefiore Hospital completed a $22.9 million capital development program, the purpose of which was to provide the Hospital with the modern facilities and equipment necessary to support a large general hospital with major medical and paramedical education, patient care, community service and biomedical research programs.

A major part of the capital development program encompassed the construction of the $19 million Frank Wing, an eleven story, 325,000 square foot facility, with 172 medical-surgical beds and supportive services.

Frank Wing

Floor	Services
Penthouse	Mechanical Equipment
6	26 medical-surgical beds
5	49 medical-surgical beds
4	49 medical-surgical beds
3	24 medical-surgical beds
2	24 medical-surgical beds
M	Main Lobby, Auditorium, Meditation Room, Medical Library, Medical Record Suite, Medical Staff Lounge, Fiscal Offices, Administrative Offices, Coffee and Gift Shop
A	Clinical Laboratories, Rehabilitation Unit, Inhalation Therapy Suite, Heart Station, Pharmacy
B	Emergency Suite, Admitting Suite, Operating Room Suite, Post-operative Recovery Suite, Central Sterile Supply, Diagnostic and Therapeutic Radiology Suite
C	Cafeteria and Dining Room, Food Service Area, Maintenance Shops, Laundry, Housekeeping Area, Purchasing and General Stores Area
D	Mechanical Equipment

In addition to the completion of the Frank Wing, the capital development program included the renovation and modernization of 20,000 square feet of space on the B level of the Katz Pavilion to provide a 24 bed intensive care unit and 12 bed coronary care unit at a cost of $1.5 million; the development of the $1.5 million Leo Lehman Research Wing, a three story, 20,000 square foot medical research facility with medical and surgical research laboratories, a vivarium and supportive facilities; and a $900,000, seven story, 42 unit house staff residence facility.

Planning Association Approval

The capital development program was reviewed and approved by the Hospital Planning Association of Allegheny County in April, 1969, as meeting a demonstrated community need and being fully in accord with accepted principles of areawide health planning.

Architect

Donald Ritchie Associates, which has its offices in Chestnut Hill, Massachusetts, was organized in 1909, and has specialized in the planning and design of health care facilities since 1950. The firm has been the architect for the Hospital since 1947. The Ritchie organization has been responsible for major hospital and health care facility development programs throughout the United States and includes among its clients the United States Veterans Administration, the United States Defense Department, Commonwealth of Massachusetts; Lahey Clinic, Boston; Albert Einstein Medical Center, Philadelphia; and the Salvation Army. In addition to Montefiore Hospital, the firm's local clients include Braddock General Hospital, Latrobe Hospital, Westmoreland Hospital, and the Henry Clay Frick Community Hospital.

Increase in Available Space

The following is a summary of the increase in gross square feet, number of beds and square feet per bed resulting from the construction program:

	Gross Square Feet of Space	Number of Beds	Square Feet per Bed
Before Construction.............	228,000	321	710
After Completion..............	602,000**	490	1,229

**Does not include 125,000 square foot integral parking garage

Sources of Capital Funds

Major financial support for the capital development program has been received from the federal government through the Hill-Burton, Appalachian Regional Development and Accelerated Public Works Programs, and the National Institutes of Health. Included in donations by the Hospital family and affiliated individual contributors and trusts are thirty gifts of more than $10,000 and five gifts of $250,000 or more. Major national corporations and foundations contributed generously to the capital development program. Long-term financing provided the balance of the funds necessary to complete the program.

Federal Government:

Hill-Burton Grant.............................	$1,520,000	
Appalachian Regional Development Grant..........	380,000	
Accelerated Public Works Grant..................	1,707,500	
National Institutes of Health Grant...............	512,500	
Housing and Home Finance Agency Bonds*........	750,000	
Subtotal..		$ 4,870,000

Hospital Family Contributions and Pledges:

Building Fund.................................	1,350,000	
Board of Trustees.............................	2,638,500	
Medical Staff.................................	458,000	
Ladies Hospital Aid Society.....................	750,000	
Hospital Employees............................	9,500	
Subtotal..		5,206,000

Public Contributions and Pledges:

(Corporations, Foundations and Individuals)........		2,781,872

Loans and Due Contractors:

Connecticut General Mortgage....................	5,542,128	
Union National Bank..........................	4,100,000	
Due Contractors..............................	400,000	
Subtotal..		10,042,128
TOTAL..		$22,900,000

*A Bond issue to be retired over 50 years through accelerated principal payments beginning with $5,000 in the first year and ending with $30,000 in the last year, and 3½ percent annual interest.

Major Corporate Contributors:

Allis-Chalmers Corp.

Aluminum Company of America

Boise Cascade Corporation

Duquesne Light Company

Equitable Gas Company

Executone Systems, Inc.

Fayette Bank and Trust Company

Gulf Corporation

Koppers Company

Mellon Bank, N.A.

National Cash Register Company

Pitney Bowes Inc.

Pittsburgh National Bank

PPG Industries, Inc.

Sealtest Foods Division of Kraftco Corp.

Union Corporation

The Union National Bank of Pittsburgh

United States Steel Corporation

Westinghouse Electric Corporation

Wheeling-Pittsburgh Steel Corp.

Major Foundation Contributors:

Addison Gibson Foundation

Allegheny Foundation

Fisher Charitable Trust

Hillman Foundation

Laurel Foundation

Richard King Mellon Charitable Trust

Sarah Mellon Scaife Foundation

Use of Capital Funds

Capital funds have been used for construction costs, architect's fees, the purchase of equipment and other contracts and payments.

Major contractors..$18,082,000

Architects Fees.. 1,229,000

Group II and III Equipment... 3,239,000

Other Contracts and Payments.. 350,000

TOTAL..$22,900,000

FUTURE DEVELOPMENT PROGRAM

Montefiore Hospital's Long Range Plan, which was approved by its Board of Trustees in April, 1969, delineates a future capital development program. This program would encompass the renovation and modernization of eight floors with 108,000 square feet in the thirteen story Katz Pavilion, which was constructed in 1929, and contains 318 of the Hospital's 490 beds, and supportive facilities. It will entail interior demolition of eight floors of the Katz Pavilion in order to provide modern air-conditioned nursing units, adequate size patient rooms, utility rooms, toilet facilities, treatment rooms, lounges, conference rooms, and supportive facilities. The electrical and mechanical systems in the building will be completely replaced. Modern elevators will replace the existing elevators. Because of complex architectural and engineering requirements and in order to maintain continuity of service to the community, the program will have to be completed in stages.

The importance of implementing the future capital development program at the earliest possible date was recognized in the approval of the program by the Comprehensive Health Planning Association of Western Pennsylvania in May, 1972. The need for the future program is further supported by the approval of a $320,000 grant and a $5.6 million reduced interest loan through the federal Hill-Burton program which will be administered locally by the Commonwealth of Pennsylvania's Department of Public Welfare.

The financial requirements for the future capital development program are estimated at $8.1 million of which $5.9 million would be obtained through a Hill-Burton grant and reduced interest loan.

CONNECTICUT GENERAL LIFE INSURANCE COMPANY MORTGAGE

The Hospital Premises are presently subject to a mortgage in favor of Connecticut General Life Insurance Company (the "Insurance Company") given to secure a Note (the "Note") in the original principal amount of $6,000,000. The Note is dated February 13, 1969, matures January 1, 1993, and at present has a balance of $5,542,128.07. The Note bears an interest rate of 7⅝% and requires the Hospital to make equal semi-annual payments in the amount of $285,976, which amount is sufficient to pay accrued interest and to amortize the principal of the Note at maturity.

The Insurance Company has agreed to permit the Hospital to prepay the Note in full upon payment of a prepayment premium in the amount of $135,000. Out of the proceeds of the bond issue, the Trustee will deliver to the Insurance Company an amount equal to the outstanding principal balance of the Note. The Hospital will pay the accrued interest and the prepayment premium of $135,000. Upon receipt of those amounts, the Insurance Company will satisfy the mortgage of record.

The original proceeds of the borrowing from the Insurance Company were used to pay a portion of the cost of the Capital Development Program.

OTHER OUTSTANDING CAPITAL INDEBTEDNESS

In order to provide for a construction loan during the Hospital's Capital Development Program, the Hospital has obtained a line of credit with the Union National Bank of Pittsburgh in the amount of $4,500,000, pursuant to which it has borrowed the sum of $4,100,000. $3,000,000 of this sum bears interest at the rate of ¼% above the current prime rate and $1,100,000 carries the prime rate. Out of the proceeds of the bond issue, the Trustee will pay to the Union National Bank of Pittsburgh sufficient amounts to satisfy the indebtedness to it in full.

In addition, the Hospital has incurred other construction costs in connection with its Capital Development Program in the form of amounts due to contractors for construction work. Payment of these amounts will also be made out of the proceeds of the bond issue.

USES OF BOND PROCEEDS

The following is a summary of the uses of the proceeds from the bond issue:

Repayment of Connecticut General Life Insurance Company Mortgage	$ 5,542,128
Repayment of Union National Bank Loan	4,100,000
Due Contractors	400,000
Hospital Equipment	500,000
Debt Service Reserve Fund	807,000
Legal, Printing, Bond Discount, Trustee, Ratings	280,872
BOND ISSUE	$11,630,000

MONTEFIORE HOSPITAL
STATEMENT OF HISTORICAL AND PROJECTED OPERATIONS
(Dollar Amounts and Patient Days in Thousands)

Year Ended June 30	*Historical*[a]					*Projected*[e]	
	1969	*1970*	*1971*	*1972*	*1973*	*1974*[b]	*1975*[c]
Patient Days	149.6	155.8	153.9	146.3	140.7	140.0	145.0
Occupancy Rate	89.1%	90.4%	87.9%	84.2%	83.9%	85.0%	85.0%
Net Patient Service Revenue	$12,390	$14,679	$16,499	$18,021	$19,079	$20,677	$21,896
Other Revenue	509	591	858	858	835	870	769
Total Revenue	$12,899	$15,270	$17,357	$18,879	$19,914	$21,547	$22,665
Less: Operating Expenses[f]	11,697	14,169	16,475	17,625	18,587	19,504	20,595
Net Revenue Before Depreciation and Interest[d]	$ 1,202	$ 1,101	$ 882	$ 1,254	$ 1,327	$ 2,043	$ 2,070

	1974	*1975*
Net Hospital Rental (estimated at 6⅜%)	$820	$820
Times Net Hospital Rental Covered	2.49X	2.52X

(a) From the financial statements of the Hospital.
(b) Derived from approved 1973-74 Hospital budget.
(c) Derived from Hospital projection.
(d) Excess revenue over expense before United Jewish Federation subsidy excluding depreciation and interest.
(e) No revenue has been projected which would require an exception from the Cost of Living Council.
(f) Operating expense is reflected net of applicable grant income.

22

MONTEFIORE HOSPITAL
STATEMENT OF REVENUE AND EXPENSE
YEARS ENDED JUNE 30, 1969 TO 1975

	Historical(a)					Projected(e)	
	1969	1970	1971	1972	1973(a)	1974(b)	1975(c)
Patient Service Revenue	$13,139,737	$15,573,219	$17,570,096	$19,245,132	$21,121,274	$22,583,000	$23,927,000
Contractual and Other Adjustments	749,642	894,079	1,071,403	1,223,817	2,041,796	1,906,000	2,031,000
Net Patient Service Revenue	$12,390,095	14,679,140	16,498,693	18,021,315	19,079,478	20,677,000	21,896,000
Operating Expense:(f)							
Wages and Salaries	6,928,622	9,315,986	11,000,985	11,710,581	12,236,966	12,736,500	13,369,700
Supplies and Expense	4,767,598	4,853,802	5,474,296	5,915,401	6,350,617	6,767,800	7,225,300
Depreciation	912,410	938,973	966,789	1,149,061	1,408,870	1,406,000	1,471,000
Interest	449,644	489,224	472,709	556,258	685,127	911,000(g)	747,000
Total Operating Expense	13,058,274	15,597,985	17,914,779	19,331,301	20,681,580	21,821,300	22,813,000
Loss from Hospital Operations	(668,179)	(918,845)	(1,416,086)	(1,309,986)	(1,602,102)	(1,144,300)	(917,000)
Other Revenue(f)	508,611	591,198	858,387	858,268	835,374	870,000	769,000
Loss from Operations	(159,568)	(327,647)	(557,699)	(451,718)	(766,728)	(274,300)	(148,000)
Add: Items Included in Above Expenses:							
Depreciation	912,410	938,973	966,789	1,149,061	1,408,870	1,406,000	1,471,000
Interest Expense	449,644	489,224	472,709	556,258	685,127	911,000(g)	747,000
Net Revenue Before Depreciation and Interest(d)	$ 1,202,486	$ 1,100,550	$ 881,799	$ 1,253,601	$ 1,327,269	$ 2,042,700	$ 2,070,000

(a) From financial statements of the Hospital.
(b) Derived from approved 1973-74 Hospital budget.
(c) Derived from Hospital projection.
(d) Excess revenue over expense before United Jewish Federation subsidy excluding depreciation and interest.
(e) No revenue has been projected which would require an exception from the Cost of Living Council.
(f) Operating expense is reflected net of applicable grant income.
(g) Includes Connecticut General Life Insurance Company prepayment premium of $135,000.

BOND AMORTIZATION SCHEDULE
$11,630,000 HOSPITAL GROSS REVENUE BONDS
SERIES C of 1973
ALLEGHENY COUNTY HOSPITAL DEVELOPMENT AUTHORITY
(The Montefiore Hospital Association of Western Pennsylvania, Sublessee)

Dated: October 1, 1973
Due: October 1

Interest Payable:
April 1 and October 1, commencing April 1, 1974

Year Ending October 1	Annual Hospital Payment	Plus Debt Service Reserve Fund Earnings[1]	Less Authority Expenses	Net Revenue Available	Interest	Principal Maturities October 1	Mandatory Sinking Fund	Total Debt Service	Cumulative Debt Service Reserve Fund ($807,000)[2]
1974	$ 760,857.00	$ 48,400	$ 4,652	$ 804,605.00	$ 649,605.00	$ 155,000		$ 804,605.00	($807,000)[3]
1975	763,494.50	48,400	4,652	807,242.50	642,242.50	165,000		807,242.50	
1976	760,657.00	48,400	4,652	804,405.00	634,405.00	170,000		804,405.00	
1977	762,497.00	48,400	4,652	806,245.00	626,245.00	180,000		806,245.00	
1978	763,767.00	48,400	4,652	807,515.00	617,515.00	190,000		807,515.00	
1979	764,457.00	48,400	4,652	808,205.00	608,205.00	200,000		808,205.00	
1980	764,557.00	48,400	4,652	808,305.00	598,305.00	210,000		808,305.00	
1981	764,057.00	48,400	4,652	807,805.00	587,805.00	220,000		807,805.00	
1982	762,947.00	48,400	4,652	806,695.00	576,695.00	230,000		806,695.00	
1983	761,217.00	48,400	4,652	804,965.00	564,965.00	240,000		804,965.00	
1984	763,857.00	48,400	4,652	807,605.00	552,605.00	255,000		807,605.00	
1985	760,724.50	48,400	4,652	804,472.50	539,472.50	265,000		804,472.50	
1986	761,944.50	48,400	4,652	805,692.50	525,692.50	280,000		805,692.50	
1987	762,384.50	48,400	4,652	806,132.50	511,132.50	295,000		806,132.50	
1988	761,897.00	48,400	4,652	805,645.00	495,645.00	310,000		805,645.00	
1989	765,622.00	48,400	4,652	809,370.00	479,370.00		$ 330,000	809,370.00	
1990	761,482.00	48,400	4,652	805,230.00	460,230.00		345,000	805,230.00	
1991	761,472.00	48,400	4,652	805,220.00	440,220.00		365,000	805,220.00	
1992	760,302.00	48,400	4,652	804,050.00	419,050.00		385,000	804,050.00	
1993	762,972.00	48,400	4,652	806,720.00	396,720.00		410,000	806,720.00	
1994	764,192.00	48,400	4,652	807,940.00	372,940.00		435,000	807,940.00	
1995	763,962.00	48,400	4,652	807,710.00	347,710.00		460,000	807,710.00	
1996	762,282.00	48,400	4,652	806,030.00	321,030.00		485,000	806,030.00	
1997	764,152.00	48,400	4,652	807,900.00	292,900.00		515,000	807,900.00	
1998	764,282.00	48,400	4,652	808,030.00	263,030.00		545,000	808,030.00	
1999	762,672.00	48,400	4,652	806,420.00	231,420.00		575,000	806,420.00	
2000	759,322.00	48,400	4,652	803,070.00	198,070.00		605,000	803,070.00	
2001	764,232.00	48,400	4,652	807,980.00	162,980.00		645,000	807,980.00	
2002	761,822.00	48,400	4,652	805,570.00	125,570.00		680,000	805,570.00	
2003	720,382.00	48,400	4,652	1,571,130.00	86,130.00	8,265,000	1,485,000	1,571,130.00	—
	$22,838,465.00	$1,452,000	$139,560	$24,957,905.00	$13,327,905.00	$11,630,000		$24,957,905.00	

[1] Estimated at 6%.

AVERAGE ANNUAL DEBT SERVICE (1974-2002)—$806,441

24

Room Rates

The following is a current schedule of daily room rate ranges for private and semi-private beds for Montefiore Hospital:

Private..................................$63.00 to $88.00
Semi-Private.............................$59.00 to $73.00

The following is a schedule of room rate ranges for hospitals in the Pittsburgh area of similar size and offering the same range of services as Montefiore Hospital:

	Private	*Semi-Private*
Allegheny General Hospital................	$76.00 to $104.00	$76.00 to $82.00
Mercy Hospital..........................	$72.00 to $100.00	$62.00 to $66.00
Presbyterian-University Hospital............	$69.50 to $ 93.50	$60.50 to $75.50
Shadyside Hospital.......................	$72.00 to $105.00	$59.00 to $72.00
West Penn Hospital......................	$75.00 to $ 91.00	$65.00 to $75.00

Third Party Payments

Payments on behalf of certain patients are made to Montefiore Hospital by commercial insurance carriers, Blue Cross of Western Pennsylvania, the Commonwealth of Pennsylvania's Medicaid Program and the Federal Government under the Medicare Program. A table showing the percentage of the hospital's total patient revenues by source of payment during Fiscal 1973 follows:

Blue Cross...33%
Medicare...43%
Medicaid...9%
    Total Cost Formula............................85%
Private...1%
Commercial...14%
    Total Revenues...............................100%

Most commercial insurance plans reimburse their insurers or make direct payments to hospitals at established rates. Patients carrying such insurance are responsible to the hospital for any deficiency between the insurance proceeds and the total charges imposed.

Within the Hospital's service area, there are now several employees whose commercial group hospitalization insurance provides various benefits to employees and their dependents while at the Hospital; these plans usually pay the prevailing area semi-private room rates plus ancillary service charges, subject to various limitations and deductibles, depending on the plan.

The Federal Medicare program reimburses the Hospital for its costs in accordance with the current Medicare principles of reimbursement. Reimbursable cost includes interest and depreciation expenses.

Blue Cross of Western Pennsylvania has approved the Hospital's current schedule of room and ancillary service rates, which are based on the cost of care and service provided. Commercial employers who provide Blue Cross group insurance plans to their employees sign separate contracts with Blue Cross for varying amounts and types of benefits depending on the plan adopted. Most of these group plans now provide for the payment of the Hospital's weighted average semi-private room costs, generally for periods up to 120 days. Most plans also provide for full payment of all covered ancillary service charges.

Medicare payments are subject to review and audit by the Social Security Administration through fiscal intermediaries. Payments to hospitals under the Medicare program began in 1966; the administration of this program, and its payment schedules, are still developing.

With respect to Blue Cross, Medicare and Medicaid, the Hospital's rental payments are not considered reimbursable costs. Instead, provision is made for depreciation of the hospital building and equipment.

THE LEASE

The Lease, dated October 1, 1973, has been entered into between the Hospital, as lessor, and the Authority, as lessee. The Lease provides that the Hospital shall lease certain real property which together with the facility to be constructed thereon by the Authority is hereinafter called the "Hospital Premises," to the Authority for a term of 30 years. As rental under the Lease, the Authority will deposit the entire proceeds of the Bond issue with the Trustee. After paying the costs of financing, $5,542,128.07 of the proceeds will be used to prepay the Hospital's indebtedness to Connecticut General Life Insurance Company (see caption entitled Connecticut General Life Insurance Company) and $4,500,000 of the proceeds will be used to repay a construction loan to the Union National Bank of Pittsburgh and to pay amounts due to contractors for work on the project. The Authority's obligation to pay rent is not a general obligation but is payable only out of the proceeds of the sale of bonds.

The Authority is granted the right to sublease the Hospital Premises to the Hospital, pursuant to the Sublease. During the term of the Lease, the Hospital will not make or permit to be made any transfer of the Hospital Premises, nor any interest therein, nor permit any liens or encumbrances (other than permitted encumbrances) to attach to the Hospital Premises.

THE SUBLEASE

The Sublease, dated October 1, 1973 has been entered into between the Authority, as lessor, and the Hospital, as lessee. The Authority has subleased the Hospital Premises to the Hospital for operation and use for a term of 30 years beginning October 1, 1973, and ending September 30, 2003.

The Hospital may cause the Sublease to be cancelled and terminated at any time during its term by paying to the Authority amounts sufficient to pay principal, interest, premium, if any, and costs of redemption required in order to pay or redeem all Bonds issued under the Indenture or any subsequent indenture under which refunding bonds are issued, and to pay any other sums payable thereunder. Such termination of the Sublease shall not take effect until the Trustee shall execute and deliver the necessary instruments to the Authority.

Hospital Rates and Charges:

The Hospital covenants that it will fix, charge and collect such rates, fees and charges for use of the entire Hospital Premises which, together with other available funds, will be sufficient in the lease year ending September 31, 1974 and in each lease year thereafter to provide the following: (a) annual Net Revenues (as defined in the Sublease) equal to at least 120% of average annual debt service requirements on all outstanding Bonds, calculated as of October 1 of each year over the remaining life of each series of Bonds on the principal amount of bonds of each series then outstanding; (such calculations of average annual debt service requirements to be computed for each series separately and then combined to determine the annual requirement) plus mandatory payments to be made to the Debt Service Reserve Fund; (b) payment of the annual administrative expenses of the Authority, not to exceed $4,652 and (c) payment of the cost of operating, maintaining and repairing the Hospital Premises. If, in any lease year, revenues shall be less than provided above, the Hospital Covenants that, within 60 days from the end of such Lease Year it will take all action necessary to cause its revenues to equal the amount provided above, or if proper action is not so taken, it immediately shall request a firm of Hospital Consultants (the "Hospital Consultants") which firm shall not be unsatisfactory to the Authority and the Trustee, to make a report and recommendations with respect to such rates, fees and charges, and upon the receipt of such report and recommendations, the Hospital shall, to the extent permitted by law, accept and implement such recommendation.

Application of Revenues:

To the extent required for the payment of rentals, the Hospital shall apply and pay to the Authority or its assignee all Gross Receipts of the Hospital (including the proceeds of its rates, fees and charges, and any moneys paid over to the Hospital from any other sources, and excluding only grants, gifts, bequests and other donations specifically restricted to other purposes by the donor and the first Two Thousand Dollars ($2,000) of the gross revenues derived each month from the ownership or operation of the Hospital Pharmacy).

Rentals and Other Payments:

The Hospital shall pay to the Authority, or its assignee, as rental the following amounts on the following dates, subject to credits provided in the Sublease:

(a) commencing on the 15th day of first month immediately following the issuance of the bonds, and on the 15th day of each month thereafter, to and including March 15, 1974, equal amounts, which, together with other moneys in the Debt Service Fund will equal of the interest due on the Bonds on April 1, 1974;

(b) commencing April 15, 1974, and on the 15th day of each month thereafter, to and including September 15, 2003, an amount equal to 1/6 of the interest due on the Bonds on the next interest payment date;

(c) commencing on the 15th day of each month, after notification by the Trustee that the amount in the Debt Service Reserve Fund is less than the average annual Debt Service requirements on the Bonds, and continuing for a period of not more than eighteen months, such amount as may be necessary to bring the total in the Debt Service Reserve Fund up that amount;

(d) commencing on the 15th day of the month following the issuance of the bonds and on the 15th day of each month thereafter, to and including September 15, 1974 equal amounts which shall be sufficient to pay principal amounts of bonds maturing by their terms on October 1, 1974, and on the 15th day of each month thereafter, to and including September 15, 1988, and on October 15, 2002 and on the fifteenth day of each month thereafter to and including September 15, 2003, an amount equal to 1/12 of the principal amount of Bonds then outstanding and maturing by their terms on the next succeeding October 1;

(e) commencing October 15, 1988, and on the 15th day of each month thereafter to and including September 15, 2002, 1/12 of the amounts hereinafter set forth so that payments equal the following amounts by September 15 of the following years:

Amount	Year
$330,000	1989
345,000	1990
365,000	1991
385,000	1992
410,000	1993
435,000	1994
460,000	1995
485,000	1996
515,000	1997
545,000	1998
575,000	1999
605,000	2000
645,000	2001
680,000	2002

(f) commencing on the date, 15th day of the first month immediately following the issuance of the Bonds, and on the 15th day of each month thereafter during the term of the Sublease, an amount equal to 1/12 of the current administration expenses of the Authority allocable to the Project, presently $4,652 annually.

Gross Receipts Pledge:

To the extent required for the payment of rentals, the Hospital shall apply and pay to the Authority or its assignee all Gross Receipts derived from the Hospital Premises (including the proceeds of its rates, fees and charges, and any moneys paid over to the Hospital from any other sources, excluding only grants, gifts, bequests and other donations specifically restricted to other purposes by the donor and the first Two Thousand Dollars ($2,000) of the gross revenues derived each month from the ownership or operation of the Hospital's Pharmacy). Rentals payable under the Sublease are payable without suspension or abatement of any kind notwithstanding that all of the Hospital Premises have been wholly or partially damaged or destroyed. The Hospital is also required to pay, out of its receipts and revenues, and as additional rentals, all taxes which may be levied or assessed by federal, state or municipal bodies against the Authority or the Hospital relating to the Hospital Premises or the operations conducted thereon during the term of the Sublease.

Insurance:

The Hospital covenants to provide and maintain certain insurance coverages, as follows:

(a) Insurance against loss or damage to the Hospital Premises covering such risks as are ordinarily insured against by similar hospitals, including fire and uniform standard extended coverage in the standard

27

form at the time in use in Pennsylvania and containing agreed amount clauses with respect to the coverage provided.

(b) Rents insurance covering the payment of rent due under the Sublease during such period when, after being damaged or destroyed by specific casualties, the Hospital Premises shall be under reconstruction, rebuilding or repair, not exceeding 12 months.

(c) Business interruption insurance covering the expense of operating the Hospital Premises during such period when, after being damaged or destroyed by specified casualties, the Hospital Premises shall be under reconstruction, rebuilding or repair, not exceeding 12 months.

(d) Public liability insurance, landlord's liability insurance and comprehensive automobile liability insurance protecting the Authority and the Hospital against liability for injuries to persons or property in the minimum amount of $300,000 to any one person for personal injury, $1,000,000 for personal injury for each occurrence and in the aggregate, and $50,000 liability for property damage for each occurrence and in an aggregate of not less than $100,000.

(e) Malpractice insurance insuring the Authority and the Hospital against liability for death, injury, loss or damage occurring in the examination, diagnosis, treatment or care of any patient of the Hospital in the minimum amount of $300,000 to any one person and to the extent of at least $1,000,000 in the aggregate.

(f) Fidelity bonds on all officers and employees of the Hospital who have access to any funds of the Hospital, in amounts customarily carried by like organizations.

(g) Workmen's compensation and employer's liability insurance meeting the Hospital's statutory obligations. If the Hospital becomes an approved self-insured, employer's liability coverage shall be purchased with limits of at least $100,000.

(h) Boiler and machinery coverages (direct damage and use and occupancy) on a replacement cost basis where deemed advisable by the Insurance Consultants, or where required by ordinance or law.

(i) Excess liability coverage, either straight excess or umbrella excess, covering excess of sections (d), (e) and (g) above, to be maintained in force so that the total coverage available under the aforementioned sections, including this section, is not less than $5,000,000 for any one occurrence.

The Hospital shall designate each year during the term of the Sublease, Insurance Consultants who shall not be unsatisfactory to the Trustee or the Authority and who may be a broker or agent who has been regularly retained by the Hospital or the Authority, to perform duties as prescribed by the Sublease. All insurance policies and bonds obtained by the Hospital shall comply with legal requirements and the recommendations of the Insurance Consultants. The Hospital covenants to furnish the Authority and the Trustee annually a certificate from the Insurance Consultants, setting forth amounts and types of insurance then in force with respect to the Hospital Premises, stating whether in the opinion of such Insurance Consultants such insurance then in force is adequate, and stating amounts and types of insurance which should be maintained during the ensuing Lease Year. The Hospital covenants to maintain such amounts and types of insurance.

Extraordinary Repairs and Capital Additions:

The Hospital may request the Authority to provide moneys for payments of all or part of the costs of extraordinary repairs or capital additions, as provided in the Sublease. Upon receipt of such request, the Authority may but shall have no obligation to requisition amounts so requested, to the extent available, from a Fund or Funds created under the Indenture and/or may but shall have no obligation to provide all or part of the amounts requested by issuance and sale of Additional Bonds under the Indenture. If the Authority does not provide the funds necessary for such purposes, the Hospital may finance the cost of such construction through other sources provided that it delivers to the Authority a Hospital Consultants' Certificate of the tenor required by the Indenture in connection with the issuance of additional bonds, as applied however to such other sources rather than to additional bonds, and further provided that the Hospital's obligations with respect to such other financing shall at all times be subordinate to the obligations of the Hospital under the Sublease.

28

Hospital to Maintain Its Tax-Exempt Status:

The Hospital shall preserve and maintain its Articles of Incorporation or Charter, By-laws and its corporate existence, organization, and operation so that it will be, to the extent permitted by law at any given time, free from Federal, state and local income, property, franchise and other taxes, and preserve its authority to do business in the Commonwealth. The Hospital covenants that it shall not (without the written consent of the Authority) initiate any proceedings or take any action whatever to dissolve, liquidate or terminate its existence as a corporation during the term of the Sublease except to consolidate or merge as permitted therein.

Without the written consent of the Authority, the Hospital shall not consolidate with or merge into any other corporation, or transfer or permit the transfer of the Sublease or the Hospital Premises unless the following conditions shall be met: (a) The successor formed by such merger, consolidation or transfer shall be a hospital which is a non-profit corporation organized under the laws of the United States or any state, district or territory, and exempt from Federal Income Taxation under Section 501 (a) of the Internal Revenue Code of 1954 as amended; (b) such successor or transferee corporation shall expressly assume in writing the full and faithful performance of the Hospital's duties, obligations and covenants under the Sublease; and (c) immediately after such consolidation, merger or transfer, the Hospital, or such successor corporation, shall not be in default in the performance or observance of any duties, obligations or covenants of the Hospital under the Sublease.

Other Covenants:

The Hospital shall maintain the Hospital Premises in good repair and operating condition, operate the same continuously in an economical and efficient manner and make all ordinary repairs, renewals, replacements and improvements.

The Hospital shall furnish the Authority and the Trustee annually, on October 1, beginning on October 1, 1974, a certificate stating the Hospital Premises are in good repair and operating condition, or indicating which portions of the Hospital Premises are not in good repair and operating condition and stating in what respects repairs and improvements are needed, and the approximate expenditures and amount of time needed to place the Hospital Premises in good repair and operating condition. In addition the Hospital shall furnish the Trustee and the Authority the annual report of the Department of Welfare and the bi-annual report of the Joint Commission On Accreditation Of Hospitals which relate to the repair and operating condition of the Hospital.

The Hospital shall keep accurate records and books of account with respect to its revenues and expenditures and annually have made a complete audit of such records by a Certified Public Accountant, with copies to be furnished to the Authority, the Trustee and the Original Underwriters.

The Hospital covenants not to create any charges upon the revenues derived from the Hospital Premises prior to or on a parity with its obligations created under the Sublease.

The Hospital covenants not to construct, permit or join in construction or operation of another hospital except to the extent that the Hospital Consultants shall certify to the Authority and the Trustee and that such construction or operation will not adversely affect the proper and economical operation of the Leased Premises.

THE TRUST INDENTURE

The Bonds have been issued under and are subject to the provisions of the Trust Indenture, dated October 1, 1973, by and between the Authority and Mellon Bank, N.A., Pittsburgh, Pennsylvania, as Trustee, to which reference is made for complete details of the terms of the Bonds. The following summarizes certain provisions of the Trust Indenture but is not to be regarded as a full statement thereof.

Pledge and Assignment:

Under the Trust Indenture, all receipts and revenues (as defined therein) derived by the Authority from the subleasing of the Hospital Premises have been pledged to the Trustee. The rights of the Authority under the Sublease have been assigned to the Trustee to secure the payment of the Bonds and the performance and observance of the covenants in the Trust Indenture.

The Authority may release from the Lease and Sublease any real or personal property or materials used in connection with the Hospital premises having a value of less than $100,000 if the Hospital certifies to the Authority that such release will not impair the operation of the Hospital Premises and the cash proceeds, if any, derived from the sale are applied to the replacement of properties so sold or deposited into the Bond Redemption and Improvement Fund. The Trust Indenture also provides for the release of other property upon certification by the Hospital and in the case of property sold for a price in excess of $100,000, certification by Hospital Consultants that the release will not impair the operation of the Hospital Premises.

Redemption:

The Bonds are subject to redemption prior to maturity on thirty days' notice as follows:

(a) Bonds maturing after October 1, 1983, at the option of the Authority, in whole, or in part in the inverse order of maturity at any time on and after October 1, 1983, at redemption prices equal to the following percentages of the principal amount redeemed, plus accrued interest to the date fixed for redemption:

Redemption Period (Both Dates Inclusive)	Redemption Price
October 1, 1983 to September 30, 1986	101%
October 1, 1986 to September 30, 1989	100½%
October 1, 1989 and thereafter	100%

(b) Bonds maturing after October 1, 1978 in part from time-to-time, in inverse order of maturity, from moneys in the Bond Redemption and Improvement Fund provided for in the Indenture, on October 1, 1978 and on any interest payment date thereafter, at redemption prices equal to the following percentages of the principal amount redeemed, plus accrued interest to the date fixed for redemption:

Redemption Period (Both Dates Inclusive)	Redemption Price
October 1, 1978 to September 30, 1984	101%
October 1, 1984 to September 30, 1989	100½%
October 1, 1989 and thereafter	100%

(c) bonds maturing on October 1, 2003 in part, on October 1 of each year from 1989 to 2002 inclusive from moneys in the 1973 Series C Bond Sinking Fund upon payment of 100% of the principal amount thereof, plus accrued interest to the redemption date.

If less than the entire unmatured portion of Bonds of a particular maturity is called for redemption at any time or from time to time, the selection of the Bonds of that maturity shall be made by lot by the Trustee.

Disposition of Proceeds: Debt Service Reserve Fund and Construction Fund:

From the proceeds of the sale of the Bonds, an amount equal to accrued interest on the Bonds will be deposited to the Debt Service Fund and $807,000 will be deposited in the Debt Service Reserve Fund. $5,542,128.07 will be paid to Connecticut General Life Insurance Company in payment of the Hospital's indebtedness to it and $4,100,000 will be used to pay the Hospital's indebtedness to the Union National Bank of Pittsburgh. The balance of the proceeds from the sale of Bonds, after paying the cost of financing, shall be deposited in the Construction Fund maintained with the Trustee under the Indenture and will be used solely to pay the cost of completing the construction of the Hospital Premises. Any such moneys which shall not be required for that purpose will be transferred to the Bond Redemption and Improvement Fund for application in accordance with the provisions summarized below. Payments shall be made by the Trustee from the Construction Fund only upon receipt of a requisition signed in the manner required by the Indenture.

Revenue Fund:

All rentals payable by the Hospital under the Sublease and any and all other moneys received by the Trustee in connection with the Hospital Premises, as provided in the Indenture, shall be deposited by the Trustee in the Revenue Fund. Moneys from time to time in the Revenue Fund shall be held by the Trustee, in trust, and shall be secured and applied as provided in the Indenture. Pending such application, the moneys will be subject to a lien and charge in favor of the bondholders.

Authority Administrative Expense:

Commencing March 20, 1974 and semi-annually thereafter, the Trustee shall transfer to the Authority the amount provided in the Sublease with respect to administrative expenses of the Authority, including the reasonable costs and expenses of the Trustee.

Debt Service Fund:

The Trustee shall transfer from the Revenue Fund and deposit in the Debt Service Fund:

(a) On or before March 20, 1974 and on or before September 20, 1974 and on each March 20 and September 20 thereafter, an amount equal to the interest becoming due on the Bonds on the next interest payment date:

(b) On or before March 20, 1974 and September 20, 1974 and on the 20th day of each March and September thereafter to and including September 20, 1988 and on March 20, 2003 and September 20, 2003 an amount equal to one-half the principal amount of Bonds then outstanding maturing on the next succeeding October 1:

(c) Such amounts on such dates as may be required by any supplemental indenture for the payment of principal of and interest on additional bonds.

No transfer is required to be made to the Debt Service Fund to the extent that such transfer would cause the amount in said fund to exceed the amounts required to be paid to the bondholders. Moneys held in the Debt Service Fund are pledged irrevocably for the payment of principal and interest on the Bonds. The Trustee shall, without further direction from the Authority, pay out the Debt Service Fund the principal and interest on the Bonds as the same shall become due and payable.

1973 Series C Bond Sinking Fund:

After having made the required transfers from the Revenue Fund to the Debt Service Fund and to the Authority for its Administrative Expenses, the Trustee will transfer to the 1973 Series C Bond Sinking Fund the following sums on or before March 20 and September 20 on each of the following years:

March 20	*September 20*	*Year*
$165,000	$165,000	1989
172,500	172,500	1990
182,500	182,500	1991
192,500	192,500	1992
205,000	205,000	1993
217,500	217,500	1994
230,000	230,000	1995
242,500	242,500	1996
257,500	257,500	1997
272,500	272,500	1998
287,500	287,500	1999
302,500	302,500	2000
322,500	322,500	2001
340,000	340,000	2002

Moneys on deposit to the credit of the 1973 Series C Bond Sinking Fund may be applied to the purchase of Bonds at a price not in excess of 100% plus accrued interest. If the amount in the 1973 Series C Bond Sinking Fund on August 10 of any year (including the deposit to be made on September 20 of such year) shall be sufficient to redeem on the next succeeding October 1 at least $25,000, principal amount, of the Bonds, the Trustee shall select and call for redemption on such October 1 such principal amount of Bonds as shall be sufficient to exhaust as nearly as practicable the moneys in the 1973 Series C Bond Sinking Fund. If on August 10 of any year the moneys in the 1973 Series C Bond Sinking Fund shall be sufficient to effect the redemption of all Bonds outstanding on the next succeeding October 1 or, at such time as there shall not be any Bonds outstanding, any moneys in the 1973 Series C Bond Sinking Fund in excess of the amount required for such redemption, or all such moneys as the case may be, shall be transferred to the Bond Redemption and Improvement Fund.

Debt Service Reserve Fund:

Out of the proceeds of the issue, $807,000 will be deposited to the Debt Service Reserve Fund. Subject to making the deposits and transfers required to be made to the Authority for its Administrative Expenses, to the Debt Service Fund and the 1973 Series C Bond Sinking Fund, the Trustee shall on March 20 and September 20 of each year in which the amount in the Debt Service Reserve Fund is less than an amount equal to the average annual debt service requirements on the Bonds beginning with the date on which the transfers are required to be made to the Debt Service Fund and continuing for a period not exceeding 18 months, transfer to the Debt Service Reserve Fund from the Revenue Fund such amounts as may be necessary to maintain in said fund an amount equal to the average annual debt service requirements on the Bonds.

Bond Redemption and Improvement Fund:

There will be deposited in the Bond Redemption and Improvement Fund any moneys which may be available for deposit therein as provided in the Indenture.

If a deficiency shall exist in the Debt Service Fund or the Debt Service Reserve Fund, and there shall be insufficient moneys in the Revenue Fund to eliminate the same, the Trustee, without further direction from the Authority, will transfer a sufficient amount or amounts, in the order of priority above set forth, as moneys shall be available, from the Bond Redemption and Improvement Fund to eliminate such deficiency or deficiencies.

Moneys in the Bond Redemption and Improvement Fund will be used or applied by the Authority, from time to time (provided there are no deficiencies in any of the Funds referred to in the preceding paragraph) for any of the following purposes, in accordance with the provisions of the Indenture:

(a) For or toward costs of extraordinary repairs, renewals, replacements, alterations or improvements; or

(b) For or toward the cost of making Capital Additions; or

(c) For redemption, retirement, or purchase of Bonds, in accordance with the terms of the Indenture; or

(d) To pay, as and when the same shall become due and payable, any expenses, debts, liabilities and obligations of the Authority in connection with the Indenture for payment of which provision otherwise shall not have been made.

Investment of Funds:

Moneys held in the Construction Fund, Revenue Fund, Debt Service Fund, Debt Service Reserve Fund and Bond Redemption and Improvement Fund may be retained uninvested as trust funds and insured or secured as required by law, or, upon written request of the Authority, may be wholly or partially deposited and redeposited in interest-bearing deposit accounts in the banking department of the Trustee, or shall be invested and reinvested by the Trustee in any bonds or obligations, which, as to principal and interest, constitute direct obligations of the United States of America, subject to the limitations as provided in the Indenture.

The interest and income received from time to time upon such deposits and investments in such Funds shall be credited to said Funds and transferred on March 20 and September 20, as the case may be, to the Revenue Fund except that interest and profit earned in the Construction Fund shall remain in the Fund and interest and profit earned in the Debt Service Reserve Fund shall remain in that Fund to the extent necessary to maintain the reserve requirement and otherwise shall be transferred to Revenue Fund.

Additional Bonds:

The Authority may issue Additional Bonds for the purpose of financing the Cost of Capital Additions or refunding outstanding bonds. No such Additional Bonds for the purpose of financing the Cost of Capital Additions shall be authenticated and delivered by the Trustee unless in each case there shall be delivered to the Trustee inter alia, a certificate of the Hospital Consultants to the effect that the issuance of Additional Bonds is necessary, desirable or advisable for the proper maintenance and/or operation of the Hospital Premises; that proceeds from the Additional Bonds together with other available moneys will be sufficient to pay the necessary costs; and that except in the case of Additional Bonds issued to pay the costs of completion of capital additions, as more fully described in the Indenture) Net Revenues of the Hospital to be received annually beginning with the second Lease year immediately following completion of the Capital Additions and during each of the next succeeding four lease years as estimated by the Hospital Consultants, will be at least equal, in each of such years, to the annual Authority administrative expense and to 120% of the average annual debt service requirements on all outstanding Bonds and the Additional Bonds to be issued and that the supplemental sublease meets the requirements of the Indenture.

Covenants of the Authority:

The Authority covenants, among other things, to pay promptly or cause to be paid, from the rentals derived from the Hospital Premises, the Bonds and interest thereon, to cause the Hospital to provide for the maintenance of the Hospital Premises in good repair and operating condition, and to require the Hospital to observe faithfully all its covenants and agreements under the Sublease. The Authority will pay or cause to be paid all taxes and assessments levied against the Authority in connection with the Hospital Premises.

Except for Permitted Liens and Title Defects and defined in the Indenture, the Authority will not create nor suffer to be created any lien or charge upon the Hospital Premises, other than the Sublease, or upon the rentals and other receipts and revenues (with the exception of the first two thousand ($2,000) derived monthly from the ownership or operation of the Hospital's Pharmacy) derived from the Hospital Premises, except the lien and charge of the Indenture and of the Bonds and liens and charges subordinate thereto imposed in connection with financing by the Hospital of extraordinary repairs and capital additions financed from sources other than the Authority.

The Authority covenants and certifies that the proceeds of the Bonds will not be used in a manner which would cause the obligations to be arbitrage bonds within the meaning of Section 103(d) of the Internal Revenue Code of 1954 as amended.

Defaults and Remedies:

The Act, which governs the Authority, provides remedies to the bondholders in the event of default or failure on the part of the Authority to fulfill its covenants.

Under the Indenture, in the event of any such default as therein defined, the Trustee may enforce, and upon the written request of the holders of 25% in principal amount of the Bonds then outstanding, accompanied by indemnity as provided in the Indenture, shall enforce for the equal benefit of all bondholders all rights provided under the Indenture and said Act, including the rights of entry, of bringing suit upon the Bonds, of protecting and enforcing by mandamus or other suit, action or proceeding at law or in equity all rights of bondholders and of having a receiver appointed.

Neither the Trustee nor any receiver, however, may sell, assign, mortgage or otherwise dispose of any assets of the Authority. For a more complete statement of rights and remedies of the bondholders and of the limitations thereon reference is made to the Indenture.

Modifications:

The Authority and the Trustee may enter into supplemental indentures in connection with the issuance of Additional Bonds (see "Additional Bonds"), to cure ambiguities, formal defects or omissions in the Indenture, or to grant additional rights, powers, and security for the benefit of Bondholders. All other supplemental indentures require the consent and approval of the holders of not less than 66⅔% in principal amount of all Bonds then outstanding, but no such supplemental indenture shall, without the consent of holders of all Bonds then outstanding (1) alter any date fixed for the payment of principal of or interest on the Bonds or otherwise modify the terms of payment of principal; (2) reduce the amount of or extend the time for making sinking fund payments; (3) alter the amount of principal of or the rate of interest or premium if any on the Bonds; (4) affect the rights of holders of less than all the Bonds of any series then outstanding; (5) permit the creation of any lien prior to or, except for additional Bonds issued under the provisions of the Indenture, on a parity with the lien of the Indenture or, (6) reduce the percentage of Bondholders required for modification as aforesaid.

SERIES C-C, 1973 BONDS

Concurrently with the authorization of the Bonds, the Authority has authorized the issuance of $5,000, principal amount, of its Series C-C, 1973 Bonds (hereinafter the "Series C-C Bonds") in the denomination of $100 each. The Series C-C Bonds were offered for sale to the general public but none were purchased.

TAX EXEMPTION

The interest on the Bonds is not subject to present Federal income taxes under existing statutes and decisions.

Under the statutes of Pennsylvania, which include the Municipality Authorities Act, the Act of August 31, 1971 (Act No. 93) and the Act of August 31, 1971 (Act No. 94), the Bonds, their transfer and the income therefrom (including any profits made on the sale thereof) shall at all times be free from taxation for State and local purposes within the Commonwealth of Pennsylvania, but this exemption does not extend to gift, succession or inheritance taxes or any other taxes not levied or assessed directly on the Bonds or the income therefrom.

The Hospital and the Authority covenant in the Sublease and the Indenture, respectively, that they shall not take any action or suffer or permit any action to be taken or condition to exist which causes or may cause the interest payable on the Bonds to be subject to Federal income taxes.

Legal matters incident to the authorization, issuance and sale of the Bonds are subject to the approval of Messrs. Berkman Ruslander Pohl Lieber & Engel and Messrs. Beck, McGinnis & Jarvis, Pittsburgh, Pennsylvania, whose approving opinion will be printed on the Bonds.

The Hospital has furnished all information in this Official Statement relating to the Hospital and the Project. The Balance Sheet of the Hospital, as of June 30, 1973 and 1972 and the statements of Revenue and Expenses and Changes in Fund Balances and Changes in Financial Position for the years ended June 30, 1973 and 1972 have been examined by Touche Ross & Co., Certified Public Accountants, auditors for the Hospital, as set forth in Exhibit C. Such financial statements have been included in reliance upon the opinion of such firm and upon the authority of such firm as experts in auditing and accounting.

The foregoing summaries or descriptions of provisions in the Lease, the Sublease and the Indenture, and the references to other materials not purporting to be quoted in full, are only brief outlines of certain provisions thereof and do not constitute complete statements of such documents or provisions and reference is hereby made to the complete documents relating to such matters for further information, copies of which will be furnished on request by the Hospital.

The Authority and the Hospital have authorized the distribution of this Official Statement.

Very truly yours,

ALLEGHENY COUNTY HOSPITAL DEVELOPMENT AUTHORITY

By: /s/John M. Arthur
Chairman

THE MONTEFIORE HOSPITAL ASSOCIATION OF
WESTERN PENNSYLVANIA

By: /s/Milton Porter
President

34

EXHIBITS:

A. MEDICAL STAFF

B. SUMMARY OF SERVICES

C. ACCOUNTANTS' REPORT AND FINANCIAL STATEMENTS

ACTIVE MEDICAL STAFF

Name	*Specialty*	*Medical School*
Adibi, Siamak A.	Gastroenterology	Thomas Jefferson University
Adler, Lawrence N.	Cardiology	University of Pittsburgh
Adler, Sheldon	Nephrology	State University of New York (Downstate)
Ahmed, Quzi	Ophthalmology	Dacca Medical College (E. Pakistan)
Alpern, A. Nathan	Internal Medicine	University of Pittsburgh
Amshel, Albert L.	Proctology	Thomas Jefferson University
Antis, Max A.	Obstetrics-Gynecology	Thomas Jefferson University
Arnhcim, Falk K.	Urologic Surgery	University of Pittsburgh
Balk, Phillip	Rheumatology	University of Pittsburgh
Bass, Lee W.	Pediatrics	Johns Hopkins University
Berkman, Ronald	Ophthalmology	University of Pittsburgh
Ismail-Beigi, Farhad	Gastroenterology	Vanderbilt University
Bilder, Milton	Internal Medicine	University of Pittsburgh
Binakonsky, Harry S.	Internal Medicine	University of Pittsburgh
Boniface, Dolores	Ophthalmology	University of Bologna (Italy)
Boas, Harry	Internal Medicine	University of Pittsburgh
Boehnke, Manfred	Radiology	Kiel Medical College (Germany)
Brasuk, John L.	Orthopedic Surgery	University of Pittsburgh
Bruns, Frank J.	Nephrology	State University of New York (Upstate)
Bress, Alan N.	Oncology	University of Pittsburgh
Bress, James C.	Oncology	University of Pittsburgh
Brostoff, Philip	Cardiology	University of Pennsylvania
Burks, Charles J.	General Medicine	University of Pittsburgh
Bushkoff, Stanley H.	Orthopedic Surgery	Hahnemann Medical College
Busis, Sidney N.	Otorhinolaryngology	University of Pittsburgh
Caplan, Paul S.	Rheumatology	University of Pittsburgh
Cavallo, Tito	Pathology	University of San Paulo (Brazil)
Chamovitz, Robert	Gastroenterology	University of Maryland
Chetlin, Stuart H.	General Surgery	University of Pittsburgh
Chetlin, Milton A.	General Surgery	Columbia University
Cohen, Manfred L.	Thoracic Surgery	Ohio State University
Cohen, Norman	Internal Medicine	University of Pittsburgh
Cohen, Peter Z.	Orthopedic Surgery	University of Pittsburgh
Cruz, Pedro A.	Pathology	University of Cartegena (Colombia)
Curtiss, Edward	Cardiology	New York University
Eisen, Howard B.	Radiology	University of Pittsburgh
Elias, Stanton B.	Ophthalmology	University of Pittsburgh
Ersoz, Namik	Anesthesiology	University of Ankara (Turkey)
Einhorn, Jerzy	Endocrinology	Poznan Medical Academy (Poland)
Fine, Joseph	Anesthesiology	University of LaPlata (Argentina)
Finegold, Aaron, N.	Urologic Surgery	University of Maryland
Finegold, Joseph	General Surgery	University of Maryland
Finegold, Richard A.	Urologic Surgery	University of Maryland
Finegold, Wilfred J.	Obstetrics-Gynecology	University of London
Finestone, Stephen C.	Anesthesiology	New York University
Flom, David M.	General Medicine	University of Pittsburgh
Fogel, Michael F.	Gastroenterology	George Washington University
Friedlander, Myron	Pulmonary Disease	University of Pittsburgh
Friedman, H. W.	Radiology	University of Michigan
Gerber, Michael L.	Thoracic Surgery	University of Pittsburgh

Name	*Specialty*	*Medical School*
Ghanooni, Sion	Anesthesiology	Pahlavi Medical School (Iran)
Goldberg, Solomon	Ophthalmology	University of Pittsburgh
Goldblum, Abraham D.	Ophthalmology	University of Pittsburgh
Goldblum, Raymond W.	Dermatology	University of Pittsburgh
Golding, Irvin M.	Psychiatry	University of Pittsburgh
Goldman, Irving S.	Ophthalmology	University of Pittsburgh
Goldstein, Morton L.	Gastroenterology	University of Pittsburgh
Granowitz, Samuel P.	Orthopedic Surgery	University of Pittsburgh
Green, Mayer A.	Allergy	University of Pittsburgh
Grossman, Charles C.	Neurology	University of Bratislava (Czech)
Harris, Barry C.	Cardiology	Duke University
Harrison, Anthony M.	General Surgery	Thomas Jefferson University
Herman, Julius	General Medicine	University of Pittsburgh
Hershenson, Lee M.	Internal Medicine	University of Pittsburgh
Hirsch, Stanley A.	General Surgery	University of Pittsburgh
Hubbard, Jeffrey	Pathology	Albany Medical College
Hydovitz, Jerrold D.	Endocrinology	University of Pittsburgh
Isaacs, Gilbert H.	Nuclear Medicine	University of Maryland
Isaacson, Stanford I.	Internal Medicine	University of Pittsburgh
Itskowitz, Alan L.	Internal Medicine	Hahnemann Medical College
Jannetta, Peter J.	Neurosurgery	University of Pennsylvania
Kalla, Richard L.	Internal Medicine	University of Pittsburgh
Kaufer, Gerald I.	General Surgery	University of Pittsburgh
Kaufman, Sidney S.	General Surgery	University of Pittsburgh
Kessler, Laibe A.	Neurosurgery	University of Pittsburgh
Kennerdell, John S.	Ophthalmology	Temple University
Krause, Seymoure	Cardiology	University of Pittsburgh
Krieger, Abbott J.	Neurosurgery	New York University
Krochmal, David H.	General Medicine	Hahnemann Medical College
Kyllonen, A. S.	Thoracic Surgery	Boston University
Kyriacopoulos, John D.	Cardiology	The National and Capodistria University (Greece)
Landerman, Nathaniel S.	Allergy	Temple University
Landy, Jules C.	General Medicine	St. Louis University
Lang, Howard N.	Internal Medicine	University of Pittsburgh
Lebovitz, Charles N.	General Surgery	University of Pittsburgh
Leff, Bernard	Otorhinolaryngology	Albert Einstein Medical School
Levick, Marvin H.	General Medicine	University of Pittsburgh
Levine, Macy I.	Allergy	University of Pittsburgh
Levinson, Julian P.	Cardiology	George Washington University
Levy, Leslie	Internal Medicine	University of Chicago
Levy, Marshall	Rheumatology	University of Pittsburgh
Levy, Reinhardt	General Medicine	University of Chicago
Lippe, Richard D.	Endocrinology	Thomas Jefferson University
Lisowitz, Gerald M.	Psychiatry	University of Pittsburgh
Lubic, Lowell G.	Neurology	University of Pittsburgh
Madoff, Henry	Thoracic Surgery	New York University
Mallit, Melvin	General Medicine	University of Pittsburgh
Maroon, Joseph C.	Neurosurgery	Indiana University
Mendelow, Harvey	Pathology	State University of New York
Meyers, Louis L.	Obstetrics-Gynecology	University of Pittsburgh
Miller, Felix H.	Obstetrics-Gynecology	University of Pittsburgh
Miller, Samuel G.	Otorhinolaryngology	University of Pittsburgh

Name	Specialty	Medical School
Miller, William B.	General Medicine	University of Pittsburgh
Minde, Norman	General Medicine	University of Buffalo
Morris, Leslie E.	Peripheral Vascular	Trinity Medical College (Ireland)
Nagabhushanam, Nunna	Internal Medicine	Kasturba Medical School (India)
Nallathambi, S. A.	Internal Medicine	Christian Medical College (India)
Nankin, Howard R.	Endocrinology	State University of New York (Upstate)
Neft, Burton H.	Plastic Surgery	University of Pittsburgh
Neiman, Lee M.	Internal Medicine	University of Chicago
Norden, Carl W.	Infectious Disease	Harvard University
Newberg, Jay A.	Ophthalmology	University of Pittsburgh
Palkovitz, Joseph	General Medicine	University of Pittsburgh
Palkovitz, Harry P.	Neurology	University of Pittsburgh
Penn, Samuel E.	Otorhinolaryngology	University of Chicago
Pincus, Jack H.	General Medicine	University of Pittsburgh
Pober, H. A.	General Medicine	Eclectic Medical College (Cincinnati)
Pochapin, Sherman W.	Psychiatry	University of Pittsburgh
Pollock, Burton H.	Rheumatology	University of Pennsylvania
Ravitch, Mark M.	General & Thoracic Surgery	Johns Hopkins University
Reel, Charles M.	Ophthalmology	University of Pittsburgh
Reese, Edward	General Surgery	St. Louis University
Richardson, Roosevelt	General Medicine	University of Pittsburgh
Rosenbach, Loren M.	Hematology	University of Pittsburgh
Rosenbloom, Stanley E.	Internal Medicine	University of Pittsburgh
Rosenthal, Phillip J.	Internal Medicine	University of Pittsburgh
Ruben, Frederick L.	Infectious Disease	Duke University
Rubenstein, Leonard S.	General Medicine	University of Pittsburgh
Ruiz, Cesar A.	Internal Medicine	San Marcos University (Peru)
Sachs, Murray	Pulmonary Disease	University of Pittsburgh
Sagone, Anita Mae	Pathology	University of Pittsburgh
Sampson, Arnold	General Surgery	University of Pittsburgh
Schachter, Allan B.	Urologic Surgery	University of Chicago
Schwartz, Henry J. H.	Obstetrics-Gynecology	University of Edinburg (U.K.)
Schwartz, Leonard	Psychiatry	University of Pittsburgh
Segall, Nathan T.	General Medicine	University of Pittsburgh
Segel, David P.	Nephrology	Harvard University
Selker, Robert G.	Neurosurgery	University of Pittsburgh
Shadduck, Robert K.	Hematology	State University of New York (Upstate)
Shapera, Richard P.	Internal Medicine	University of Pittsburgh
Sherman, Samuel	Physical Med. & Rehabilitation	St. Louis University
Shonberg, Irving L.	Proctology	University of Chicago
Siew, Shirley	Pathology	University of Witwatersrand (S. Africa)
Silverberg, Jay H.	Hematology	University of Pittsburgh
Silverblatt, Marvin L.	Cardiology	University of Pittsburgh
Silverman, Jerry D.	Pulmonary Disease	University of Pittsburgh
Snitzer, Arnold	General Medicine	University of Pittsburgh
Super, Benjamin	General Medicine	University of Pittsburgh
Steichen, Felicien M.	General & Thoracic Surgery	University of Lausanne (Switzerland)
Steinberg, Abraam	Ophthalmology	University of Michigan
Stept, Leonard A.	Urologic Surgery	University of Pittsburgh
Stept, Raymond	Urologic Surgery	University of Pittsburgh
Stewart, Mervin S.	Psychiatry	University of Pittsburgh

Name	*Specialty*	*Medical School*
Stolzer, Bertrand L.	Rheumatology	New York University
Tanning, Howard M.	Ophthalmology	University of Chicago
Tauberg, Herbert R.	Orthopedic Surgery	University of Pittsburgh
Temeles, Roy S.	Orthopedic Surgery	Medical College of Virginia
Tenenouser, Barry	General Medicine	University of Pittsburgh
Terner, Irwin S.	Ophthalmology	University of Pittsburgh
Treger, Albert	Cardiology	New York University
Troen, Philip	Endocrinology	Harvard University
Vagnucci, Anthony	Endrocrinology	Genoa University (Italy)
Varat, Murray A.	Cardiology	State University of New York (Downstate)
Wald, Michael E.	Pulmonary Disease	University of Chicago
Wechsler, Richard	Gastroenterology	University of Pittsburgh
Weigler, Richard	Allergy	Rush Medical College
Weill, David R.	Internal Medicine	University of Pennsylvania
Whitman, Robert S.	General Medicine	University of Pittsburgh
Williams, Norman	Radiology	Tufts Medical College
Winkelstein, Alan	Clinical Immunology	State University of New York (Downstate)
Wing, Edward J.	Internal Medicine	Harvard University
Wishnev, Martin	Gastroenterology	Thomas Jefferson University
Wolfe, Joseph D.	General Surgery	University of Pittsburgh
Wolfson, Jerome H.	Pediatrics	State University of New York (Downstate)
Wolfson, Sidney K.	Neurosurgery	University of Chicago
Zangwill, Donald P.	Infectious Disease	Harvard University
Zeigler, Zella R.	Hematology	University of Pittsburgh
Ziskind, Zelda	Pediatrics	Women's Medical College of Pennsylvania
Baraff, Louis	Dentistry	University of Pittsburgh
Bauhammers, Andrejs	Dentistry	University of Pittsburgh
Beirne, Vincent	Dentistry	University of Pittsburgh
Blow, Clarence C.	Dentistry	University of Pittsburgh
Browdie, Gerald	Dentistry	University of Pittsburgh
Catone, Gaeteano	Oral Surgery	University of Pittsburgh
Davis, Harold	Dentistry	University of Pittsburgh
Dixon, Reginald W.	Dentistry	University of Pittsburgh
Finder, Moses	Oral Surgery	University of Pittsburgh
Gottlieb, Marcus A.	Dentistry	University of Pittsburgh
Guggenheimer, James	Dentistry	Columbia University
Hammermeister, Rudolf O.	Dentistry	University of Pittsburgh
Kahn, Michael R.	Oral Surgery	University of Pittsburgh
Kanterman, Larry	Dentistry	University of Pittsburgh
Lautman, Martin	Dentistry	University of Pittsburgh
Levine, Donald Louis	Dentistry	University of Pittsburgh
Lindner, Robert T.	Oral Surgery	University of Pittsburgh
Meyers, Herbert E.	Dentistry	University of Pittsburgh
Michanowicz, Andrew E.	Dentistry	University of Pittsburgh
Michanowicz, John P.	Dentistry	University of Pittsburgh
Polk, Joseph L.	Dentistry	University of Pittsburgh

Name	Specialty	Medical School
Roscow, Asher B.	Dentistry	University of Pittsburgh
Rosenthal, Arnold M.	Dentistry	University of Pittsburgh
Rubenstein, Daniel F.	Dentistry	University of Pittsburgh
Schechter, Murray P.	Dentistry	University of Pittsburgh
Samuels, Marc	Dentistry	University of Pittsburgh
Seltman, M. A.	Dentistry	University of Pittsburgh
Shensa, David R.	Oral Surgery	University of Pittsburgh
Smoller, Joseph H.	Dentistry	University of Pittsburgh
Sobel, Michael	Dentistry	University of Pittsburgh
Spatz, Sherman	Oral Surgery	University of Pittsburgh
Spatz, Sidney	Oral Surgery	University of Pittsburgh
Stockton, William	Dentistry	Howard University
Waldholtz, Harvey A.	Dentistry	University of Pittsburgh
Waller, Wilvor C.	Dentistry	University of Pittsburgh
Werrin, Samuel R.	Dentistry	Temple University
Yocca, John A.	Dentistry	University of Pittsburgh
Zubrow, Harold J.	Oral Surgery	University of Pittsburgh
Kelsky, Albert J.	Podiatry	Ohio College of Podiatry
Persky, Bernard	Podiatry	Ohio College of Podiatry
Schindler, Samuel	Podiatry	Ohio College of Podiatry
Slotsky, Malcolm A.	Podiatry	Ohio College of Podiatry
Stein, Emanuel	Podiatry	Illinois College of Chiropody and Foot Surgery
Stolzenberg, Harold	Podiatry	Illinois College of Chiropody and Foot Surgery
Stone, Arthur B.	Podiatry	Ohio College of Podiatry

EMERITUS MEDICAL STAFF

Name	Specialty	Medical School
Berenfield, Simon	Otorhinolaryngology	Emory University
Berger, Benjamin	Psychiatry	St. Louis University
Boharas, Saul	Internal Medicine	University of Pittsburgh
Callomon, Verner B.	Respiratory Disease	University of Pennsylvania
Canter, Hyman E.	Obstetrics-Gynecology	Temple University
Criep, Leo H.	Allergy	University of Pittsburgh
DeRoy, Mayer S.	Orthopedic	University of Pittsburgh
Friedman, Louis L.	Otorhinolaryngology	University of Pittsburgh
Goldman, M. R.	Ophthalmology	Thomas Jefferson University
Goldstein, Samuel	Obstetrics-Gynecology	University of Pittsburgh
Golomb, Milton W.	Rheumatology	University of Pittsburgh
Koskoff, Yale D.	Neurosurgery	Yale University
Krause, Gilbert	General Medicine	University of Pittsburgh
Landay, Louis H.	Cardiology	Columbia University
Lebovitz, Edward	Respiratory Disease	Thomas Jefferson University
Lenchner, A. Leonard	Dentistry	University of Pittsburgh
Margolis, H. M.	Rheumatology	University of Pittsburgh
Marks, Pauline	Obstetrics-Gynecology	University of Pittsburgh
Marmins, A. R.	Otorhinolaryngology	George Washington University
Miller, Harry I.	Internal Medicine	University of Pittsburgh

Name	*Specialty*	*Medical School*
Morgan, Irving J.	Ophthalmology	University of Maryland
Odle, Sidney	Internal Medicine	University of Pittsburgh
Pachtman, Isadore	Ophthalmology	University of Maryland
Rosenburg, Sidney A.	General Surgery	University of Pittsburgh
Rubel, Theodore	General Medicine	University of Vienna
Sapira, Harry A.	General Medicine	University of Pittsburgh
Saul, Sydney M.	Pediatrics	University of Pittsburgh
Steinman, David	Pediatrics	University of Pittsburgh
Stutz, Irving L.	Cardiology	University of Pittsburgh
Thorpe, Harvey E.	Ophthalmology	University of Pittsburgh
Weber, Morris B.	General Medicine	University of Pittsburgh
Wechsler, Sylvia	Allergy	University of Pittsburgh
Weiner, Sidney E.	Neurology	Royal College of Physicians & Surgeons (U.K.)
Weintraub, Fred S.	Pediatrics	University of Maryland
Yardumian, Krikor	Pathology	American University of Beirut
Zimmerman, Irwin E.	Dentistry	University of Pittsburgh

CONSULTING MEDICAL STAFF

Bahnson, Henry T.	General & Thoracic Surgery	Harvard University
Grauer, Robert C.	Endocrinology	University of Pittsburgh
Gumerman, Lewis	Nuclear Medicine	University of Pennsylvania
Higman, Henry	Neurology	University of Pittsburgh
Leonard, James J.	Cardiology	Georgetown University
Myers, Jack	Internal Medicine	University of Pittsburgh
Sanes, Gilmore M.	Thoracic Surgery	University of Pittsburgh
Smudski, James W.	Dentistry	University of Pittsburgh
Stockdale, Robert H.	Radiology	Thomas Jefferson University
Wholey, Mark H.	Radiology	Hahnemann Medical College
Verbin, Robert S.	Dentistry (Pathology)	University of Pittsburgh

COURTESY MEDICAL STAFF

Barr, James H., Jr.	Rheumatology	Western Reserve University
Binstock, Harold	Industrial Medicine	University of Pittsburgh
Childs, Elizabeth	General Medicine	University of Pittsburgh
Cohen, Harold M.	Obstetrics-Gynecology	University of Pittsburgh
Eisenbeis, Carl H.	Rheumatology	University of Pittsburgh
Felman, Israel	General Medicine	University of Virginia
Heineman, Arthur C., Jr.	Endocrinology	University of Pittsburgh
Kaufman, I. Leonard	General Medicine	Thomas Jefferson University
Lebovitz, Jerome J.	Respiratory Disease	Thomas Jefferson University
Michaels, Milton	Hematology	University of Pittsburgh
Pretter, Paul	Internal Medicine	University of Louvain (Belgium)
Reswick, Murray	Radiology	University of Paris
Rosen, Samuel J.	Orthopedic Surgery	University of Pittsburgh
Rosenberg, Harvey W.	General Medicine	University of Pittsburgh
Rosenbloom, Meyer A.	Obstetrics-Gynecology	University of Pittsburgh
Schulman, Benjamin L.	General Medicine	University of Louisville
Schultz, Edward M.	Radiology	University of Pittsburgh

MONTEFIORE HOSPITAL
SUMMARY OF SERVICES
FISCAL YEARS 1973, 1968, 1963

STATISTICAL HIGHLIGHTS	1973	1968	1963
Ambulatory Care Visits			
Emergency Room	20,964	14,322	13,475
Outpatient Department	33,749	24,930	25,133
Hazelwood Health Center	5,094	—	—
Private Outpatient	35,010	28,633	27,512
Total Ambulatory Care Visits	94,817	67,885	66,120
Inpatient Care			
Total Patient Days	140,748	147,310	109,802
Admissions	12,287	12,585	11,641
Average Daily Census	386	402	287
Average Length of Stay	11.5	11.7	9.4
Services			
Anesthetics	6,920	6,108	2,455
Blood Transfusions	3,737	3,240	1,530
Cardiovascular Laboratory Procedures	421	1,082	—
Dietary (Meals Served)	1,119,718	928,931	644,707
Electroencephalograms	529	805	441
Electrocardiograms	31,478	20,441	9,473
Endocrine Studies	7,665	1,130	921
Home Care Days	25,503	33,364	2,104
Inhalation Therapy Treatments	82,480	2,684	—
Laboratory Tests	2,033,993	545,878	221,300
Laundry (lbs. of Linen Processed)	2,395,276	2,097,142	1,682,805
Maintenance Calls	40,159	20,825	11,229
Nursing Service Hours of Care	1,054,055	886,360	538,720
Pharmacy Prescriptions Filled	268,719	228,012	149,154
Pulmonary Laboratory Tests	821	244	136
Radioactive Isotope Studies	3,441	2,302	673
Recovery Room Patients	6,511	5,702	4,646
Rehabilitation:			
Physical Therapy Treatments	39,342	26,067	16,141
Occupational Therapy Treatments	1,745	2,049	3,979
Recreational Therapy Occasions	4,761	9,859	6,672
Speech & Hearing Evaluations & Treatments	598	501	—
Bureau of Vocational Rehabilitation Patients Served	346	133	—
Social Service Patients Served	2,740	4,734	6,252
Surgical Procedures	8,519	8,326	6,336
Volunteer Service Hours	41,536	46,708	33,694
X-Ray Diagnostic Examinations	59,277	43,859	32,654
X-Ray Therapy Treatments	7,892	8,984	5,439

EXHIBIT C

ACCOUNTANTS' REPORT

TOUCHE ROSS & CO.
Pittsburgh, Pennsylvania

The Board of Trustees
The Montefiore Hospital Association of Western Pennsylvania
Pittsburgh, Pennsylvania

We have examined the balance sheet of The Montefiore Hospital Association of Western Pennsylvania as of June 30, 1973 and 1972 and the related statement of revenues and expenses—unrestricted fund, statement of changes in fund balances and statement of changes in financial position—unrestricted fund for the years then ended. Our examination was made in accordance with generally accepted auditing standards and accordingly included such tests of the accounting records and such other auditing procedures as we considered necessary in the circumstances.

In our opinion, the aforementioned financial statements present fairly the financial position of The Montefiore Hospital Association of Western Pennsylvania at June 30, 1973 and 1972, and the results of its operations, changes in its fund balances and financial position for the years then ended, in conformity with generally accepted accounting principles consistently applied during the period subsequent to the changes, with which we concur, made as of July 1, 1971 as described in Note 1 to the financial statements.

We did not assist in the preparation of the projected results of operations for the years ended June 30, 1974 and June 30, 1975 as set forth on pages 22 and 23 of this "Official Statement" and accordingly express no opinion thereon.

TOUCHE ROSS & CO.
Certified Public Accountants

September 14, 1973

THE MONTEFIORE HOSPITAL ASSOCIATION OF WESTERN PENNSYLVANIA
BALANCE SHEET

UNRESTRICTED FUND

ASSETS

	June 30 1973	June 30 1972*
CURRENT ASSETS:		
Cash and short-term securities, at cost	$ 674,174	$ 344,523
Accounts receivable from patients less estimated uncollectible accounts and contractual allowances of $402,753 in 1973 and $290,000 in 1972	3,418,003	3,293,748
Retroactive adjustments receivable (Note 1):		
Medicare	1,160,000	818,966
Blue Cross	340,000	357,507
Medicaid	158,079	103,070
Other accounts receivable	306,652	216,087
Prepaid expenses	154,986	260,421
Inventories, at cost	236,549	199,625
Due from Restricted Fund	—	57,298
TOTAL CURRENT ASSETS	6,448,443	5,651,245
OTHER:		
Investment in University Health Center of Pittsburgh Central Pharmacy, at cost	72,652	72,652
Investment in University Health Center of Pittsburgh Land Bank Program (Note 2)	443,600	443,600
Other investments	8,680	8,680
Property, plant and equipment, at cost, less accumulated depreciation of $11,370,200 in 1973 and $9,951,626 in 1972 (Notes 1, 3 and 5)	21,388,088	21,526,143
	21,913,020	22,051,075
	$28,361,463	$27,702,320

RESTRICTED FUND

	1973	1972*
Cash and short-term investments, at cost	$ 296,903	$ 308,758
Securities, at cost (quoted market approximately $505,000 in 1973 and $548,000 in 1972)	425,042	438,594
Bond indenture escrow account, House Staff Residence Building, at cost (Note 3)	75,000	75,000
Pledges receivable, less allowance for doubtful collection of $100,000	1,406,103	1,709,945
Accounts and loans receivable	211,413	189,097
Construction grants receivable	57,486	98,876
Due from Unrestricted Fund	126,324	—
	$ 2,598,271	$ 2,820,270

Restated (Note 1)

See notes to financial statements.

THE MONTEFIORE HOSPITAL ASSOCIATION OF WESTERN PENNSYLVANIA
BALANCE SHEET

UNRESTRICTED FUND

LIABILITIES AND FUND BALANCE

	June 30	
	1973	1972*
CURRENT LIABILITIES:		
Demand notes payable (Notes 4 and 8)............................	$ 4,100,000	$ 3,150,000
Trade accounts payable..	453,082	526,206
Construction accounts payable (Note 8).........................	422,136	775,322
Advances on billings:		
Blue Cross...	420,000	330,000
Medicare..	538,860	555,000
Accrued payroll...	282,233	237,542
Current portion of long-term debt..............................	160,000	160,000
Due to Restricted Fund..	126,324	—
TOTAL CURRENT LIABILITIES...............................	6,502,635	5,734,070
DEFERRED INCOME:		
Advance reimbursement, Medicare accelerated depreciation (Note 1)..	1,164,420	990,000
LONG-TERM DEBT (Note 8):		
3½ % Bonds payable, Housing and Home Finance Agency, payable serially to 2012, less $10,000 included in current liabilities (Note 3)...	669,000	679,000
Mortgage payable, less $150,000 included in current liabilities (Note 5)...	5,392,128	5,533,366
	6,061,128	6,212,366
UNRESTRICTED FUND BALANCE.....................................	14,633,280	14,765,884
	$28,361,463	$27,702,320
Due to Unrestricted Fund.......................................	$ —	$ 57,298
Restricted Fund Balance...	2,598,271	2,762,972
	$ 2,598,271	$ 2,820,270

THE MONTEFIORE HOSPITAL ASSOCIATION OF WESTERN PENNSYLVANIA
STATEMENT OF REVENUES AND EXPENSES — UNRESTRICTED FUND

	Year Ended June 30	
	1973	*1972**
GROSS REVENUE FROM PATIENTS............................	$ 21,121,274	$ 19,245,132
CONTRACTUAL ADJUSTMENTS, ALLOWANCES AND UNCOLLECTIBLE ACCOUNTS.........................	2,041,796	1,223,817
NET REVENUE FROM PATIENTS.............................	19,079,478	18,021,315
OTHER OPERATING REVENUE..............................	1,384,380	1,237,319
Total Operating Revenues............................	20,463,858	19,258,634
OPERATING EXPENSES:		
Medical and Special services....................................	8,694,022	7,962,982
Nursing services...	3,897,423	3,740,485
Operation of plant...	2,268,085	2,060,273
Dietary..	1,358,270	1,378,797
Housekeeping and laundry.....................................	821,116	793,381
Outpatient department..	260,260	289,925
Social services...	505,848	412,423
Fiscal services...	720,227	708,012
Administrative services.......................................	272,828	313,250
Data processing services......................................	338,510	345,505
Depreciation...	1,408,870	1,149,061
Interest..	685,127	556,258
Total Operating Expenses.............................	21,230,586	19,710,352
LOSS FROM OPERATIONS....................................	(766,728)	(451,718)
OTHER NONOPERATING REVENUE:		
Subsidy from United Jewish Federation.........................	248,970	248,981
EXCESS OF EXPENSES OVER REVENUES.....................	$ (517,758)	$ (202,737)

**Restated (Note 1)*

See notes to financial statements.

46

THE MONTEFIORE HOSPITAL ASSOCIATION OF WESTERN PENNSYLVANIA
STATEMENT OF CHANGES IN FINANCIAL POSITION — UNRESTRICTED FUND

	Year Ended June 30	
	1973	1972*
FUNDS PROVIDED:		
Loss from operations...	$ (766,728)	$ (451,718)
Add items not requiring outlay of funds:		
Depreciation..	1,408,870	1,149,061
Increase in advance reimbursement, Medicare..................	174,420	120,000
Funds provided from operations................................	816,562	817,343
Nonoperating revenue..	248,970	248,981
Decrease in other investment..................................	—	7,015
Decrease in working capital....................................	—	792,377
	$ 1,065,532	$ 1,865,716
FUNDS APPLIED:		
Decrease in long-term debt.....................................	$ 151,238	$ 326,634
Increase in investments in University Health Center of Pittsburgh.....	—	167,847
Additions to property, plant and equipment, net of transfer from		
Restricted Fund..	885,661	1,371,235
Increase in working capital....................................	28,633	—
	$ 1,065,532	$ 1,865,716
INCREASE (DECREASE) IN WORKING CAPITAL		
COMPONENTS:		
Cash and short-term securities.................................	$ 329,651	$ (597,638)
Accounts receivable from patients..............................	224,255	191,564
Retroactive adjustments receivable.............................	278,536	321,557
Other accounts receivable......................................	90,565	92,287
Prepaid expenses..	(105,435)	70,283
Inventories..	36,924	14,566
Demand notes payable..	(950,000)	(1,150,000)
Accounts payable..	426,310	(110,726)
Advances on billings..	(73,860)	(218,000)
Accrued payroll...	(44,691)	233,647
Interfund accounts..	(183,622)	360,083
INCREASE (DECREASE) IN WORKING CAPITAL........	$ 28,633	$ (792,377)

Restated (Note 1)

See notes to financial statements.

THE MONTEFIORE HOSPITAL ASSOCIATION OF WESTERN PENNSYLVANIA
STATEMENT OF CHANGES IN FUND BALANCES

	Operating Fund	Special Funds	Capital Account	Unrestricted Fund	Restricted Fund
BALANCE, June 30, 1971, as previously reported	$641,950	$697,594	$13,601,980	$ —	$ —
Reclassification to comply with recommendations of American Institute of Certified Public Accountants' Hospital Audit Guide	(641,950)	(697,594)	(13,601,980)	13,686,267	1,255,257
Retroactive effect on prior years of change in accounting method (Note 1)				—	2,649,317
BALANCE, June 30, 1971, as restated	$ —	$ —	$ —	13,686,267	3,904,574
Additions:					
Transfer from restricted fund				1,282,354	—
Donations, bequests and grants				—	470,528
Income from investments				—	37,371
Membership dues				—	5,793
				1,282,354	513,692
Deductions:					
Net loss				202,737	—
Expended for designated purposes				—	372,940
Transfer to unrestricted fund				—	1,282,354
				202,737	1,655,294
BALANCE, June 30, 1972, as restated				14,765,884	2,762,972
Additions:					
Transfer from restricted fund				385,154	—
Donations, bequests and grants				—	559,370
Income from investments				—	42,892
Membership dues				—	5,416
				385,154	607,678
Deductions:					
Net loss				517,758	—
Expended for designated purposes				—	387,225
Transfer to unrestricted fund				—	385,154
				517,758	772,379
BALANCE, June 30, 1973				$14,633,280	$2,598,271

See notes to financial statements

48

THE MONTEFIORE HOSPITAL ASSOCIATION OF WESTERN PENNSYLVANIA
NOTES TO FINANCIAL STATEMENTS
Years Ended June 30, 1973 and 1972

1. Summary of Significant Accounting Policies:

a. Basis of Presentation—In accordance with the recommendations of the American Institute of Certified Public Accountants' Hospital Audit Guide, the Hospital has made certain reclassifications in its balance sheet and statements of revenues and expenses, changes in fund balances and changes in financial position for the year ended June 30, 1972.

In the year ended June 30, 1973, the method of accounting for pledge income and reimbursements from government agencies for construction costs was changed from the cash to the accrual basis. The cumulative effect on prior periods of this change which was made to conform to the Audit Guide has been retroactively recorded at June 30, 1971 and resulted in an increase of $2,649,317 in the restricted fund balance.

b. Restatement—The Hospital has retroactively adjusted certain estimated construction costs which were recorded in the year ended June 30, 1972. The effect of this change is a decrease of $296,691 in property, plant and equipment and construction accounts payable at June 30, 1972.

c. Retroactive Adjustments Receivable—Retroactive adjustments receivable from Medicare, Blue Cross and Medicaid are based on currently available information. These amounts are subject to adjustment and final settlement will result from examinations by the respective agencies.

d. Depreciation—Property, plant and equipment is carried at cost, less allowance for depreciation which is based on useful lives recommended by the American Hospital Association.

The Hospital uses accelerated depreciation in determining reimbursable costs under Medicare cost reimbursement agreements, whereas depreciation is recorded on a straight-line basis for financial reporting purposes. The Hospital recognizes the effect of this difference by reflecting as deferred income the excess of Medicare reimbursement received over the amount which would have been received on the basis of straight-line depreciation. The amount deferred during 1973 and 1972 was $174,420 and $120,000, respectively.

2. Affiliation with University Health Center of Pittsburgh:

The Hospital is a party to an agreement of affiliation with the University of Pittsburgh School of Health Professions. Under this agreement the Hospital associated itself with other similar institutions in the University Health Center of Pittsburgh.

In this connection the Hospital is committed to an initial investment of not more than $500,000 in the Land Bank Program of the Health Center. The purpose of the Program is to acquire land adjacent to the Health Center Hospitals for future development.

3. Property, Plant and Equipment:

Property, plant and equipment consisted of the following:

	June 30	
	1973	*1972*
Land and land improvements	$ 784,851	$ 778,210
Buildings	13,510,339	13,366,577
Equipment	18,463,098	17,278,266
Construction in progress	—	54,716
	32,758,288	31,477,769
Less accumulated depreciation	11,370,200	9,951,626
	$21,388,088	$21,526,143

The property, plant and equipment includes the House Staff Residence Building which is pledged as collateral for the bonds payable. The carrying value of the building is $548,163.

THE MONTEFIORE HOSPITAL ASSOCIATION OF WESTERN PENNSYLVANIA
NOTES TO FINANCIAL STATEMENTS
Years Ended June 30, 1973 and 1972
(Continued)

4. Demand Notes Payable:

The Hospital has lines of credit totaling $4,500,000 with the Union National Bank of Pittsburgh. Interest rates varied from 7½% to 7¾% at June 30, 1973. Borrowings under these lines of credit are used to finance the Hospital's Capital Development Program and are expected to be repaid by proceeds from long-term financing.

5. Mortgage Payable:

The mortgage is payable to Connecticut General Life Insurance Company and is secured by substantially all Hospital property except the House Staff Residence Building (see Note 3). The mortgage bears interest at 7⅝% and provides for semi-annual payments, including interest, of $285,976 through 1989. The provisions of the mortgage requires, among other things, that net income plus depreciation and interest shall not be less than 150% of the annual principal and interest payable. This provision was met for the years ending June 30, 1973 and 1972.

6. Pension Plan:

The Hospital has a noncontributory pension plan for its eligible employees. The total pension expense for the years 1973 and 1972 is $201,350 and $178,800, respectively, which includes amortization of prior service cost over 40 years. The Hospital's policy is to fund pension costs accrued. The actuarially computed value of vested benefits as of January 1, 1973 exceeded the total value of the pension fund by approximately $393,389.

7. Arbitration Proceedings:

The general contractor for a portion of the Hospital's Capital Development Program has filed a claim against the Hospital with the American Arbitration Association for approximately $718,000 for damages resulting from alleged delays, interruptions and interferences by the Hospital in its performance under the contract. The Hospital has filed a counterclaim of approximately $1,256,000 based on uncompleted construction work and consequential damages as a result of the delays. In the opinion of legal counsel the Hospital has an adequate defense against the claim of the contractor. However, it is too early in the arbitration process to determine the eventual outcome of these proceedings.

8. Proposed Refinancing:

The Hospital is currently negotiating agreements with the Allegheny County Hospital Development Authority under the terms of which, the Hospital will lease certain hospital facilities to the Authority for a 30 year period. As rental under this lease, the Authority will deposit the proceeds of a $11,705,000 bond issue with a trustee. The trustee will disburse these funds to pay the mortgage payable of $5,542,128 and the demand notes payable of $4,100,000, to pay contractors on the project, to purchase equipment, to establish a debt service reserve fund and to pay the costs of this financing.

The Hospital will in turn sublease the facilities for 30 years for a net annual rental sufficient to cover the debt service costs and administrative costs of the Authority reduced by income earned by the debt service reserve fund.

APPENDIX 12

TAX-EXEMPT BOND RATINGS

Key to Moody's Municipal Ratings

Aaa

ds which are rated **Aaa** are judged to be of the best quality. They the smallest degree of investment risk and are generally referred to lt edge." Interest payments are protected by a large or by an excep- ly stable margin and principal is secure. While the various protective nts are likely to change, such changes as can be visualized are most ely to impair the fundamentally strong position of such issues.

Aa

ds which are rated **Aa** are judged to be of high quality by all ards. Together with the **Aaa** group they comprise what are generally n as high grade bonds. They are rated lower than the best bonds se margins of protection may not be as large as in **Aaa** securities or ation of protective elements may be of greater amplitude or there be other elements present which make the long-term risks appear what larger than in **Aaa** securities.

A

ds which are rated **A** possess many favorable investment attributes are to be considered as upper medium grade obligations. Factors g security to principal and interest are considered adequate, but nts may be present which suggest a susceptibility to impairment ime in the future. See General Note below.

Baa

nds which are rated **Baa** are considered as medium grade ations; i.e., they are neither highly protected nor poorly secured. est payments and principal security appear adequate for the present ertain protective elements may be lacking or may be characteris- y unreliable over any great length of time. Such bonds lack outstand- nvestment characteristics and in fact have speculative characteristics ell. See General Note below.

Ba

nds which are rated **Ba** are judged to have speculative elements; future cannot be considered as well-assured. Often the protection of est and principal payments may be very moderate, and thereby not

well safeguarded during both good and bad times over the future. Un- certainty of position characterizes bonds in this class.

B

Bonds which are rated **B** generally lack characteristics of the desirable investment. Assurance of interest and principal payments or of mainte- nance of other terms of the contract over any long period of time may be small.

Caa

Bonds which are rated **Caa** are of poor standing. Such issues may be in default or there may be present elements of danger with respect to prin- cipal or interest.

Ca

Bonds which are rated **Ca** represent obligations which are speculative in a high degree. Such issues are often in default or have other marked shortcomings.

C

Bonds which are rated **C** are the lowest rated class of bonds, and issues so rated can be regarded as having extremely poor prospects of ever attaining any real investment standing.

Con. (...)

Bonds for which the security depends upon the completion of some act or the fulfillment of some condition are rated conditionally. These are bonds secured by (a) earnings of projects under construction, (b) earnings of projects unseasoned in operating experience, (c) rentals which begin when facilities are completed, or (d) payments to which some other limit- ing condition attaches. Parenthetical rating denotes probable credit stature upon completion of construction or elimination of basis of con- dition.

neral Note: Those bonds in the **A** and **Baa** groups which Moody's believes possess the strongest investment attributes are designated by the ols **A 1** and **Baa 1**. Other **A** and **Baa** bonds comprise the balance of their respective groups. These rankings (1) designate the bonds which offer the mum in security within their quality group, (2) designate bonds which can be bought for possible upgrading in quality and (3) additionally afford nvestor an opportunity to gauge more precisely the relative attractiveness of offerings in the market place. nerally speaking, bonds in Moody's highest rating categories can be characterized as follows: **Aaa** obligations, their safety is so absolute that the occasional exception of oversupply in a few specific instances, characteristically, their market value is affected solely by money market fluc- ons; **Aa** bonds, their market value is virtually immune to all but money market influences, with the occasional exception of oversupply in a few tic instances; **A**-rated bonds may be influenced to some degree by economic performance during a sustained period of depressed business condi- ring to some bonds of this class. **Baa** issues will move in parallel with **Aaa**, **Aa**, and **A** obligations during periods of economic normalcy, except in nces of oversupply. **Ba** bonds are speculative, their market value may be affected by varying economic circumstances not necessarily geared to the less cycle; **B**-rated bonds are usually quite sensitive to day-to-day circumstances affecting the borrower's ability to service debt on schedule, es- lly during down trending economic cycle; **Caa** bonds reflect the market's concept of the probability and imminence of a workout; **Ca** bonds are lative in high degree and usually indicate nominal workout value; and **C**-rated bonds appear to be hopelessly in default and usually have only a nal speculative market value.

less otherwise noted, municipal ratings are for "general obligations" which are defined as validly issued and legally binding evidences of indebted- secured by the full faith, credit and taxing powers of the issuer.

STANDARD & POOR'S CORPORATION

AAA-Prime—These are obligations of the highest quality. They have the strongest capacity for timely payment of debt service.

> General Obligation Bonds—In a period of economic stress, the issuers will suffer the smallest declines in income and will be least susceptible to autonomous decline. Debt burden is mod- erate. A strong revenue structure appears more than adequate to meet future expenditure requirements. Quality of manage- ment appears superior.

> Revenue Bonds—Debt service coverage has been and is ex- pected to remain substantial. Stability of the pledged revenues is also exceptionally strong, due to the competitive position of the municipal enterprise or to the nature of the revenues. Basic security provisions (including rate covenant, earnings test for issuance of additional bonds, debt service reserve requirements) are rigorous. There is evidence of superior management.

AA-High Grade—The investment characteristics of general obliga- tion and revenue bonds in this group are only slightly less marked than those of the prime quality issues. Bonds rated "AA" have the second strongest capacity for payment of debt service.

A-Good Grade—Principal and interest payments on bonds in this category are regarded as safe. This rating describes the third strongest capacity for payment of debt service. It differs from the two higher ratings because:

> General Obligation Bonds—There is some weakness, either in the local economic base, in debt burden, in the balance between revenues and expenditures, or in quality of management. Under certain adverse circumstances, any one such weakness might impair the ability of the issuer to meet debt obligations at some future date.

> Revenue Bonds—Debt service coverage is good, but not excep- tional. Stability of the pledged revenues could show some varia- tions because of increased competition or economic influences on revenues. Basic security provisions, while satisfactory, are less stringent. Management performance appears adequate.

BBB-Medium Grade—This is the lowest investment grade security rating.

> General Obligation Bonds—Under certain adverse conditions, several of the above factors could contribute to a lesser capacity for payment of debt service. The difference between "A" and "BBB" ratings is that the latter shows more than one fundamental weakness, or one very substantial fundamental weakness, whereas the former shows only one deficiency among the factors considered.

> Revenue Bonds—Debt coverage is only fair. Stability of the pledged revenues could show substantial variations, with the revenue flow possibly being subject to erosion over time. Basic security provisions are no more than adequate. Management performance could be stronger.

BB-Lower Medium Grade—Bonds in this group have some in- vestment characteristics, but they no longer predominate. For the most part this rating indicates a speculative, non-investment grade obligation.

B-Low Grade—Investment characteristics are virtually nonexistent and default could be imminent.

D-Defaults—Payment of interest and/or principal is in arrears.

> In order to provide more detailed indications of credit quality, our traditional bond letter ratings may be modified by the addition of a plus or a minus sign, when appropriate, to show relative stand- ing within the major rating categories, the only exceptions being in the "AAA"—Prime Grade category and in the lesser categories below "BB."

NCR—No contract rating No ratings are assigned to new offerings unless a contract rating is applied for.

Provisional Ratings—The letter "p" following a rating indicates the rating is provisional, where payment of debt service requirement will be largely or entirely dependent upon the timely completion of the project.

213

THE TAX-FREE FUND GLOSSARY

It is always good to know what a salesman is talking about when you buy bonds. It is no different with tax-free funds. The following definitions should be helpful to any investor who is thinking about tax-free funds but is sometimes confused by the various terms.

FUND—The fund is an investment trust formed for the purpose of obtaining tax-free income through investment in a portfolio of bonds (usually rated BBB by Standard & Poor's and Baa or better by Moody's) issued on behalf of states, towns, cities, territories, and authorities or political subdivisions in the United States. The interest on the bonds in the portfolio is exempt from all federal income taxes (and some state taxes if they are bonds of a state or one of its subdivisions where there is an income tax law) per the legal opinions of various recognized bond counsel to the issuing governmental bodies.

UNIT—This is what you buy. It represents a certain fractional undivided interest in the overall principal amount of the fund. A unit is usually issued in $1,000 pieces.

SPONSOR—The sponsor corresponds to an underwriter. The sponsor has the responsibility for assembling the portfolio and monitoring the progress of the various issues in the fund. The sponsor can direct the trustee to dispose of bonds when he feels the bonds are not acting well or are in default.

TRUSTEE—The trustee is a bank and its job is to hold the bonds and act as a general disburser of principal and interest. It also pays the various charges incurred by the fund. It redeems units when called upon to do so by unit holders or when the sponsor has a bid for the outstanding units.

EVALUATOR—In most funds available, Standard & Poor's acts as the evaluator. However, this is not necessarily the case in all funds. The evaluator's job is to establish the price of the units in the fund. The evaluator also evaluates the bonds in the portfolio, usually on the last business day of a week. This evaluated price becomes effective for the following week. The evaluator also makes an evaluation twice a year, usually on the last business day of June and December.

SALES CHARGE—This is the charge that is added to the price of the units (which was set by the evaluator) and is the compensation that the sponsor and other dealers distributing a particular fund receive. It is used to pay sales commissions and is then sales profit. It usually runs from 3½ to 4 percent or $35.00 to $40.00 per $1,000 unit.

MONTHLY DISTRIBUTION—Many funds (especially the recent ones) make a monthly interest distribution.